THE LOGIC OF SOLIDARITY

THE LOGIC OF SOLIDARITY

Commentaries on Pope John Paul II's Encyclical
On Social Concern

Edited by Gregory Baum and Robert Ellsberg

with the complete text of the Encyclical

ORBIS BOOKS

Maryknoll, New York 10545

The Catholic Foreign Mission Society of America (Maryknoll) recruits and trains people for overseas missionary service. Through Orbis Books Maryknoll aims to foster the international dialogue that is essential to mission. The books published, however, reflect the opinions of their authors and are not meant to represent the official position of the society.

Copyright © 1989 by Orbis Books
All rights reserved
Published by Orbis Books, Maryknoll, N.Y. 10545
Manufactured in the United States of America

The essay by Bishop Francisco F. Claver, S.J. originally appeared in *Sollicitudo Rei Socialis: Philippine Reflections and Response* © 1988, published by Bahay Maria, 95 Amapola St., Bel-Air, Makati, Metro Manila, Philippines. The essay by Ricardo Antoncich, S.J. appeared in a much longer version in *La encíclica Sollicitudo Rei Socialis: Sus Proyecciones en América Latina* © 1988, published by Latinoamérica Libros srl, Junín 969 - 10ºp. "C", 1113 Buenos Aires, Argentina. Both essays are used with permission of the authors.

The text of *Sollicitudo Rei Socialis* reproduced in this volume is the official Vatican English translation.

Manuscript editor and indexer: William E. Jerman

Library of Congress Cataloging-in-Publication Data

The Logic of solidarity: commentaries on Pope John Paul II's
  encyclical On social concern/edited by Gregory Baum and Robert
  Ellsberg: with the complete text of the encyclical.
      p.   cm.
  Includes bibliographical references.
  ISBN 0-88344-578-6
  1. Catholic Church. Pope (1978-   : John Paul II).   Sollicitudo rei
socialis.   2. Sociology, Christian (Catholic) — Papal documents.
3. Sociology, Christian (Catholic)   4. Church and social problems
— Catholic Church.   5. Catholic Church — Doctrines.   I. Baum,
Gregory, 1923-   .   II. Ellsberg, Robert, 1955-   .   III. Catholic
Church.   Pope (1978-   : John Paul II).   Sollicitudo rei socialis.
English.   1990.
BX1753.C34   1990
261.8 — dc20   89-27941
                                                                    CIP

Contents

Introduction

Robert Ellsberg

On December 30, 1987, Pope John Paul II issued his second encyclical devoted to Catholic social teaching, *Sollicitudo Rei Socialis*, or "On Social Concern." A theological reflection on issues of global poverty and development, the encyclical provoked unusually strong reactions. While the *National Catholic Reporter* welcomed *Sollicitudo* as "the first encyclical of the twenty-first century," the response of many conservative North Americans bordered on shock and outrage. William Safire warned that the pope risked "becoming known as the foremost political moral relativist of our time." According to William F. Buckley, the whole document was "swamped by a theological version of the kind of historical revisionism generally associated with modern nihilists." As a tenable and useful description of the contemporary world, Peter Berger was inclined to grade this document "somewhere between a C+ and a B−."

What provoked such heated response? The major source of contention centered on the pope's rejection of what he calls "the logic of blocs," the division of the world between East and West, each side harboring a tendency to imperialism, and each in part responsible for the widening gap between the world's rich and poor. This encyclical aims at shifting the social concern of the church and world attention away from the East-West ideological orbit and toward the ultimately more fateful division between the rich nations of the North and the so-called underdeveloped nations of the South.

This is a sentiment often expressed by representatives of the Third World and just as often ignored by those for whom the key to all history is contained in the opposition between the U.S. and the U.S.S.R. But it carries a different weight when spoken by the pope. In part this is because of the common, well-founded impression that in the ideological struggle between East and West the church has been no disinterested bystander. Since the days of Leo XIII the social teaching of the church has been regarded by most Catholics as a bulwark against Marxist social-ism. Successive American leaders, for their part, have encour-aged the belief that the cause of the West is the church's cause. Only a few years ago most American Catholics would not have hesitated to embrace this equation. For many it remains an ar-ticle of faith—so much so that any doubt or disagreement is liable to the charge of "moral equivalence."

In this encyclical the pope registers more than doubt. He flatly rejects a view of the world in which all problems are re-duced to the contest between East and West. Such a perspective, in his view, not only impedes the solution to the real problems confronting the majority of the human race; such a perspective is, indeed, a major part of the problem.

Of course, the habit of grading the pope on the degree of his approval of the United States is not the exclusive prerogative of conservatives. But in this case, concerning a document that spe-cifically invites the reader to assume a global perspective, it is especially appropriate to consider the pope's counsel in a wider frame of reference. That is the motive behind the present col-lection.

SOCIAL TEACHING FOR THE WORLD CHURCH

No previous pope has traveled so widely or so far from Eu-rope. His pilgrimages have symbolized the universality of the church. But they have also dramatized the diversity of cultures and historical challenges to which the gospel is addressed. One might say that the particular challenge faced by John Paul II, the first non-Italian pontiff of the modern age, has been the arrival of what Karl Rahner termed, in a famous phrase, "the world church." According to Rahner, the transition from a Eu-ropean church to a truly world church is as momentous a de-velopment as the first-century transition from a predominantly

Jewish church to a church of the gentiles. This transition raises questions concerning all aspects of the life of the church, including, inevitably, its social teaching.

Catholic social teaching, defined here by John Paul II as "the application of the word of God to people's lives and the life of society," is a body of official church teaching that began a century ago with Leo XIII's historic encyclical, *Rerum Novarum* (1891). For most of the century which followed, Catholic social teaching presupposed a European audience, focusing on such problems as industrialization, labor relations, and secularization. It was only at Vatican II that there arose a consciousness that the church was not essentially European. To be truly catholic the church must do more than seek geographical extension; it must become incarnate in the cultures, the hopes, and the struggles of the entire human race. Subsequent church teaching began to reflect the concerns of the underdeveloped nations, where the critical social issues are hunger, extreme poverty, the denial of basic human rights, and the challenge of revolution.

It was in this context that Paul VI wrote his encyclical *Populorum Progressio* (1967), which focused on the gap between the rich and poor nations of the world. Pope Paul addressed with urgency the sufferings of the poor and firmly committed the church to the project of authentic development, "the transition from less than human conditions to truly human ones." Perhaps the most memorable line of that encyclical was "Development is the new name for peace."

Sollicitudo Rei Socialis was issued to commemorate the twentieth anniversary of *Populorum Progressio*, and the pope has used this occasion to reaffirm the global perspective of Catholic social teaching. The intervening decades have only underlined the conviction of many that the future strength and vitality of the Catholic Church is to be found in the Third World. Demographic trends alone would support this prediction. But apart from population figures, the last two decades have seen an extraordinary renewal of the church in the Third World, reflected in religious vocations as well as in new forms of ministry and community, a rediscovery of the Bible, and an outpouring of theological reflection and activity. Unquestionably, the focus of this renewal has been the insertion of the church into the world of the poor.

Priests and religious in many countries have left their rectories and convents to live in the slums and among the rural poor. Theologians have engaged in a systematic review of Christian faith from the starting point of God's option for the poor. Evangelization has been linked to the promotion of justice, and the church, which had in the past served as an ally of the status quo, has identified with the cause of progressive social change.

But if these developments have fostered grounds for hope, the years since *Populorum Progressio* have undermined the rather optimistic tone of Paul VI's encyclical. In the 1960s it was easier to assume that good will, foreign aid and investment, and technical know-how would gradually reduce the gap between the developed and underdeveloped nations. In fact, as John Paul observes, the gap has steadily widened: "One cannot deny that the present situation of the world, from the point of view of development, offers a rather negative impression." In one indicator after another, the pope cites evidence of a deteriorating situation: hunger, illiteracy, unemployment, massive debt, ecological ruin, war, the expenditure on arms, the increase in refugees, torture, and the abuse of human rights.

Without endorsing a particular analysis of the causes of these problems, the pope supports a position shared by many Third World theologians. According to this argument, the divisions between the rich and poor nations are not simply accidental, a matter of differing rates of development. Rather, as the pope suggests, there are deep structural and moral connections between the affluence of the rich countries of the North and the poverty or underdevelopment of the nations of the South. We all live in a global economy, the rules of which are devised and enforced by the privileged players to serve and protect their existing advantage.

The solutions to the problems of underdevelopment will entail more than paternalistic aid. They will require a change of some kind in the overall structure of relations between rich and poor countries—a change in the "rules." How this is to be achieved is a topic beyond the scope of *Sollicitudo*. But according to the pope, one of the critical factors is the need for a profound awakening to the deep interdependence that is a feature of our common humanity. There is no solution to the problems surveyed in this encyclical that does not involve a recovery of the bonds of loyalty reflected in the ancient teaching of the church: we are all "members one of another."

But there are obstacles in the way of this necessary transformation. Chief among them, according to the pope, is the current division of the world into the opposing blocs of East and West, partners as much as adversaries in the so-called Cold War. Nothing is so injurious to the recognition of basic human interdependence as this "logic of blocs." Not only does it determine the allocation of precious scientific, economic and political resources; it enters into our consciousness and corrupts our imaginations. It renders the developing countries "parts of a machine, cogs on a gigantic wheel."

This, of course, is the aspect of the encyclical that has sparked such vigorous debate in the United States. Both East and West, according to the pope, represent models of development in need of reform. Both reflect forms of idolatry—whether of money or of power—that distort the relations among human beings, and undermine the possibility of authentic development. In place of this logic, the pope proposes an alternative, *the logic of solidarity*, which is the moral counterpart to the fact of global interdependence. The word "solidarity" is not original to John Paul II, despite its resonance with the popular struggle in his native Poland. It has appeared in previous encyclicals. But in *Sollicitudo* it attains a new depth and prominence, representing the intersection of theology and a new kind of political morality demanded by our age. It is this new "logic" that is the subject of this volume.

CRITICAL PERSPECTIVES

Philip Land and Peter Henriot begin by examining the methodology of *Sollicitudo*. Much of the distinctive evolution of recent Catholic social teaching may be credited to the inductive, history-centered approach established at Vatican II. Pope John XXIII's attention to the "signs of the times" marked a shift from the tendency of previous Catholic teaching to begin with *a priori* principles, which had then to be applied in deductive fashion to society. The result of this shift is a much more dynamic approach to society and its problems, and a greater sensitivity to the urgency of social change.

Gregory Baum and John Coleman examine aspects of the encyclical that have been particularly controversial in North America: the pope's rejection of liberal capitalism and his critique of certain Western cultural attributes. Many Americans have assumed that the pope's intimate experience of communism would induce a more favorable opinion of the West and its dominant values and institutions. Baum shows, however, that the critique of liberal capitalism is in fact well established in traditional Catholic teaching. Coleman, likewise, shows how deeply rooted in John Paul II's personalist philosophy is his rejection of individualism, consumerism, and materialism—in their own ways, perhaps, more invidious threats to spiritual values than the cruder affronts of atheism.

In another essay, Gregory Baum examines the pope's treatment of what he calls "structures of sin." This renewed attention to the social dimension of sin represents a significant development in Catholic teaching, and one which has been particularly urged by theologians and bishops from the Third World. It rejects a view of religion as a private matter of concern to the individual alone. While denying neither the personal dimension of sin, nor the responsibility of individuals, the pope here recognizes the extent to which selfishness and injustice are embodied in social structures that systematically deny the dignity of human beings. In this view, all economic and social situations have a theological dimension, a status in the light of God's plan for creation, which must be carefully discerned. And if sin has a social or structural dimension, then the same may be said of conversion—a step which the pope appears to take in his treatment of solidarity. This is a development of great importance for the church's understanding of the relation between salvation and the struggle within history for justice and freedom, a major concern of liberation theology.

Pope Paul wrote, "Development is the new name for peace." Part of John Paul's purpose in *Sollicitudo* is to re-examine that statement in light of the disappointing accomplishments in the field of development in the past two decades. Much of the blame, in the pope's view, stems from a too-narrow concept of development. Two essays, by an economist and a theologian, explore the pope's understanding of this key theme. Denis Goulet situates the pope within an emerging consensus of social scientists, ethicists, and economists who reject a definition of development in purely economic terms. What is proposed is a new paradigm of development which would, in the pope's words, "respect and promote all the dimensions of the human person." Donal Dorr explores the theological overtones of the pope's understanding of "authentic human development," especially the key role of solidarity. In light of this encyclical it might be appropriate to amend Pope Paul's words to read, "Solidarity is the new name for development."

Several authors, while sympathetic to the pope's intentions, question the adequacy of his analysis or the assumptions that underlie it. Obviously the Catholic Church does not formally espouse a particular school of socio-economic analysis, but it is just as obvious that any analysis that goes beneath the level of symptoms to an understanding of underlying structures involves a particular understanding of the world and how it functions. Differing forms of analysis support different strategies for change.

William Tabb, an economist, faults the encyclical for its overly general approach and its inadequate attention to the mechanisms of dependence and underdevelopment. The pope, he charges, relies too much on moral exhortation addressed to the elites, rather than on the empowerment of the poor as agents of social change. Similar points are made by Mary Hobgood, who examines the underlying social analysis in the encyclical and charges that it represents a departure from more radical tendencies in Catholic social teaching. Although the pope speaks of structures of sin, he actually puts less emphasis than his predecessor on the structural roots of poverty. Hobgood is further critical of John Paul's prescriptions for overcoming poverty, charging that he prefers top-down, voluntaristic approaches that rely on the good will of those in power. Does the pope, she asks, propose a form of "solidarity without struggle"?

A number of authors raise questions about the credibility of papal teaching. The synod of bishops in 1971 declared that the church, which describes itself as "an expert in humanity," must be held accountable to the standards of justice and freedom which it prescribes for the world at large. Is there a tendency among the hierarchy to be less tolerant of open dialogue and consultation within the church than is deemed healthy and necessary for secular society?

According to Dominican Sister Maria Riley, one of the factors that undermines the credibility of papal teaching is the church's attitude toward the role of women. Given the composition of the magisterium, women's voices and experience are, by definition, excluded from any role in authoritative Catholic teaching. This is particularly unfortunate in an encyclical concerned with the problem of global poverty and development, given the importance of women in local economies, and the extent to which women represent the poorest of the poor. Considerable literature has linked the advancement of women and the cause of development, and Riley describes the ways in which familiarity with this perspective would have enhanced the pope's analysis.

It is particularly appropriate, given the aims of *Sollicitudo*, to conclude this collection with two perspectives from the Third World. Bishop Francisco Claver from the Philippines and Peruvian Jesuit Ricardo Antoncich examine the encyclical in terms of its relevance to their respective continents. Their apparent indifference to the supposedly key issue of "moral equivalence" serves to indicate how different the encyclical appears when read outside the glare of East-West rivalry, which has so conditioned its reception in North America.

Bishop Claver finds a document that seems particularly addressed to the Philippines. In a country which has recently seen a popular struggle against a dictator, and yet still finds itself beset by unresolved political, economic, and social conflicts, the pope's holistic approach to social transformation strikes a resonant chord. Antoncich expresses an appreciation for the methodology of the encyclical, finding analogies between the pope's approach and the method of pastoral discernment common in Latin America: the so-called *see-judge-act* method. Of all the contributors, he is the one most interested in the theological value of temporal struggle — the relation between the Reign of God and historical progress. He is particularly concerned that the church itself reflect the values of God's Reign, highlighting a passage in which the pope seems to call on the church to divest itself of superfluous wealth.

In the time since *Sollicitudo* was first issued momentous developments have occurred in the world. Many of these may be credited to the initiative of the Soviet president, Mikhail Gorbachev. In the space of a few years he has introduced changes in the Soviet Union that would have seemed impossible at any time in recent history. In light of these developments it has become possible to ask whether the Cold War is over. In other parts of the world, too, dramatic events have unfolded: China, the Middle East, Poland, southern Africa, Central America. . . . Some of these developments represent the upsurge of popular movements from below, inspired in many cases by values celebrated in *Sollicitudo* – a commitment to human dignity, freedom and justice.

In both the East and the West there is a rising defiance of the "logic of blocs," and the assertion of new loyalties and political aspirations. If anything, the passage of time has only enhanced the relevance of the pope's theme. We may hope that the reduction of East-West tensions prompts a shift in concern to the urgent needs of the poor. But this is hardly an inevitable outcome. Ingrained patterns of thinking are slow to die, especially when they are sustained by powerful economic and political interests. The examples above serve to remind us that no change comes without a price. But regardless of the policies of the world powers, *Sollicitudo* provides a perspective and an agenda that deserves the serious reflection and response of Christians throughout the world, and of all men and women concerned for the future of our world.

One way or another, that future is being written in the choices and actions of today. It may be that the future of our world is best reflected in the oppression of the poor, in the havoc unleashed on the environment, or in the thousands of thermonuclear warheads that remain poised and aimed at the heart of humanity. But perhaps in our midst there are the seeds of a different future. One day it may appear that today's struggles for liberation, and for peace, for a defense of the earth, for a spirit of community that transcend barriers of nationality – all these movements inspired by an instinct for human *solidarity* – were simply the first draft of history.

Encyclical Letter

SOLLICITUDO REI SOCIALIS

of the Supreme Pontiff
John Paul II
to the Bishops,
Priests,
Religious Families,
Sons and Daughters
of the Church,
and All People of Good Will
for the
Twentieth Anniversary of
Populorum Progressio

On Social Concern

*Venerable Brothers
and dear Sons and Daughters,
Health and the Apostolic Blessing!*

I. INTRODUCTION

1. The social concern of the Church, directed towards an authentic development of man and society which would respect and promote all the dimensions of the human person, has always expressed itself in the most varied ways. In recent years, one of the special means of intervention has been the Magisterium of the Roman Pontiffs which, beginning with the Encyclical *Rerum Novarum* of Leo XIII as a point of reference,[1] has frequently dealt with the question and has sometimes made the dates of publication of the various social documents coincide with the anniversaries of that first document.[2]

The Popes have not failed to throw fresh light by means of those messages upon new aspects of the social doctrine of the Church. As a result, this doctrine, beginning with the outstanding contribution of Leo XIII and enriched by the successive contributions of the Magisterium, has now become an updated doctrinal "corpus." It builds up gradually, as the Church, in the fullness of the word revealed by Christ Jesus[3] and with the assistance of the Holy Spirit (cf. Jn 14:16, 26; 16:13–15), reads events as they unfold in the course of history. She thus seeks to lead people to respond, with the support also of rational reflection and the human sciences, to their vocation as responsible builders of earthly society.

2. Part of this large body of social teaching is the distinguished Encyclical *Populorum Progressio*,[4] which my esteemed predecessor Paul VI published on March 26, 1967.

The enduring relevance of this Encyclical is easily recognized if we note the series of commemorations which took place during 1987 in various forms and in many parts of the ecclesiastical and civil world. For this same purpose, the Pontifical Commission *Iustitia et Pax* sent a circular letter to the Synods of the Oriental Catholic Churches and to the Episcopal Conferences, asking for

3

ideas and suggestions on the best way to celebrate the Encyclical's anniversary, to enrich its teachings and, if need be, to update them. At the time of the twentieth anniversary, the same Commission organized a solemn commemoration in which I myself took part and gave the concluding address.[5] And now, also taking into account the replies to the above-mentioned circular letter, I consider it appropriate, at the close of the year 1987, to devote an Encyclical to the theme of *Populorum Progressio*.

3. In this way I wish principally to achieve *two objectives* of no little importance: on the one hand, to pay homage to this historic document of Paul VI and to its teaching; on the other hand, following in the footsteps of my esteemed predecessors in the See of Peter, to reaffirm the *continuity* of the social doctrine as well as its constant *renewal*. In effect, continuity and renewal are a proof of the *perennial value* of the teaching of the Church.

This twofold dimension is typical of her teaching in the social sphere. On the one hand it is *constant*, for it remains identical in its fundamental inspiration, in its "principles of reflection," in its "criteria of judgment," in its basic "directives for action,"[6] and above all in its vital link with the Gospel of the Lord. On the other hand, it is ever *new*, because it is subject to the necessary and opportune adaptations suggested by the changes in historical conditions and by the unceasing flow of the events which are the setting of the life of people and society.

4. I am convinced that the teachings of the Encyclical *Populorum Progressio*, addressed to the people and the society of the '60s, retain all their force as an *appeal to conscience* today in the last part of the '80s, in an effort to trace the major lines of the present world always within the context of the aim and inspiration of the "development of peoples," which are still very far from being exhausted. I therefore propose to extend the impact of that message by bringing it to bear, with its possible applications, upon the present historical moment, which is no less dramatic than that of twenty years ago.

As we well know, time maintains a constant and unchanging rhythm. Today however we have the impression that it is passing *ever more quickly*, especially by reason of the multiplication and complexity of the phenomena in the midst of which we live. Consequently, the *configuration of the world* in the course of the last twenty years, while preserving certain fundamental constants, has undergone notable changes and presents some totally new aspects.

The present period of time, on the eve of the third Christian millennium, is characterized by a widespread expectancy, rather like a new "Advent"[7] which to some extent touches everyone. It offers an opportunity to study the teachings of the Encyclical in greater detail and to see their possible future developments.

The aim of the present *reflection* is to emphasize, through a theological investigation of the present world, the need for a fuller and more nuanced concept of development, according to the suggestions contained in the Encyclical. Its aim is also to indicate some ways of putting it into effect.

II. ORIGINALITY OF THE ENCYCLICAL
POPULORUM PROGRESSIO

5. As soon as it appeared, the document of Pope Paul VI captured the attention of public opinion by reason of its *originality*. In a concrete manner and with great clarity, it was possible to identify the above mentioned characteristics of *continuity* and *renewal* within the Church's social doctrine. The intention of rediscovering numerous aspects of this teaching, through a careful rereading of the Encyclical, will therefore constitute the main thread of the present reflections.

But first I wish to say a few words about the *date* of publication: the year 1967. The very fact that Pope Paul VI chose to publish a *social Encyclical* in that year invites us to consider the document in relationship to the Second Vatican Ecumenical Council, which had ended on December 8, 1965.

6. We should see something more in this than simple chronological *proximity*. The Encyclical *Populorum Progressio* presents itself, in a certain way, as *a document which applies the teachings of the Council*. It not only makes continual reference to the texts of the Council,[8] but it also flows from the same concern of the Church which inspired the whole effort of the Council—and in a particular way the Pastoral Constitution *Gaudium et Spes*—to coordinate and develop a number of themes of her social teaching.

We can therefore affirm that the Encyclical *Populorum Progressio* is a kind of response to the *Council's appeal* with which the Constitution *Gaudium et Spes* begins: "The joys and the hopes, the griefs and the anxieties of the people of this age, especially those who are poor or in any way afflicted, these too are the joys and hopes, the griefs and anxieties of the followers of Christ. Indeed, nothing genuinely human fails to raise an echo in their hearts."[9] These words express the *fundamental motive* inspiring the great document of the Council, which begins by noting the situation of *poverty* and of *underdevelopment* in which millions of human beings live.

This *poverty* and *underdevelopment* are, under another name, the "griefs and the anxieties" of today, of "especially those who are poor." Before this vast panorama of pain and suffering, the Council wished to suggest horizons of joy and hope. The Encyclical of Paul VI has the same purpose, in full fidelity to the inspiration of the Council.

7. There is also the *theme* of the Encyclical which, in keeping with the great tradition of the Church's social teaching, takes up again in a direct manner the *new exposition* and *rich synthesis* which the Council produced, notably in the Constitution *Gaudium et Spes*.

With regard to the content and themes once again set forth by the Encyclical, the following should be emphasized: the awareness of the duty of the Church, as "an expert in humanity," "to scrutinize the signs of the times and to interpret them in the light of the Gospel"[10]; the awareness, equally profound, of her mission of "service," a mission distinct from the function of the State, even when she is concerned with people's concrete situation[11]; the reference to the notorious inequalities in the situations of those same people[12]; the confirmation of the Council's teaching, a faithful echo of the centuries-old tradition of the Church regarding the "universal purpose of goods"[13]; the appreciation of the culture and the technological civilization which contribute to human liberation,[14] without failing to recognize their limits[15]; finally, on the specific theme of development, which is precisely the theme of the Encyclical, the insistence on the "most serious duty" incumbent on the more developed nations "to help the developing countries."[16] The same idea of the development proposed by the Encyclical flows directly from the approach which the Pastoral Constitution takes to this problem.[17]

These and other explicit references to the Pastoral Constitution lead one to conclude that the Encyclical presents itself as an *application* of the Council's teaching in social matters to the specific problem of the *development* and the *underdevelopment of peoples*.

8. This brief analysis helps us to appreciate better the *originality* of the Encyclical, which can be stated in *three* points.

The *first* is constituted by the *very fact* of a document, issued by the highest authority of the Catholic Church and addressed both to the Church herself and "to all people of good will,"[18] on a matter which at first sight is solely *economic* and *social*: the *development* of peoples. The term "development" is taken from the vocabulary of the social and economic sciences. From this point of view, the Encyclical *Populorum Progressio* follows directly in the line of the Encyclical *Rerum Novarum*, which deals with the "condition of the workers."[19] Considered superficially, both themes could seem extraneous to the legitimate concern of the Church seen as a *religious institution* — and "development" even more so than the "condition of the workers."

In continuity with the Encyclical of Leo XIII, it must be recognized that the document of Paul VI possesses the merit of having emphasized the *ethical* and *cultural character* of the problems connected with development, and likewise the legitimacy and necessity of the Church's intervention in this field.

In addition, the social doctrine of the Church has once more demonstrated its character as an *application* of the word of God to people's lives and the life of society, as well as to the earthly realities connected with them, offering "principles for reflection," "criteria of judgment" and "directives for action."[20] Here, in the document of Paul VI, one finds these three elements with a prevalently practical orientation, that is, directed towards *moral conduct*.

In consequence, when the Church concerns herself with the "development of peoples," she cannot be accused of going outside her own specific field of competence and, still less, outside the mandate received from the Lord.

9. The *second* point of *originality* of *Populorum Progressio* is shown by the *breadth of outlook* open to what is commonly called the "social question."

In fact, the Encyclical *Mater et Magistra* of Pope John XXIII had already entered into this wider outlook,[21] and the Council had echoed the same in the Constitution *Gaudium et Spes*.[22] However, the social teaching of the Church had not yet reached the point of affirming with such clarity that the social question has acquired a worldwide dimension,[23] nor had this affirmation and the accompanying analysis yet been made into a "directive for action," as Paul VI did in his Encyclical.

Such an explicit taking up of a position offers a *great wealth* of content, which it is appropriate to point out.

In the first place a *possible misunderstanding* has to be eliminated. Recognition that the "social question" has assumed a worldwide dimension does not at all mean that it has lost its *incisiveness* or its national and local importance. On the contrary, it means that the problems in industrial enterprises or in the workers' and union movements of a particular country or region are not to be considered as isolated cases with no connection. On the contrary they depend more and more on the influence of factors beyond regional boundaries and national frontiers.

Unfortunately, from the economic point of view, the developing countries are much more numerous than the developed ones; the multitudes of human beings who lack the goods and services offered by development are *much more numerous* than those who possess them.

We are therefore faced with a serious problem of *unequal distribution* of the means of subsistence originally meant for everybody, and thus also an unequal distribution of the benefits deriving from them. And this happens not through the *fault* of the needy people, and even less through a sort of *inevitability* dependent on natural conditions or circumstances as a whole.

The Encyclical of Paul VI, in declaring that the social question has acquired worldwide dimensions, first of all points out a *moral fact*, one which has its foundation in an objective analysis of reality. In the words of the Encyclical itself, "each one must be conscious" of this fact,[24] precisely because it directly concerns the conscience, which is the source of moral decisions.

In this framework, the *originality* of the Encyclical consists not so much in the affirmation, historical in character, of the universality of the social question, but rather in the *moral evaluation* of this reality. Therefore political leaders, and citizens of rich countries considered as individuals, especially if they are Christians, have *the moral obligation*, according to the degree of each one's responsibility, to *take into consideration*, in personal decisions and decisions of government, this relationship of universality, this interdependence which exists between their conduct and the poverty and underdevelopment of so many millions of people. Pope Paul's Encyclical translates more succinctly the moral obligation as the "duty of solidarity"[25]; and this affirmation, even though many situations have changed in the world, has the same force and validity today as when it was written.

On the other hand, without departing from the lines of this moral vision, the *originality* of the Encyclical also consists in the basic insight that the *very concept* of development, if considered in the perspective of universal interdependence, changes notably. True development *cannot* consist in the simple accumulation of wealth and in the greater availability of goods and services, if this is gained at the expense of the development of the masses, and without due consideration for the social, cultural and spiritual dimensions of the human being.[26]

10. As a *third point*, the Encyclical provides a very original contribution to the social doctrine of the Church in its totality and to the very concept of development. This originality is recognizable in a phrase of the document's concluding paragraph, which can be considered as its summary, as well as its historic label: "Development is the new name for peace."[27]

In fact, if the social question has acquired a worldwide dimension, this is because *the demand for justice* can only be satisfied on that level. To ignore this demand could encourage the temptation among the victims of injustice to respond with violence, as happens at the origin of many wars. Peoples excluded from the fair distribution of the goods originally destined for all could ask themselves: why not respond with violence to those who first treat us with violence? And if the situation is examined in the light of the division of the world into ideological blocs —

a division already existing in 1967—and in the light of the subsequent economic and political repercussions and dependencies, the danger is seen to be much greater.

The first consideration of the striking content of the Encyclical's historic phrase may be supplemented by a second consideration to which the document itself alludes[28]: how can one justify the fact that *huge sums of money*, which could and should be used for increasing the development of peoples, are instead utilized for the enrichment of individuals or groups, or assigned to the increase of stockpiles of weapons, both in developed countries and in the developing ones, thereby upsetting the real priorities? This is even more serious given the difficulties which often hinder the direct transfer of capital set aside for helping needy countries. If "development is the new name for peace," war and military preparations are the major enemy of the integral development of peoples.

In the light of this expression of Pope Paul VI, we are thus invited to re-examine the *concept of development*. This of course is not limited to merely satisfying material necessities through an increase of goods, while ignoring the sufferings of the many and making the selfishness of individuals and nations the principal motivation. As the Letter of St. James pointedly reminds us: "What causes wars, and what causes fightings among you? Is it not your passions that are at war in your members? You desire and do not have" (Js 4:1–2).

On the contrary, in a different world, ruled by concern for the *common good* of all humanity, or by concern for the "spiritual and human development of all" instead of by the quest for individual profit, peace would be *possible* as the result of a "more perfect justice among people."[29]

Also this new element of the Encyclical has a *permanent and contemporary value*, in view of the modern attitude which is so sensitive to the close link between respect for justice and the establishment of real peace.

III. SURVEY OF THE CONTEMPORARY WORLD

11. In its own time *the fundamental teaching* of the Encyclical *Populorum Progressio* received great acclaim for its novel character. The social context in which we live today cannot be said

to be completely *identical* to that of twenty years ago. For this reason, I now wish to conduct a brief review of some of the characteristics of today's world, in order to develop the teaching of Paul VI's Encyclical, once again from the point of view of the "development of peoples."

12. The *first fact* to note is that the *hopes for development*, at that time so lively, today appear very far from being realized.

In this regard, the Encyclical had no illusions. Its language, grave and at times dramatic, limited itself to stressing the seriousness of the situation and to bringing before the conscience of all the urgent obligation of contributing to its solution. In those years there was a *certain* widespread *optimism* about the possibility of overcoming, without excessive efforts, the economic backwardness of the poorer peoples, of providing them with infrastructures and assisting them in the process of industrialization.

In that historical context, over and above the efforts of each country, the United Nations Organization promoted consecutively *two decades of development*.[30] In fact, some measures, bilateral and multilateral, were taken with the aim of helping many nations, some of which had already been independent for some time, and others—the majority—being States just born from the process of decolonization. For her part, the Church felt the duty to deepen her understanding of the problems posed by the new situation, in the hope of supporting these efforts with her religious and human inspiration, in order to give them a "soul" and an effective impulse.

13. It cannot be said that these various religious, human, economic and technical initiatives have been in vain, for they have succeeded in achieving certain results. But in general, taking into account the various factors, one cannot deny that the present situation of the world, from the point of view of development, offers a *rather negative* impression.

For this reason, I wish to call attention to a number of *general indicators*, without excluding other specific ones. Without going into an analysis of figures and statistics, it is sufficient to face squarely the reality of an *innumerable multitude of people*—children, adults and the elderly—in other words, real and unique human persons, who are suffering under the intolerable burden of poverty. There are many millions who are deprived of hope due to the fact that, in many parts of the world, their situation has noticeably worsened. Before these tragedies of total indigence and need, in which so many of *our brothers and sisters* are living, it is the Lord Jesus himself who comes to question us (cf. Mt 25:31–46).

14. The first *negative observation* to make is the persistence and often the widening of the *gap* between the areas of the so-called developed North and the developing South. This geographical terminology is only indicative, since one cannot ignore the fact that the frontiers of wealth and poverty intersect within the societies themselves, whether developed or developing. In fact, just as social inequalities down to the level of poverty exist in rich countries, so, in parallel fashion, in the less developed countries one often sees manifestations of selfishness and a flaunting of wealth which is as disconcerting as it is scandalous.

The abundance of goods and services available in some parts of the world, particularly in the developed North, is matched in the South by an unacceptable delay, and it is precisely in this geopolitical area that the major part of the human race lives.

Looking at all the various sectors — the production and distribution of foodstuffs, hygiene, health and housing, availability of drinking water, working conditions (especially for women), life expectancy and other economic and social indicators — the general picture is a disappointing one, both considered in itself and in relation to the corresponding data of the more developed countries. The word "gap" returns spontaneously to mind.

Perhaps this is not the appropriate word for indicating the true reality, since it could give the impression of a *stationary* phenomenon. This is not the case. The *pace of progress* in the developed and developing countries in recent years has differed, and this serves to widen the distances. Thus the developing countries, especially the poorest of them, find themselves in a situation of very serious delay.

We must also add the *differences of culture* and *value systems* between the various population groups, differences which do not always match the degree of *economic development*, but which help to create distances. These are elements and aspects which render *the social question much more complex*, precisely because this question has assumed a universal dimension.

As we observe the various parts of the world separated by this widening gap, and note that each of these parts seems to follow its own path with its own achievements, we can understand the current usage which speaks of different worlds within our *one world*: the First World, the Second World, the Third World and at times the Fourth World.[31] Such expressions, which obviously do not claim to classify exhaustively all countries, are significant: they are a sign of a widespread sense that the *unity of the world*, that is, *the unity of the human race*, is seriously compromised. Such phraseology, beyond its more or less objective value, undoubtedly conceals a *moral content*, before which the Church, which is a "sacrament or sign and instrument . . . of the unity of the whole human race,"[32] cannot remain indifferent.

15. However, the picture just given would be incomplete if one failed to add to the "economic and social indices" of underdevelopment other indices which are equally negative and indeed even more disturbing, beginning with the cultural level. These are *illiteracy*, the difficulty or impossibility of obtaining *higher education*, the inability to share in the *building of one's own nation*, the *various forms of exploitation* and of economic, social, political and even religious *oppression of* the individual and his or her rights, *discrimination of every type*, especially the exceptionally odious form based on difference of race. If some of these scourges are noted with regret in areas of the more developed North, they are undoubtedly more frequent, more lasting and more difficult to root out in the developing and less advanced countries.

It should be noted that in today's world, among other rights, *the right of economic initiative* is often suppressed. Yet it is a right which is important not only for the individual but also for the common good. Experience shows us that the denial of this right, or its limitation in the name of an alleged "equality" of everyone in society, diminishes, or in practice absolutely destroys the spirit of initiative, that is to say *the creative subjectivity of the citizen*. As a consequence, there arises, not so much a true equality as a "leveling down." In the place of creative initiative there appears passivity, dependence and submission to the bureaucratic apparatus which, as the only "ordering" and "decision-making" body—if not also the "owner"—of the entire totality of goods and the means of production, puts everyone in a position of almost absolute dependence, which is similar to the traditional dependence of the worker-proletarian in capitalism. This provokes a sense of frustration or desperation and predisposes people to opt out of national life, impelling many to emigrate and also favoring a form of "psychological" emigration.

Such a situation has its consequences also from the point of view of the "rights of the individual nations." In fact, it often happens that a nation is deprived of its subjectivity, that is to say the "sovereignty" which is its right, in its economic, political-social and in a certain way cultural significance, since in a national community all these dimensions of life are bound together.

It must also be restated that no social group, for example a political party, has the right to usurp the role of sole leader, since this brings about the destruction of the true subjectivity of society of the individual citizens, as happens in every form of totalitarianism. In this situation the individual and the people become "objects," in spite of all declarations to the contrary and verbal assurances.

We should add here that in today's world there are many other *forms of poverty*. For are there not certain privations or deprivations which deserve this name? The denial or the limitation of human rights—as for example the right to religious freedom, the right to share in the building of society, the freedom to organize and to form unions, or to take initiatives in economic matters—do these not impoverish the human person as much as, if not more than, the deprivation of material goods? And is development which does not take into account the full affirmation of these rights really development on the human level?

In brief, modern underdevelopment is not only economic but also cultural, political and simply human, as was indicated twenty years ago by the Encyclical *Populorum Progressio*. Hence at this point we have to ask ourselves if the sad reality of today might not be, at least in part, the result of a *too narrow idea* of development, that is, a mainly economic one.

16. It should be noted that in spite of the praiseworthy efforts made in the last two decades by the more developed or developing nations and the international organizations to find a way out of the situation, or at least to remedy some of its symptoms, the conditions have become *notably worse*.

Responsibility for this deterioration is due to various causes. Notable among them are undoubtedly grave instances of omissions on the part of the developing nations themselves, and especially on the part of those holding economic and political power. Nor can we pretend not to see the responsibility of the developed nations, which have not always, at least in due measure, felt the duty to help countries separated from the affluent world to which they themselves belong.

Moreover, one must denounce the existence of economic, financial and social *mechanisms* which, although they are manipulated by people, often function almost automatically, thus accentuating the situation of wealth for some and poverty for the rest. These mechanisms, which are maneuvered directly or indirectly by the more developed countries, by their very functioning favor the interests of the people manipulating them. But in the end they suffocate or condition the economies of the less developed countries. Later on these mechanisms will have to be subjected to a careful analysis under the ethical-moral aspect.

Populorum Progressio already foresaw the possibility that under such systems the wealth of the rich would increase and the poverty of the poor would remain.[33] A proof of this forecast has been the appearance of the so-called Fourth World.

17. However much society worldwide shows signs of fragmentation, expressed in the conventional names First, Second, Third and even Fourth World, their *interdependence* remains close. When this interdependence is separated from its ethical requirements, it has *disastrous consequences* for the weakest. Indeed, as a result of a sort of internal dynamic and under the impulse of mechanisms which can only be called perverse, this *interdependence* triggers *negative effects* even in the rich countries. It is precisely within these countries that one encounters, though on a lesser scale, the *more specific manifestations* of underdevelopment. Thus it should be obvious that development either becomes shared in *common* by every part of the world or it

undergoes a *process of regression* even in zones marked by constant progress. This tells us a great deal about the nature of *authentic* development: either *all* the nations of the world participate, or it will not be true development.

Among the *specific signs* of underdevelopment which increasingly affect the developed countries also, there are two in particular that reveal a tragic situation. The *first* is the *housing crisis*. During this International Year of the Homeless proclaimed by the United Nations, attention is focused on the millions of human beings lacking adequate housing or with no housing at all, in order to awaken everyone's conscience and to find a solution to this serious problem with its negative consequences for the individual, the family and society.[34]

The lack of housing is being experienced *universally* and is due in large measure to the growing phenomenon of urbanization.[35] Even the most highly developed peoples present the sad spectacle of individuals and families literally struggling to survive, without a *roof* over their heads or with a roof *so inadequate* as to constitute no roof at all.

The lack of housing, an extremely serious problem in itself, should be seen as a sign and summing-up of a whole series of shortcomings: economic, social, cultural or simply human in nature. Given the extent of the problem, we should need little convincing of how far we are from an authentic development of peoples.

18. *Another indicator* common to the vast majority of nations is the phenomenon of *unemployment* and *underemployment.*

Everyone recognizes the *reality* and *growing seriousness* of this problem in the industrialized countries.[36] While it is alarming in the developing countries, with their high rate of population growth and their large numbers of young people, in the countries of high economic development the *sources of work* seem to be shrinking, and thus the opportunities for employment are decreasing rather than increasing.

This phenomenon too, with its series of negative consequences for individuals and for society, ranging from humiliation to the loss of that self-respect which every man and woman should have, prompts us to question seriously the type of development which has been followed over the past twenty years.

Here the words of the Encyclical *Laborem Exercens* are extremely appropriate: "It must be stressed that the constitutive element in the *progress* and also the most adequate *way to verify it* in a spirit of justice and peace, which the Church proclaims and for which she does not cease to pray ... is *the continual reappraisal of man's work*, both in the aspect of its objective finality and in the aspect of the dignity of the subject of all work, that is to say, man." On the other hand, "we cannot fail to be struck by *a disconcerting fact* of immense proportions: the fact that ... there are huge numbers of people who are unemployed ... a fact that without any doubt demonstrates that both within the individual political communities and in their relationships on the continental and world level there is something wrong with the organization of work and employment, precisely at the most critical and socially most important points."[37]

This second phenomenon, like the previous one, because it is *universal* in character and tends to *proliferate*, is a very telling negative sign of the state and the quality of the development of peoples which we see today.

19. A *third phenomenon*, likewise characteristic of the most recent period, even though it is not met with everywhere, is without doubt equally indicative of the *interdependence* between developed and less developed countries. It is the question of the *international debt*, concerning which the Pontifical Commission *Iustitia et Pax* has issued a document.[38]

At this point one cannot ignore the *close connection* between a problem of this kind—the growing seriousness of which was already foreseen in *Populorum Progressio*[39]—and the question of the development of peoples.

The reason which prompted the developing peoples to accept the offer of abundantly available capital was the hope of being able to invest it in development projects. Thus the availability of capital and the fact of accepting it as a loan can be considered a contribution to development, something desirable and legitimate in itself, even though perhaps imprudent and occasionally hasty.

Circumstances have changed, both within the debtor nations and in the international financial market; the instrument chosen to make a contribution to development has turned into a *counter-*

productive mechanism. This is because the debtor nations, in order to service their debt, find themselves obliged to export the capital needed for improving or at least maintaining their standard of living. It is also because, for the same reason, they are unable to obtain new and equally essential financing.

Through this mechanism, the means intended for the development of peoples has turned into a *brake* upon development instead, and indeed in some cases has even *aggravated underdevelopment.*

As the recent document of the Pontifical Commission *Iustitia et Pax* states,[40] these observations should make us reflect on the *ethical character* of the interdependence of peoples. And along similar lines, they should make us reflect on the requirements and conditions, equally inspired by ethical principles, for cooperation in development.

20. If at this point we examine the *reasons* for this serious delay in the process of development, a delay which has occurred contrary to the indications of the Encyclical *Populorum Progressio*, which had raised such great hopes, our attention is especially drawn to the *political* causes of today's situation.

Faced with a combination of factors which are undoubtedly complex, we cannot hope to achieve a comprehensive analysis here. However, we cannot ignore a striking fact about the *political picture* since the Second World War, a fact which has considerable impact on the forward movement of the development of peoples.

I am referring to the *existence of two opposing blocs,* commonly known as the East and the West. The reason for this description is not purely political but is also, as the expression goes, *geopolitical.* Each of the two blocs tends to assimilate or gather around it other countries or groups of countries, to different degrees of adherence or participation.

The opposition is first of all *political,* inasmuch as each bloc identifies itself with a system of organizing society and exercising power which presents itself as an alternative to the other. The political opposition, in turn, takes its origin from a deeper opposition which is *ideological* in nature.

In the West there exists a system which is historically inspired by the principles of the *liberal capitalism* which developed with industrialization during the last century. In the East there exists a system inspired by the *Marxist collectivism* which sprang from an interpretation of the condition of the proletarian classes made in the light of a particular reading of history. Each of the two ideologies, on the basis of two very different visions of man and of his freedom and social role, has proposed and still promotes, on the economic level, antithetical forms of the organization of labor and of the structures of ownership, especially with regard to the so-called means of production.

It was inevitable that by developing antagonistic systems and centers of power, each with its own forms of propaganda and indoctrination, the *ideological opposition* should evolve into a growing *military opposition* and give rise to two blocs of armed forces, each suspicious and fearful of the other's domination.

International relations, in turn, could not fail to feel the effects of this "logic of blocs" and of the respective "spheres of influence." The tension between the two blocs which began at the end of the Second World War has dominated the whole of the subsequent forty years. Sometimes it has taken the form of "*cold war*," sometimes of "*wars by proxy*," through the manipulation of local conflicts, and sometimes it has kept people's minds in suspense and anguish by the threat of an *open and total war*.

Although at the present time this danger seems to have receded, yet without completely disappearing, and even though an initial agreement has been reached on the destruction of one type of nuclear weapon, the existence and opposition of the blocs continue to be a real and worrying fact which still colors the world picture.

21. This happens with particularly negative effects in international relations which concern the developing countries. For as we know the tension *between East and West* is not in itself an opposition between two different *levels* of development but rather between two *concepts* of the development of individuals and peoples, both concepts being imperfect and in need of radical correction. This opposition is transferred to the developing countries themselves, and thus helps to widen the gap already existing on the economic level between *North and South* and which results from the distance between the two *worlds*: the

more developed one and the less developed one.

This is one of the reasons why the Church's social doctrine adopts a critical attitude towards both liberal capitalism and Marxist collectivism. For from the point of view of development the question naturally arises: in what way and to what extent are these two systems capable of changes and updatings such as to favor or promote a true and integral development of individuals and peoples in modern society? In fact, these changes and updatings are urgent and essential for the cause of a development common to all.

Countries which have recently achieved independence, and which are trying to establish a cultural and political identity of their own, and need effective and impartial aid from all the richer and more developed countries, find themselves involved in, and sometimes overwhelmed by, ideological conflicts, which inevitably create internal divisions, to the extent in some cases of provoking full civil war. This is also because investments and aid for development are often diverted from their proper purpose and in opposition to the interests of the countries which ought to benefit from them. Many of these countries are becoming more and more aware of the danger of falling victim to a form of neo-colonialism and are trying to escape from it. It is this awareness which in spite of difficulties, uncertainties and at times contradictions gave rise to the *International Movement of Non-Aligned Nations*, which, in its positive aspect, would like to affirm in an effective way the right of every people to its own identity, independence and security, as well as the right to share, on a basis of equality and solidarity, in the goods intended for all.

22. In the light of these considerations, we easily arrive at a clearer picture of the last twenty years and a better understanding of the conflicts in the northern hemisphere, namely between East and West, as an important cause of the retardation or stagnation of the South.

The developing countries, instead of becoming *autonomous nations* concerned with their own progress towards a just sharing in the goods and services meant for all, become parts of a machine, cogs on a gigantic wheel. This is often true also in the field of social communications, which, being run by centers mostly in the northern hemisphere, do not always give due consideration to the priorities and problems of such countries or respect their cultural make-up. They frequently impose a distorted vision of life and of man and thus fail to respond to the demands of true development.

Each of the two *blocs* harbors in its own way a tendency towards *imperialism*, as it is usually called, or towards forms of neo-colonialism: an easy temptation to which they frequently succumb, as history, including recent history, teaches.

It is this abnormal situation, the result of a war and of an unacceptably exaggerated concern *for security*, which deadens the impulse towards united cooperation by all for the common good of the human race, to the detriment especially of peaceful peoples who are impeded from their rightful access to the goods meant for all.

Seen in this way, the present division of the world is a *direct obstacle* to the real transformation of the conditions of underdevelopment in the developing and less advanced countries. However, peoples do not always resign themselves to their fate. Furthermore, the very needs of an economy stifled by military expenditure and by bureaucracy and intrinsic inefficiency now seem to favor processes which might mitigate the existing opposition and make it easier to begin a fruitful dialogue and genuine collaboration for peace.

23. The statement in the Encyclical *Populorum Progressio* that the resources and investments devoted to arms production ought to be used to alleviate the misery of impoverished peoples[41] makes more urgent the appeal to overcome the opposition between the two blocs.

Today, the reality is that these resources are used to enable each of the two blocs to overtake the other and thus guarantee its own security. Nations which historically, economically and politically have the possibility of playing a leadership role are prevented by this fundamentally flawed distortion from adequately fulfilling their duty of solidarity for the benefit of peoples which aspire to full development.

It is timely to mention—and it is no exaggeration—that a leadership role among nations can only be justified by the possibility and willingness to contribute widely and generously to the common good.

If a nation were to succumb more or less deliberately to the temptation to close in upon itself and failed to meet the responsibilities following from its superior position in the community of nations, it *would fall seriously short* of its clear ethical duty. This is readily apparent in the circumstances of history, where believers discern the dispositions of Divine Providence, ready to make use of the nations for the realization of its plans, so as to render "vain the designs of the peoples" (cf. Ps 33[32]:10).

When the West gives the impression of abandoning itself to forms of growing and selfish isolation, and the East in its turn seems to ignore for questionable reasons its duty to cooperate in the task of alleviating human misery, then we are up against not only a betrayal of humanity's legitimate expectations—a betrayal that is a harbinger of unforeseeable consequences—but also a real desertion of a moral obligation.

24. If arms production is a serious disorder in the present world with regard to true human needs and the employment of the means capable of satisfying those needs, *the arms trade* is equally to blame. Indeed, with reference to the latter it must be added that the *moral judgment is even more severe*. As we all know, this is a trade without frontiers, capable of crossing even the barriers of the blocs. It knows how to overcome the division between East and West, and above all the one between North and South, to the point—and this is more serious—of pushing its way into the *different sections* which make up the southern hemisphere. We are thus confronted with a strange phenomenon: while economic aid and development plans meet with the obstacle of insuperable ideological barriers, and with tariff and trader barriers, *arms* of whatever origin circulate with almost total freedom all over the world. And as the recent document of the Pontifical Commission *Iustitia et Pax* on the international debt points out,[42] everyone knows that in certain cases the capital lent by the developed world has been used in the underdeveloped world to buy weapons.

If to all this we add the *tremendous* and universally acknowledged *danger* represented by *atomic weapons* stockpiled on an incredible scale, the logical conclusion seems to be this: in to-day's world, including the world of economics, the prevailing picture is one destined to lead us more quickly *towards death* rather than one of concern for *true development* which would lead all towards a "more human" life, as envisaged by the En-cyclical *Populorum Progressio*.[43]

The consequences of this state of affairs are to be seen in the festering of a *wound* which typifies and reveals the imbalances and conflicts of the modern world: *the millions of refugees* whom war, natural calamities, persecution and discrimination of every kind have deprived of home, employment, family and homeland. The tragedy of these multitudes is reflected in the hopeless faces of men, women and children who can no longer find a home in a divided and inhospitable world.

Nor may we close our eyes to another painful wound in to-day's world: the phenomenon of *terrorism*, understood as the intention to kill people and destroy property indiscriminately, and to create a climate of terror and insecurity, often including the taking of hostages. Even when some ideology or the desire to create a better society is adduced as the motivation for this inhuman behavior, acts of terrorism are never justifiable. Even less so when, as happens today, such decisions and such actions, which at times lead to real massacres, and to the abduction of innocent people who have nothing to do with the conflicts, claim to have a propaganda purpose for furthering a cause. It is still worse when they are an end in themselves, so that murder is committed merely for the sake of killing. In the face of such horror and suffering, the words I spoke some years ago are still true, and I wish to repeat them again: "What Christianity forbids is to seek solutions . . . by the ways of hatred, by the murdering of defenseless people, by the methods of terrorism."[44]

25. At this point something must be said about the *demo-graphic problem* and the way it is spoken of today, following what Paul VI said in his Encyclical[45] and what I myself stated at length in the Apostolic Exhortation *Familiaris Consortio*.[46]

One cannot deny the existence, especially in the southern hemisphere, of a demographic problem which creates difficulties for development. One must immediately add that in the north-ern hemisphere the nature of this problem is reversed: here, the cause for concern is the *drop in the birthrate*, with repercussions on the aging of the population, unable even to renew itself biologically. In itself, this is a phenomenon capable of hindering development. Just as it is incorrect to say that such difficulties stem solely from demographic growth, neither is it proved that *all* demographic growth is incompatible with orderly development.

On the other hand, it is very alarming to see governments in many countries launching *systematic campaigns* against birth, contrary not only to the cultural and religious identity of the countries themselves but also contrary to the nature of true development. It often happens that these campaigns are the result of pressure and financing coming from abroad, and in some cases they are made a condition for the granting of financial and economic aid and assistance. In any event, there is an *absolute lack of respect* for the freedom of choice of the parties involved, men and women often subjected to intolerable pressures, including economic ones, in order to force them to submit to this new form of oppression. It is the poorest populations which suffer such mistreatment, and this sometimes leads to a tendency towards a form of racism, or the promotion of certain equally racist forms of eugenics.

This fact too, which deserves the most forceful condemnation, is a *sign* of an erroneous and perverse *idea* of true human development.

26. This mainly negative overview of the *actual situation* of development in the contemporary world would be incomplete without a mention of the coexistence of *positive aspects*.

The *first* positive note is the *full awareness* among large numbers of men and women of their own dignity and of that of every human being. This awareness is expressed, for example, in the more *lively concern* that *human rights should be respected*, and in the more vigorous rejection of their violation. One sign of this is the number of recently established private associations, some worldwide in membership, almost all of them devoted to monitoring with great care and commendable objectivity what is happening *internationally* in this sensitive field.

At this level one must acknowledge the *influence* exercised by the *Declaration of Human Rights*, promulgated some forty years ago by the United Nations Organization. Its very existence and gradual acceptance by the international community are signs of a growing awareness. The same is to be said, still in the field of human rights, of other juridical instruments issued by the United Nations Organization or other international organizations.[47]

The awareness under discussion applies not only to *individuals* but also to *nations* and *peoples*, which, as entities having a specific cultural identity, are particularly sensitive to the preservation, free exercise and promotion of their precious heritage.

At the same time, in a world divided and beset by every type of conflict, the *conviction* is growing of a radical *interdependence* and consequently of the need for a solidarity which will take up interdependence and transfer it to the moral plane. Today perhaps more than in the past, people are realizing that they are linked together by a *common destiny*, which is to be constructed together, if catastrophe for all is to be avoided. From the depth of anguish, fear and escapist phenomena like drugs, *typical of the contemporary world*, the idea is slowly emerging that the good to which we are all called and the happiness to which we aspire cannot be obtained without an *effort and commitment on the part of all*, nobody excluded, and the consequent renouncing of personal selfishness.

Also to be mentioned here, as a sign of *respect for life* — despite all the temptations to destroy it by abortion and euthanasia — is a *concomitant concern* for peace, together with an awareness that peace is *indivisible*. It is either *for all* or *for none*. It demands an ever greater degree of rigorous respect for *justice* and consequently a fair distribution of the results of true development.[48]

Among today's *positive signs* we must also mention a greater realization of the limits of available resources, and of the need to respect the integrity and the cycles of nature and to take them into account when planning for development, rather than sacrificing them to certain demagogic ideas about the latter. Today this is called *ecological concern*.

It is also right to acknowledge the generous commitment of statesmen, politicians, economists, trade unionists, people of science and international officials — many of them inspired by religious faith — who at no small personal sacrifice try to resolve the world's ills and who give of themselves in every way so as to ensure that an ever increasing number of people may enjoy the benefits of peace and a quality of life worthy of the name.

The great *international organizations*, and a number of the regional organizations, *contribute* to this *in no small measure*. Their united efforts make possible more effective action.

It is also through these contributions that some Third World countries, despite the burden of many negative factors, have succeeded in reaching a *certain self-sufficiency in food*, or a degree of industrialization which makes it possible to survive with dignity and to guarantee sources of employment for the active population.

Thus, *all is not negative* in the contemporary world, nor would it be, for the Heavenly Father's providence lovingly watches over even our daily cares (cf. Mt 6:25–32; 10:23–31; Lk 12:6–7, 22–30). Indeed, the positive values which we have mentioned testify to a new moral concern, particularly with respect to the great human problems such as development and peace.

This fact prompts me to turn my thoughts to the *true nature* of the development of peoples, along the lines of the Encyclical which we are commemorating, and as a mark of respect for its teaching.

IV. AUTHENTIC HUMAN DEVELOPMENT

27. The examination which the Encyclical invites us to make of the contemporary world leads us to note in the first place that development *is not* a straightforward process, *as it were automatic* and *in itself limitless*, as though, given certain conditions, the human race were able to progress rapidly towards an undefined perfection of some kind.[49]

Such an idea — linked to a notion of "progress" with philosophical connotations deriving from the Enlightenment, rather than to the notion of "development"[50] which is used in a specifically economic and social sense — now seems to be seriously called into doubt, particularly since the tragic experience of the two world wars, the planned and partly achieved destruction of whole peoples, and the looming atomic peril. A naive *mechanistic optimism* has been replaced by a well-founded anxiety for the fate of humanity.

28. At the same time, however, the "economic" concept itself, linked to the word development, has entered into crisis. In fact there is better understanding today that the *mere accumulation* of goods and services, even for the benefit of the majority, is not enough for the realization of human happiness. Nor, in consequence, does the availability of the many *real benefits* provided in recent times by science and technology, including the computer sciences, bring freedom from every form of slavery. On the contrary, the experience of recent years shows that unless all the considerable body of resources and potential at man's disposal is guided by a *moral understanding* and by an orientation towards the true good of the human race, it easily turns against man to oppress him.

A *disconcerting conclusion* about the most recent period should serve to enlighten us: side-by-side with the miseries of underdevelopment, themselves unacceptable, we find ourselves up against a form of *superdevelopment*, equally inadmissible, because like the former it is contrary to what is good and to true happiness. This superdevelopment, which consists in an *excessive* availability of every kind of material goods for the benefit of certain social groups, easily makes people slaves of "possession" and of immediate gratification, with no other horizon than the multiplication or continual replacement of the things already owned with others still better. This is the so-called civilization of "consumption" or "consumerism," which involves so much "throwing-away" and "waste." An object already owned but now superseded by something better is discarded, with no thought of its possible lasting value in itself, nor of some other human being who is poorer.

All of us experience firsthand the sad effects of this blind submission to pure consumerism: in the first place a crass materialism, and at the same time a *radical dissatisfaction*, because one quickly learns—unless one is shielded from the flood of publicity and the ceaseless and tempting offers of products—that the more one possesses the more one wants, while deeper aspirations remain unsatisfied and perhaps even stifled.

The Encyclical of Pope Paul VI pointed out the difference, so often emphasized today, between "having" and "being,"[51] which had been expressed earlier in precise words by the Second

Vatican Council.[52] To "have" objects and goods does not in itself perfect the human subject, unless it contributes to the maturing and enrichment of that subject's "being," that is to say unless it contributes to the realization of the human vocation as such.

Of course, the difference between "being" and "having," the danger inherent in a mere multiplication or replacement of things possessed compared to the value of "being," need not turn into a *contradiction*. One of the greatest injustices in the contemporary world consists precisely in this: that the ones who possess much are relatively *few* and those who possess almost nothing are *many*. It is the injustice of the poor distribution of the goods and services originally intended for all.

This then is the picture: there are some people — the few who possess much — who do not really succeed in "being" because, through a reversal of the hierarchy of values, they are hindered by the cult of "having"; and there are others — the many who have little or nothing — who do not succeed in realizing their basic human vocation because they are deprived of essential goods.

The evil does not consist in "having" as such, but in possessing without regard for the *quality* and the *ordered hierarchy* of the goods one has. *Quality and hierarchy* arise from the subordination of goods and their availability to man's "being" and his true vocation.

This shows that although *development* has a *necessary economic dimension*, since it must supply the greatest possible number of the world's inhabitants with an availability of goods essential for them "to be," it is not limited to that dimension. If it is limited to this, then it turns against those whom it is meant to benefit.

The characteristics of full development, one which is "more human" and able to sustain itself at the level of the true vocation of men and women without denying economic requirements, were described by Paul VI.[53]

29. Development which is not only economic must be measured and oriented according to the reality and vocation of man seen in his totality, namely, according to his *interior dimension*. There is no doubt that he needs created goods and the products of industry, which is constantly being enriched by scientific and

technological progress. And the ever greater availability of material goods not only meets needs but also opens new horizons. The danger of the misuse of material goods and the appearance of artificial needs should in no way hinder the regard we have for the new goods and resources placed at our disposal and the use we make of them. On the contrary, we must see them as a gift from God and as a response to the human vocation, which is fully realized in Christ.

However, in trying to achieve true development we must never lose sight of that *dimension* which is in the *specific nature* of man, who has been created by God in his image and likeness (cf. Gen 1:26). It is a bodily and a spiritual nature, symbolized in the second creation account by the two elements: the *earth*, from which God forms man's body, and the *breath of life* which he breathes into man's nostrils (cf. Gen 2:7).

Thus man comes to have a certain affinity with other creatures: he is called to use them, and to be involved with them. As the Genesis account says (cf. Gen 2:15), he is placed in the garden with the duty of cultivating and watching over it, being superior to the other creatures placed by God under his dominion (cf. Gen 1:25–26). But at the same time man must remain subject to the will of God, who imposes limits upon his use and dominion over things (cf. Gen 2:16–17), just as he promises him immortality (cf. Gen 2:9; Wis 2:23). Thus man, being the image of God, has a true affinity with him too.

On the basis of this teaching, development cannot consist only in the use, dominion over and *indiscriminate* possession of created things and the products of human industry, but rather in *subordinating* the possession, dominion and use to man's divine likeness and to his vocation to immortality. This is the *transcendent reality* of the human being, a reality which is seen to be shared from the beginning by a couple, a man and a woman (cf. Gen 1:27), and is therefore fundamentally social.

30. According to Sacred Scripture therefore, the notion of development is not only "lay" or "profane," but it is also seen to be, while having a socio-economic dimension of its own, the *modern expression* of an essential dimension of man's vocation.

The fact is that man was not created, so to speak, immobile and static. The first portrayal of him, as given in the Bible, certainly presents him as a *creature* and *image, defined* in his deepest reality by the *origin* and *affinity* that constitute him. But all this plants within the human being—man and woman—the *seed* and the *requirement* of a special task to be accomplished by each individually and by them as a couple. The task is "to have dominion" over the other created beings, "to cultivate the garden." This is to be accomplished within the framework of *obedience* to the divine law and therefore with respect for the image received, the image which is the clear foundation of the power of dominion recognized as belonging to man as the means to his perfection (cf. Gen 1:26–30; 2:15–16; Wis 9:2–3).

When man disobeys God and refuses to submit to his rule, nature rebels against him and no longer recognizes him as its "master," for he has tarnished the divine image in himself. The claim to ownership and use of created things remains still valid, but after sin its exercise becomes difficult and full of suffering (cf. Gen 3:17–19).

In fact, the following chapter of Genesis shows us that the descendants of Cain build "a city," engage in sheep farming, practice the arts (music) and technical skills (metallurgy); while at the same time people began to "call upon the name of the Lord" (cf. Gen 4:17–26).

The story of the human race described by Sacred Scripture is, even after the fall into sin, a story of *constant achievements*, which, although always called into question and threatened by sin, are nonetheless repeated, increased and extended in response to the divine vocation given from the beginning to man and woman (cf. Gen 1:26–28) and inscribed in the image which they received.

It is logical to conclude, at least on the part of those who believe in the word of God, that today's "development" is to be seen as a moment in the story which began at creation, a story which is constantly endangered by reason of infidelity to the Creator's will, and especially by the temptation to idolatry. But this "development" fundamentally corresponds to the first premise. Anyone wishing to renounce the *difficult yet noble task* of improving the lot of man in his totality, and of all people, with the excuse that the struggle is difficult and that constant effort is required, or simply because of the experience of defeat and the need to begin again, that person would be betraying the will of God the Creator. In this regard, in the Encyclical *Laborem Exercens* I referred to man's vocation to work, in order to emphasize the idea that it is always man who is the protagonist of development.[54]

Indeed, the Lord Jesus himself, in the parable of the talents, emphasizes the severe treatment given to the man who dared to hide the gift received: "You wicked and slothful servant! You knew that I reap where I have not sowed and gather where I have not winnowed? ... So take the talent from him, and give it to him who has the ten talents" (Mt 25:26–28). It falls to us, who receive the gifts of God in order to make them fruitful, to "sow" and "reap." If we do not, even what we have will be taken away from us.

A deeper study of these harsh words will make us commit ourselves more resolutely to the *duty*, which is urgent for everyone today, to work together for the full development of others: "development of the whole human being and of all people."[55]

31. *Faith in Christ the Redeemer*, while it illuminates from within the nature of development, also guides us in the task of collaboration. In the Letter of St. Paul to the Colossians, we read that Christ is "the first-born of all creation," and that "all things were created through him" and for him (1:15–16). In fact, "all things hold together in him," since "in him all the fullness of God was pleased to dwell, and through him to reconcile to himself all things" (v. 20).

A part of this divine plan, which begins from eternity in Christ, the perfect "image" of the Father, and which culminates in him, "the first-born from the dead" (v. 18), *is our own history*, marked by our personal and collective effort to raise up the human condition and to overcome the obstacles which are continually arising along our way. It thus prepares us to share in the fullness which "dwells in the Lord" and which he communicates "to his body, which is the Church" (v. 18; cf. Eph 1:22–23). At the same time sin, which is always attempting to trap us and which jeopardizes our human achievements, is conquered and redeemed by the "reconciliation" accomplished by Christ (cf. Col 1:20).

Here the perspectives widen. The dream of "unlimited progress" reappears, radically transformed by the *new outlook* created by Christian faith, assuring us that progress is possible only because God the Father has decided from the beginning to make man a sharer of his glory in Jesus Christ risen from the dead, in whom "we have redemption through his blood ... the forgiveness of our trespasses" (Eph 1:7). In him God wished to conquer sin and make it serve our greater good,[56] which infinitely surpasses what progress could achieve.

We can say therefore — as we struggle amidst the obscurities and deficiencies of *underdevelopment* and *superdevelopment* — that one day this corruptible body will put on incorruptibility, this mortal body immortality (cf. 1 Cor 15:54), when the Lord "delivers the Kingdom to God the Father" (v. 24) and all the works and actions that are worthy of man will be redeemed.

Furthermore, the concept of faith makes quite clear the reasons which impel the *Church* to concern herself with the problems of development, to consider them a *duty of her pastoral ministry*, and to urge all to think about the nature and characteristics of authentic human development. Through her commitment she desires, on the one hand, to place herself at the service of the divine plan which is meant to order all things to the fullness which dwells in Christ (cf. Col 1:19) and which he communicated to his body; and on the other hand she desires to respond to her fundamental vocation of being a "sacrament," that is to say "a sign and instrument of intimate union with God and of the unity of the whole human race."[57]

Some Fathers of the Church were inspired by this idea to develop in original ways a concept of the *meaning of history* and of *human work*, directed towards a goal which surpasses this meaning and which is always defined by its relationship to the work of Christ. In other words, one can find in the teaching of the Fathers an *optimistic vision* of history and work, that is to say of the *perennial value* of authentic human achievements, inasmuch as they are redeemed by Christ and destined for the promised Kingdom.[58]

Thus, part of the *teaching* and most ancient *practice* of the Church is her conviction that she is obliged by her vocation — she herself, her ministers and each of her members — to relieve the misery of the suffering, both far and near, not only out of

her "abundance" but also out of her "necessities." Faced by
cases of need, one cannot ignore them in favor of superfluous
church ornaments and costly furnishings for divine worship; on
the contrary it could be obligatory to sell these goods in order
to provide food, drink, clothing and shelter for those who lack
these things.[59] As has been already noted, here we are shown a
"hierarchy of values" — in the framework of the right to property — between "having" and "being," especially when the "having" of a few can be to the detriment of the "being" of many
others.

In his Encyclical Pope Paul VI stands in the line of this teaching, taking his inspiration from the Pastoral Constitution *Gaudium et Spes*.[60] For my own part, I wish to insist once more on
the seriousness and urgency of that teaching, and I ask the Lord
to give all Christians the strength to put it faithfully into practice.

32. The obligation to commit oneself to the development of
peoples is not just an *individual* duty, and still less an *individualistic* one, as if it were possible to achieve this development
through the isolated efforts of each individual. It is an imperative which obliges *each and every* man and woman, as well as
societies and nations. In particular, it obliges the Catholic
Church and the other Churches and Ecclesial Communities,
with which we are completely willing to collaborate in this field.
In this sense, just as we Catholics invite our Christian brethren
to share in our initiatives, so too we declare that we are ready
to collaborate in theirs, and we welcome the invitations presented to us. In this pursuit of integral human development we
can also do much with the members of other religions, as in fact
is being done in various places.

Collaboration in the development of the whole person and
of every human being is in fact a duty of *all towards all*, and
must be shared by the four parts of the world: East and West,
North and South; or, as we say today, by the different "worlds."
If, on the contrary, people try to achieve it in only one part, or
in only one world, they do so at the expense of the others; and,
precisely because the others are ignored, their own development
becomes exaggerated and misdirected.

Peoples or *nations* too have a right to their own full development, which while including — as already said — the economic

and social aspects, should also include individual cultural identity and openness to the transcendent. Not even the need for development can be used as an excuse for imposing on others one's own way of life or own religious belief.

33. Nor would a type of development which did not respect and promote *human rights* — personal and social, economic and political, including the *rights of nations and peoples* — be really *worthy of man*.

Today, perhaps more than in the past, the *intrinsic contradiction* of a development limited *only* to its economic element is seen more clearly. Such development easily subjects the human person and his deepest needs to the demands of economic planning and selfish profit.

The *intrinsic connection* between authentic development and respect for human rights once again reveals the *moral* character of development: the true elevation of man, in conformity with the natural and historical vocation of each individual, is not attained *only* by exploiting the abundance of goods and services, or by having available perfect infrastructures.

When individuals and communities do not see a rigorous respect for the moral, cultural and spiritual requirements, based on the dignity of the person and on the proper identity of each community, beginning with the family and religious societies, then all the rest — availability of goods, abundance of technical resources applied to daily life, a certain level of material well-being — will prove unsatisfying and in the end contemptible. The Lord clearly says this in the Gospel, when he calls the attention of all to the true hierarchy of values: "For what will it profit a man, if he gains the whole world and forfeits his life?" (Mt 16:26).

True development, in keeping with the *specific* needs of the human being — man or woman, child, adult or old person — implies, especially for those who actively share in this process and are responsible for it, a lively *awareness* of the *value* of the rights of all and of each person. It likewise implies a lively awareness of the need to respect the right of every individual to the full use of the benefits offered by science and technology.

On the *internal level* of every nation, respect for all rights takes on great importance, especially: the right to life at every stage of its existence; the rights of the family, as the basic social community, or "cell of society"; justice in employment relationships; the rights inherent in the life of the political community as such; the rights based on the *transcendent vocation* of the human being, beginning with the right of freedom to profess and practice one's own religious belief.

On the *international level*, that is, the level of relations between States or, in present-day usage, between the different "worlds," there must be complete *respect* for the identity of each people, with its own historical and cultural characteristics. It is likewise essential, as the Encyclical *Populorum Progressio* already asked, to recognize each people's equal right "to be seated at the table of the common banquet,"[61] instead of lying outside the door like Lazarus, while "the dogs come and lick his sores" (cf. Lk 16:21). Both peoples and individuals must enjoy the *fundamental equality*[62] which is the basis, for example, of the Charter of the United Nations Organization: the equality which is the basis of the right of all to share in the process of full development.

In order to be genuine, development must be achieved within the framework of *solidarity* and *freedom*, without ever sacrificing either of them under whatever pretext. The moral character of development and its necessary promotion are emphasized when the most rigorous respect is given to all the demands deriving from the order of *truth* and *good* proper to the human person. Furthermore the Christian who is taught to see that man is the image of God, called to share in the truth and the good which is *God himself*, does not understand a commitment to development and its application which excludes regard and respect for the unique dignity of this "image." In other words, true development must be based on *love of God and neighbor*, and must help to promote the relationships between individuals and society. This is the "civilization of love" of which Paul VI often spoke.

34. Nor can the moral character of development exclude respect *for the beings which constitute* the natural world, which the ancient Greeks — alluding precisely to the *order* which distinguishes it — called the "cosmos." Such realities also demand re-

spect, by virtue of a threefold consideration which it is useful to reflect upon carefully.

The *first* consideration is the appropriateness of acquiring a *growing awareness* of the fact that one cannot use with impunity the different categories of beings, whether living or inanimate — animals, plants, the natural elements — simply as one wishes, according to one's own economic needs. On the contrary, one must take into account *the nature of each being* and of its *mutual connection* in an ordered system, which is precisely the "cosmos."

The *second consideration* is based on the realization — which is perhaps more urgent — that *natural resources* are limited; some are not, as it is said, *renewable*. Using them as if they were inexhaustible, with *absolute dominion*, seriously endangers their availability not only for the present generation but above all for generations to come.

The *third consideration* refers directly to the consequences of a certain type of development on the *quality of life* in the industrialized zones. We all know that the direct or indirect result of industrialization is, ever more frequently, the pollution of the environment, with serious consequences for the health of the population.

Once again it is evident that development, the planning which governs it, and the way in which resources are used must include respect for moral demands. One of the latter undoubtedly imposes limits on the use of the natural world. The dominion granted to man by the Creator is not an absolute power, nor can one speak of a freedom to "use and misuse," or to dispose of things as one pleases. The limitation imposed from the beginning by the Creator himself and expressed symbolically by the prohibition not to "eat of the fruit of the tree" (cf. Gen 2:16–17) shows clearly enough that, when it comes to the natural world, we are subject not only to biological laws but also to moral ones, which cannot be violated with impunity.

A true concept of development cannot ignore the use of the elements of nature, the renewability of resources and the consequences of haphazard industrialization — three considerations which alert our consciences to the *moral dimension* of development.[63]

V. A THEOLOGICAL READING OF MODERN PROBLEMS

35. Precisely because of the essentially moral character of development, it is clear that the *obstacles* to development likewise have a moral character. If in the years since the publication of Pope Paul's Encyclical there has been no development—or very little, irregular, or even contradictory development—the reasons are not only economic. As has already been said, political motives also enter in. For the decisions which either accelerate or slow down the development of peoples are really political in character. In order to overcome the misguided mechanisms mentioned earlier and to replace them with new ones which will be more just and in conformity with the common good of humanity, an effective political will is needed. Unfortunately, after analyzing the situation we have to conclude that this political will has been insufficient.

In a document of a pastoral nature such as this, an analysis limited exclusively to the economic and political causes of underdevelopment (and, *mutatis mutandis,* of so-called superdevelopment) would be incomplete. It is therefore necessary to single out the *moral causes* which, with respect to the behavior of *individuals* considered as *responsible persons,* interfere in such a way as to slow down the course of development and hinder its full achievement.

Similarly, when the scientific and technical resources are available which, with the necessary concrete political decisions, ought to help lead peoples to true development, the main obstacles to development will be overcome only by means of *essentially moral decisions.* For believers, and especially for Christians, these decisions will take their inspiration from the principles of faith, with the help of divine grace.

36. It is important to note therefore that a world which is divided into blocs, sustained by rigid ideologies, and in which instead of interdependence and solidarity different forms of imperialism hold sway, can only be a world subject to structures of sin. The sum total of the negative factors working against a true awareness of the universal *common good,* and the need to

further it, gives the impression of creating, in persons and institutions, an obstacle which is difficult to overcome.[64]

If the present situation can be attributed to difficulties of various kinds, it is not out of place to speak of "structures of sin," which, as I stated in my Apostolic Exhortation *Reconciliatio et Paenitentia,* are rooted in personal sin, and thus always linked to the *concrete acts* of individuals who introduce these structures, consolidate them and make them difficult to remove.[65] And thus they grow stronger, spread, and become the source of other sins, and so influence people's behavior.

"Sin" and "structures of sin" are categories which are seldom applied to the situation of the contemporary world. However, one cannot easily gain a profound understanding of the reality that confronts us unless we give a name to the root of the evils which afflict us.

One can certainly speak of "selfishness" and of "shortsightedness," of "mistaken political calculations" and "imprudent economic decisions." And in each of these evaluations one hears an echo of an ethical and moral nature. Man's condition is such that a more profound analysis of individuals' actions and omissions cannot be achieved without implying, in one way or another, judgments or references of an ethical nature.

This evaluation is in itself *positive,* especially if it is completely consistent and if it is based on faith in God and on his law, which commands what is good and forbids evil.

In this consists the difference between socio-political analysis and formal reference to "sin" and the "structures of sin." According to this latter viewpoint, there enter in the will of the Triune God, his plan for humanity, his justice and his mercy. The God who is *rich in mercy, the Redeemer of man, the Lord and giver of life,* requires from people clear-cut attitudes which express themselves also in actions or omissions toward one's neighbor. We have here a reference to the "second tablet" of the Ten Commandments (cf. Ex 20:12–17; Dt 5:16–21). Not to observe these is to offend God and hurt one's neighbor, and to introduce into the world influences and obstacles which go far beyond the actions and brief life span of an individual. This also involves interference in the process of the development of peoples, the delay or slowness of which must be judged also in this light.

37. This *general analysis,* which is religious in nature, can be supplemented by *a number of particular considerations* to demonstrate that among the actions and attitudes opposed to the will of God, the good of neighbor and the "structures" created by them, two are very typical: on the one hand, the *all-consuming desire for profit,* and on the other, *the thirst for power,* with the intention of imposing one's will upon others. In order to characterize better each of these attitudes, one can add the expression: "at any price." In other words, we are faced with the *absolutizing* of human attitudes with all its possible consequences.

Since these attitudes can exist independently of each other, they can be separated; however in today's world both are *indissolubly united,* with one or the other predominating.

Obviously, not only individuals fall victim to this double attitude of sin; nations and blocs can do so too. And this favors even more the introduction of the "structures of sin" of which I have spoken. If certain forms of modern "imperialism" were considered in the light of these moral criteria, we would see that hidden behind certain decisions, apparently inspired only by economics or politics, are real forms of idolatry: of money, ideology, class, technology.

I have wished to introduce this type of analysis above all in order to point out the true *nature* of the evil which faces us with respect to the development of peoples: it is a question of a *moral evil,* the fruit of *many sins* which lead to "structures of sin." To diagnose the evil in this way is to identify precisely, on the level of human conduct, *the path to be followed* in order *to overcome it.*

38. This path is *long and complex,* and what is more it is constantly threatened because of the intrinsic frailty of human resolutions and achievements, and because of the *mutability* of very unpredictable and external circumstances. Nevertheless, one must have the courage to set out on this path, and, where some steps have been taken or a part of the journey made, the courage to go on to the end.

In the context of these reflections, the decision to set out or to continue the journey involves, above all, a *moral* value which men and women of faith recognize as a demand of God's will, the only true foundation of an absolutely binding ethic.

One would hope that also men and women without an explicit faith would be convinced that the obstacles to integral development are not only economic but rest on *more profound attitudes* which human beings can make into absolute values. Thus one would hope that all those who, to some degree or other, are responsible for ensuring a "more human life" for their fellow human beings, whether or not they are inspired by a religious faith, will become fully aware of the urgent need to *change* the *spiritual attitudes* which define each individual's relationship with self, with neighbor, with even the remotest human communities, and with nature itself; and all of this in view of higher values such as the *common good* or, to quote the felicitous expression of the Encyclical *Populorum Progressio,* the full development "of the whole individual and of all people."[66]

For *Christians,* as for all who recognize the precise theological meaning of the word "sin," a change of behavior or mentality or mode of existence is called "conversion," to use the language of the Bible (cf. Mk 13:3, 5; Is 30:15). This conversion specifically entails a relationship to God, to the sin committed, to its consequences and hence to one's neighbor, either an individual or a community. It is God, in "whose hands are the hearts of the powerful"[67] and the hearts of all, who according to his own promise and by the power of his Spirit can transform "hearts of stone" into "hearts of flesh" (cf. Ezek 36:26).

On the path toward the desired conversion, toward the overcoming of the moral obstacles to development, it is already possible to point to the *positive* and *moral value* of the growing awareness of *interdependence* among individuals and nations. The fact that men and women in various parts of the world feel personally affected by the injustices and violations of human rights committed in distant countries, countries which perhaps they will never visit, is a further sign of a reality transformed into *awareness,* thus acquiring a *moral* connotation.

It is above all a question of *interdependence,* sensed as a *system determining* relationships in the contemporary world, in its economic, cultural, political and religious elements, and accepted as a *moral category.* When interdependence becomes recognized in this way, the correlative response as a moral and social attitude, as a "virtue," is *solidarity.* This then is not a feeling of vague compassion or shallow distress at the misfortunes of so many people, both near and far. On the contrary, it is *a firm and persevering determination* to commit oneself to the *common good*; that is to say to the good of all and of each individual, because we are *all* really responsible *for all.* This determination is based on the *solid* conviction that what is hindering full development is that desire for profit and that thirst for power already mentioned. These attitudes and "structures of sin" are only conquered—presupposing the help of divine grace—by a *diametrically opposed attitude*: a commitment to the good of one's neighbor with the readiness, in the gospel sense, to "lose oneself" for the sake of the other instead of exploiting him, and to "serve him" instead of oppressing him for one's own advantage (cf. Mt 10:40–42; 20:25; Mk 10:42–45; Lk 22:25–27).

39. The exercise of solidarity *within each society* is valid when its members recognize one another as persons. Those who are more influential, because they have a greater share of goods and common services, should feel *responsible* for the weaker and be ready to share with them all they possess. Those who are weaker, for their part, in the same spirit of *solidarity,* should not adopt a purely *passive* attitude or one that is *destructive* of the social fabric, but, while claiming their legitimate rights, should do what they can for the good of all. The intermediate groups, in their turn, should not selfishly insist on their particular interests, but respect the interests of others.

Positive signs in the contemporary world are the *growing awareness* of the solidarity of the poor among themselves, their *efforts to support one another,* and their *public demonstrations* on the social scene which, without recourse to violence, present their own needs and rights in the face of the inefficiency or corruption of the public authorities. By virtue of her own evangelical duty the Church feels called to take her stand beside the poor, to discern the justice of their requests, and to help satisfy them, without losing sight of the good of groups in the context of the common good.

The same criterion is applied by analogy in international relationships. Interdependence must be transformed into *solidarity,* based upon the principle that the goods of creation *are meant for all.* That which human industry produces through the processing of raw materials, with the contribution of work, must serve equally for the good of all.

Surmounting every type of *imperialism* and determination to preserve their *own hegemony,* the stronger and richer nations must have a sense of moral *responsibility* for the other nations, so that a *real international system* may be established which will rest on the foundation of the *equality* of all peoples and on the necessary respect for their legitimate differences. The economically weaker countries, or those still at subsistence level, must be enabled, with the assistance of other peoples and of the international community, to make a contribution of their own to the common good with their treasures of *humanity* and *culture,* which otherwise would be lost for ever.

Solidarity helps us to see the "other" — whether a *person, people or nation* — not just as some kind of instrument, with a work capacity and physical strength to be exploited at low cost and then discarded when no longer useful, but as our "neighbor," a "helper" (cf. Gen 2:18–20), to be made a sharer, on a par with ourselves, in the banquet of life to which all are equally invited by God. Hence the importance of reawakening the *religious awareness* of individuals and peoples.

Thus the exploitation, oppression and annihilation of others are excluded. These facts, in the present division of the world into opposing blocs, combine to produce the *danger of war* and an excessive preoccupation with personal security, often to the detriment of the autonomy, freedom of decision, and even the territorial integrity of the weaker nations situated within the so-called "areas of influence" or "safety belts."

The "structures of sin" and the sins which they produce are likewise radically opposed to *peace and development,* for development, in the familiar expression of Pope Paul's encyclical, is "the new name for peace."[68]

In this way, the solidarity which we propose is the *path to peace and at the same time to development.* For world peace is inconceivable unless the world's leaders come to recognize that *interdependence* in itself demands the abandonment of the politics of blocs, the sacrifice of all forms of economic, military or political imperialism, and the transformation of mutual distrust into *collaboration.* This is precisely the *act proper* to solidarity among individuals and nations.

The motto of the pontificate of my esteemed predecessor Pius XII was *Opus iustitiae pax,* peace as the fruit of justice. Today one could say, with the same exactness and the same power of biblical inspiration (cf. Is 32:17; Jas 3:18): *Opus solidaritatis pax,* peace as the fruit of solidarity.

The goal of peace, so desired by everyone, will certainly be achieved through the putting into effect of social and international justice, but also through the practice of the virtues which favor togetherness, and which teach us to live in unity, so as to build in unity, by giving and receiving, a new society and a better world.

40. *Solidarity* is undoubtedly a *Christian virtue.* In what has been said so far it has been possible to identify many points of contact between solidarity and *charity,* which is the distinguishing mark of Christ's disciples (cf. Jn 13:35).

In the light of faith, solidarity seeks to go beyond itself, to take on the *specifically Christian* dimension of total gratuity, forgiveness and reconciliation. One's neighbor is then not only a human being with his or her own rights and a fundamental equality with everyone else, but becomes the *living image* of God the Father, redeemed by the blood of Jesus Christ and placed under the permanent action of the Holy Spirit. One's neighbor must therefore be loved, even if an enemy, with the same love with which the Lord loves him or her; and for that person's sake one must be ready for sacrifice, even the ultimate one: to lay down one's life for the brethren (cf. 1 Jn 3:16).

At that point, awareness of the common fatherhood of God, of the brotherhood of all in Christ — "children in the Son" — and of the presence and life-giving action of the Holy Spirit will bring to our vision of the world *a new criterion* for interpreting it. Beyond human and natural bonds, already so close and strong, there is discerned in the light of faith a new *model* of the *unity* of the human race, which must ultimately inspire our *solidarity.* This supreme *model of unity,* which is a reflection of the intimate life of God, one God in three Persons, is what we Christians mean by the word "communion." This specifically Christian communion, jealously preserved, extended and enriched with the Lord's help, is the *soul* of the Church's vocation to be a "sacrament," in the sense already indicated.

Solidarity therefore must play its part in the realization of this divine plan, both on the level of individuals and on the level of national and international society. The "evil mechanisms" and "structures of sin" of which we have spoken can be overcome only through the exercise of the human and Christian solidarity to which the Church calls us and which she tirelessly promotes. Only in this way can such positive energies be fully released for the benefit of development and peace.

Many of the Church's canonized saints offer a *wonderful witness* of such solidarity and can serve as examples in the present difficult circumstances. Among them I wish to recall St. Peter Claver and his service to the slaves at Cartagena de Indias, and St. Maximilian Maria Kolbe, who offered his life in place of a prisoner unknown to him in the concentration camp at Auschwitz.

VI. SOME PARTICULAR GUIDELINES

41. The Church does not have *technical solutions* to offer for the problem of underdevelopment as such, as Pope Paul VI already affirmed in his Encyclical.[69] For the Church does not propose economic and political systems or programs, nor does she show preference for one or the other, provided that human dignity is properly respected and promoted, and provided she herself is allowed the room she needs to exercise her ministry in the world.

But the Church is an "expert in humanity,"[70] and this leads her necessarily to extend her religious mission to the various fields in which men and women expend their efforts in search of the always relative happiness which is possible in this world, in line with their dignity as persons.

Following the examples of my predecessors, I must repeat that whatever affects the dignity of individuals and peoples, such as authentic development, cannot be reduced to a "technical" problem. If reduced in this way, development would be emptied of its true content, and this would be an act of *betrayal* of the individuals and peoples whom development is meant to serve.

This is why the Church has *something to say* today, just as twenty years ago, and also in the future, about the nature, conditions, requirements and aims of authentic development, and also about the obstacles which stand in its way. In doing so the Church fulfills her mission to *evangelize,* for she offers her *first* contribution to the solution of the urgent problem of development when she proclaims the truth about Christ, about herself and about man, applying this truth to a concrete situation.[71]

As her *instrument* for reaching this goal, the Church uses her *social doctrine.* In today's difficult situation, a *more exact awareness and a wider diffusion* of the "set of principles for reflection, criteria for judgment and directives for action" proposed by the Church's teaching[72] would be of great help in promoting both the correct definition of the problems being faced and the best solution to them.

It will thus be seen at once that the questions facing us are above all moral questions; and that neither the analysis of the problem of development as such nor the means to overcome the present difficulties can ignore this essential dimension.

The Church's social doctrine is *not* a "third way" between *liberal capitalism* and *Marxist collectivism,* nor even a possible alternative to other solutions less radically opposed to one another: rather, it constitutes a *category of its own.* Nor is it an *ideology,* but rather the *accurate formulation* of the results of a careful reflection on the complex realities of human existence, in society and in the international order, in the light of faith and of the church's tradition. Its main aim is to *interpret* these realities, determining their conformity with or divergence from the lines of the Gospel teaching on man and his vocation, a vocation which is at once earthly and transcendent; its aim is thus to *guide* Christian behavior. It therefore belongs to the field, not of *ideology,* but of *theology* and particularly of moral theology.

The teaching and spreading of her social doctrine are part of the Church's evangelizing mission. And since it is a doctrine aimed at guiding *people's behavior,* it consequently gives rise to a "commitment to justice," according to each individual's role, vocation and circumstances.

The *condemnation* of evils and injustices is also part of that *ministry of evangelization* in the social field which is an aspect of the Church's *prophetic role.* But it should be made clear that *proclamation* is always more important than *condemnation,* and the latter cannot ignore the former, which gives it true solidity and the force of higher motivation.

42. Today more than in the past, the Church's social doctrine must be open to an *international outlook,* in line with the Second Vatican Council,[73] the most recent Encyclicals,[74] and particularly in line with the encyclical which we are commemorating.[75] It will not be superfluous therefore to reexamine and further clarify in this light the characteristic themes and guidelines dealt with by the Magisterium in recent years.

Here I would like to indicate one of them: the *option* or *love of preference* for the poor. This is an option, or a *special form* of primacy in the exercise of Christian charity, to which the whole tradition of the Church bears witness. It affects the life of each Christian inasmuch as he or she seeks to imitate the life of Christ, but it applies equally to our *social responsibilities* and hence to our manner of living, and to the logical decisions to be made concerning the ownership and use of goods.

Today, furthermore, given the worldwide dimension which the social question has assumed,[76] this love of preference for the poor, and the decisions which it inspires in us, cannot but embrace the immense multitudes of the hungry, the needy, the homeless, those without medical care and, above all, those without hope of a better future. It is impossible not to take account of the existence of these realities. To ignore them would mean becoming like the "rich man" who pretended not to know the beggar Lazarus lying at his gate (cf. Lk 16:19–31).[77]

Our *daily life* as well as our decisions in the political and economic fields must be marked by these realities. Likewise the *leaders* of nations and the heads of *international bodies,* while they are obliged always to keep in mind the true human dimension as a priority in their development plans, should not forget to give precedence to the phenomenon of growing poverty. Unfortunately, instead of becoming fewer the poor are becoming more numerous, not only in less developed countries but—and this seems no less scandalous—in the more developed ones too.

It is necessary to state once more the characteristic principle of Christian social doctrine: the goods of this world are *originally meant for all.*[78] The right to private property is *valid and necessary,* but it does not nullify the value of this principle. Private property, in fact, is under a "social mortgage,"[79] which means that it has an intrinsically social function, based upon and justified precisely by the principle of the universal destination of goods. Likewise, in this concern for the poor, one must not overlook that *special form of poverty* which consists in being deprived of fundamental human rights, in particular the right to religious freedom and also the right to freedom of economic initiative.

43. The motivating concern for the poor—who are, in the very meaningful term, "the Lord's poor"[80]—must be translated at all levels into concrete actions, until it decisively attains a series of necessary reforms. Each local situation will show what reforms are most urgent and how they can be achieved. But those demanded by the situation of international imbalance, as already described, must not be forgotten.

In this respect I wish to mention specifically: the *reform of the international trade system,* which is mortgaged to protectionism and increasing bilateralism; the *reform of the world monetary and financial system,* today recognized as inadequate; the *question of technological exchanges* and their proper use; the *need* for a *review of the structure of the existing international organizations,* in the framework of an international juridical order.

The *international trade system* today frequently discriminates against the products of the young industries of the developing countries and discourages the producers of raw materials. There exists, too, a kind of *international division of labor,* whereby the low-cost products of certain countries which lack effective labor laws or which are too weak to apply them are sold in other parts of the world at considerable profit for the companies engaged in this form of production, which knows no frontiers.

The *world monetary and financial system* is marked by an excessive fluctuation of exchange rates and interest rates, to the detriment of the balance of payments and the debt situation of the poorer countries.

Forms of technology and their transfer constitute today one of the major problems of international exchange and of the grave damage deriving therefrom. There are quite frequent cases of developing countries being denied needed forms of technology or sent useless ones.

In the opinion of many, the *international organizations* seem to be at a stage of their existence when their operating methods, operating costs and effectiveness need careful review and possible correction. Obviously, such a delicate process cannot be put into effect without the collaboration of all. This presupposes the overcoming of political rivalries and the renouncing of all desire to manipulate these organizations, which exist solely for *the common good.*

The existing institutions and organizations have worked well for the benefit of peoples. Nevertheless, humanity today is in a new and more difficult phase of its genuine development. It needs a *greater degree of international ordering,* at the service of the societies, economies and cultures of the whole world.

44. Development demands above all a spirit of initiative on the part of the countries which need it.[81] Each of them must act in accordance with its own responsibilities, *not expecting everything* from the more favored countries, and acting in collaboration with others in the same situation. Each must discover and use to the best advantage its *own area of freedom.* Each must make itself capable of initiatives responding to its own needs as a society. Each must likewise realize its true needs, as well as the rights and duties which oblige it to respond to them. The development of peoples begins and is most appropriately accomplished in the dedication of each people to its own development, in collaboration with others.

It is important then that as far as possible *the developing nations themselves* should favor the *self-affirmation* of each citizen, through access to a wider culture and a free flow of information. Whatever promotes *literacy* and the *basic education* which completes and deepens it is a direct contribution to true development, as the encyclical *Populorum Progressio* proposed.[82] These goals are still far from being reached in so many parts of the world.

In order to take this path, *the nations themselves* will have to identify their own *priorities* and clearly recognize their own needs, according to the particular conditions of their people, their geographical setting and their cultural traditions.

Some nations will have to increase *food production,* in order to have always available what is needed for subsistence and daily life. In the modern world — where starvation claims so many victims, especially among the very young — there are examples of not particularly developed nations which have nevertheless achieved the goal of *food self-sufficiency* and have even become food exporters.

Other nations need to reform certain unjust structures, and in particular their *political institutions,* in order to replace corrupt, dictatorial and authoritarian forms of government by *democratic* and *participatory* ones. This is a process which we hope will spread and grow stronger. For the "health" of a political community — as expressed in the free and responsible participation of all citizens in public affairs, in the rule of the law and in respect for the promotion of human rights — is the *necessary condition and sure guarantee* of the development of "the whole individual and of all people."

45. None of what has been said can be achieved *without the collaboration of all* — especially the international community — in the framework of a *solidarity* which includes everyone, beginning with the most neglected. But the developing nations themselves have the duty to practice *solidarity among themselves* and with the neediest countries of the world.

It is desirable, for example, that nations of the *same geographical area* should establish *forms of cooperation* which will make them less dependent on more powerful producers; they should open their frontiers to the products of the area; they should examine how their products might complement one another; they should combine in order to set up those services which each one separately is incapable of providing; they should extend cooperation to the monetary and financial sector.

Interdependence is already a reality in many of these countries. To acknowledge it, in such a way as to make it more operative, represents an alternative to excessive dependence on richer and more powerful nations, as part of the hoped-for development, without opposing anyone, but discovering and making best use of the country's *own potential.* The developing countries belonging to one geographical area, especially those included in the term "South," can and ought to set up *new regional organizations* inspired by criteria of *equality, freedom and participation* in the comity of nations — as is already happening with promising results.

An essential condition for global *solidarity* is autonomy and free self-determination, also within associations such as those indicated. But at the same time solidarity demands a readiness to accept the sacrifices necessary for the good of the whole world community.

VII. CONCLUSION

46. Peoples and individuals aspire to be free: their search for full development signals their desire to overcome the many obstacles preventing them from enjoying a "more human life."

Recently, in the period following the publication of the encyclical *Populorum Progressio,* a new way of confronting the problems of poverty and underdevelopment has spread in some areas of the world, especially in Latin America. This approach makes *liberation* the fundamental category and the first principle of action. The positive values, as well as the deviations and risks of deviation, which are damaging to the faith and are connected with this form of theological reflection and method, have been appropriately pointed out by the Church's Magisterium.[83]

It is fitting to add that the aspiration to freedom from all forms of slavery affecting the individual and society is something *noble* and *legitimate.* This in fact is the purpose of development, or rather liberation and development, taking into account the intimate connection between the two.

Development which is merely economic is incapable of setting man free; on the contrary, it will end by enslaving him further. Development that does not include the *cultural, transcendent and religious dimensions* of man and society, to the extent that it does not recognize the existence of such dimensions and does not endeavor to direct its goals and priorities toward the same, is *even less* conducive to authentic liberation. Human beings are totally free only when they are completely *themselves,* in the fullness of their rights and duties. The same can be said about society as a whole.

The principal obstacle to be overcome on the way to authentic liberation is *sin* and the *structures* produced by sin as it multiplies and spreads.[84]

The freedom with which Christ has set us free (cf. Gal 5:1) encourages us to become the *servants* of all. Thus the process of *development* and *liberation* takes concrete shape in the exercise of *solidarity,* that is to say in the love and service of neighbor, especially of the poorest: "For where truth and love are missing, the process of liberation results in the death of a freedom which will have lost all support."[85]

47. In the context of the *sad experiences* of recent years and of the *mainly negative picture* of the present moment, the Church must strongly affirm the *possibility* of overcoming the obstacles which, by excess or by defect, stand in the way of development. And she must affirm her confidence in a *true liberation.* Ultimately, this confidence and this possibility are based on the *Church's awareness* of the divine promise guaranteeing that our present history does not remain closed in upon itself but is open to the Kingdom of God.

The Church has *confidence also in man,* though she knows the evil of which he is capable. For she well knows that—in spite of the heritage of sin, and the sin which each one is capable of committing—there exist in the human person sufficient qualities and energies, a fundamental "goodness" (cf. Gen 1:31), because he is the image of the Creator, placed under the redemptive influence of Christ, who "united himself in some fashion with every man,"[86] and because the efficacious action of the Holy Spirit "fills the earth" (Wis 1:7).

There is no justification then for despair or pessimism or inertia. Though it be with sorrow, it must be said that just as one may sin through selfishness and the desire for excessive profit and power, *one may also be found wanting* with regard to the urgent needs of multitudes of human beings submerged in conditions of underdevelopment, through *fear, indecision* and, basically, through *cowardice.* We are *all* called, indeed *obliged,* to face the tremendous challenge of the last decade of the second Millennium, also because the present dangers threaten everyone: a world economic crisis, a war without frontiers, without winners or losers. In the face of such a threat, the distinction between rich individuals and countries and poor individuals and countries *will have little value,* except that a greater responsibility rests on those who have more and can do more.

This is not however the *sole motive or even the most important one.* At stake is the *dignity of the human person,* whose *defense* and *promotion* have been entrusted to us by the Creator, and to whom the men and women at every moment of history are strictly and responsibly *in debt.* As many people are already more or less clearly aware, the present situation *does not seem to correspond to* this dignity. *Every individual* is called upon to play his or her part in this *peaceful* campaign, a campaign to be conducted by *peaceful* means, in order to secure *development in peace,* in order to safeguard nature itself and the world about us. The Church too feels profoundly involved in this enterprise, and she hopes for its ultimate success.

Consequently, following the example of Pope Paul VI with his Encyclical *Populorum Progressio,*[87] I wish *to appeal* with simplicity and humility to *everyone,* to all men and women without exception. I wish to ask them to be convinced of the seriousness of the present moment and of each one's individual responsibility, and to implement—by the way they live as individuals and as families, by the use of their resources, by their civic activity, by contributing to economic and political decisions and by personal commitment to national and international undertakings—the *measures* inspired by solidarity and love of preference for the poor. This is what is demanded by the present moment and above all by the very dignity of the human person, the indestructible image of God the Creator, which is *identical* in each one of us.

In this commitment, the sons and daughters of the Church must serve as examples and guides, for they are called upon, in conformity with the program announced by Jesus himself in the synagogue at Nazareth, to "preach good news to the poor . . . to proclaim release to the captives and recovering of sight to the blind, to set at liberty those who are oppressed, to proclaim the acceptable year of the Lord" (Lk 4:18–19). It is appropriate to emphasize the *preeminent role* that belongs to the *laity,* both men and women, as was reaffirmed in the recent Assembly of the Synod. It is their task to animate temporal realities with Christian commitment, by which they show that they are witnesses and agents of peace and justice.

I wish to address especially those who, through the sacrament of Baptism and the profession of the same Creed, *share* a *real,* though imperfect, *communion* with us. I am certain that the concern expressed in this Encyclical as well as the motives inspiring it *will be familiar to them,* for these motives are inspired by the Gospel of Jesus Christ. We can find here a new invitation *to bear witness together* to our *common convictions* concerning the dignity of man, created by God, redeemed by Christ, made holy by the Spirit and called upon in this world to live a life in conformity with this dignity.

I likewise address this appeal to the Jewish people, who share with us the inheritance of Abraham, "our father in faith" (cf. Rm 4:11f.)[88] and the tradition of the Old Testament, as well as to the Muslims who, like us, believe in a just and merciful God. And I extend it to all the followers of *the world's great religions.*

The meeting held last October 27 in Assisi, the city of St. Francis, in order to pray for and commit ourselves to *peace* — each one in fidelity to his own religious profession — showed how much peace and, as its necessary condition, the development of the whole person and of all peoples, are also a *matter of religion,* and how the full achievement of both the one and the other depends on our *fidelity* to our vocation as men and women of faith. For it depends, above all, *on God.*

48. The Church well knows that *no temporal achievement* is to be identified with the Kingdom of God, but that all such achievements simply *reflect* and in a sense *anticipate* the glory of the Kingdom, the Kingdom which we await at the end of history, when the Lord will come again. But that expectation can never be an excuse for lack of concern for people in their concrete personal situations and in their social, national and international life, since the former is conditioned by the latter, especially today.

However imperfect and temporary are all the things that can and ought to be done through the combined efforts of everyone and through divine grace, at a given moment of history, in order to make people's lives "more human," nothing will be *lost* or *will have been in vain.* This is the teaching of the Second Vatican Council, in an enlightening passage of the Pastoral Constitution *Gaudium et Spes*: "When we have spread on earth the fruits of our nature and our enterprise—human dignity, fraternal communion, and freedom—according to the command of the Lord and in his Spirit, we will find them once again, cleansed this time from the stain of sin, illumined and transfigured, when Christ presents to his Father an eternal and universal kingdom ... here on earth that kingdom is already present in mystery."[89]

The Kingdom of God becomes *present* above all in the celebration of the *sacrament of the Eucharist,* which is the Lord's Sacrifice. In that celebration the fruits of the earth and the work of human hands—the bread and wine—are transformed mysteriously, but really and substantially, through the power of the Holy Spirit and the words of the minister, *into the Body and Blood* of the Lord Jesus Christ, the Son of God and Son of Mary, through whom the *Kingdom of the Father* has been made present in our midst.

The goods of this world and the work of our hands—the bread and wine—serve for the coming of the *definitive Kingdom,* since the Lord, through his Spirit, takes them up into himself in order to offer himself to the Father and to offer us with himself in the renewal of his one Sacrifice, which anticipates God's Kingdom and proclaims its final coming.

Thus the Lord *unites us with himself* through the Eucharist—Sacrament and Sacrifice—and he *unites us with himself and with one another* by a bond stronger than any natural union; and thus united, *he sends us* into the whole world to bear witness, through faith and works, to God's love, preparing the coming of his Kingdom and anticipating it, though in the obscurity of the present time.

All of us who take part in the Eucharist are called to discover, through this sacrament, the profound *meaning* of our actions in the world in favor of development and peace; and to receive from it the strength to commit ourselves ever more generously, following the example of Christ, who in this sacrament lays down his life for his friends (cf. Jn 15:13). Our personal commitment, like Christ's and in union with his, will not be in vain but certainly fruitful.

49. I have called the current *Marian* Year in order that the Catholic faithful may look more and more to Mary, who goes before us on the pilgrimage of faith[90] and with maternal care intercedes for us before her Son, our Redeemer. I wish to *entrust to her* and to *her intercession* this *difficult moment* of the modern world, and the efforts that are being made and will be made, often with great suffering, in order to contribute to the true development of peoples proposed and proclaimed by my predecessor Paul VI.

In keeping with Christian piety through the ages, we present to the Blessed Virgin difficult individual situations, so that she may place them before her Son, asking that he *alleviate and change* them. But we also present to her *social situations* and *the international crisis* itself, in their worrying aspects of poverty, unemployment, shortage of food, the arms race, contempt for human rights, and situations or dangers of conflict, partial or total. In a filial spirit we wish to place all this before her "eyes of mercy," repeating once more with faith and hope the ancient antiphon: "Holy Mother of God, despise not our petitions in our necessities, but deliver us always from all dangers, O glorious and blessed Virgin."

Mary most holy, our Mother and Queen, is the one who turns to her Son and says: "They have no more wine" (Jn 2:3). She is also the one who praises God the Father, because "he has put down the mighty from their thrones and exalted those of low degree; he has filled the hungry with good things, and the rich he has sent empty away" (Lk 1:52–53). Her maternal concern extends to the *personal* and *social* aspects of people's life on earth.[91]

Before the Most Blessed Trinity, I entrust to Mary all that I have written in this Encyclical, and I invite all to reflect and actively commit themselves to promoting the true development of peoples, as the prayer of the Mass for this intention states so well: "Father, you have given all peoples one common origin, and your will is to gather them as one family in yourself. Fill the hearts of all with the fire of your love, and the desire to ensure justice for all their brothers and sisters. By sharing the good things you give us, may we secure justice and equality for every human being, an end to all division and a human society built on love and peace."[92]

This, in conclusion, is what I ask in the name of all my brothers and sisters, to whom I send a special blessing as a sign of greeting and good wishes.

Given in Rome, at St. Peter's, on December 30 of the year 1987, the tenth of my Pontificate.

JOANNES PAULUS PP. II

NOTES

1. Leo XIII, Encyclical *Rerum Novarum* (May 15, 1891): *Leonis XIII P.M. Acta*, XI, Romae 1892, pp. 97–144.

2. Pius XI, Encyclical *Quadragesimo Anno* (May 15, 1931): *AAS* 23 (1931), pp. 177–228; John XXIII, Encyclical *Mater et Magistra* (May 15, 1961): *AAS* 53 (1961), pp. 401–464; Paul VI, Apostolic Letter *Octogesima Adveniens* (May 14, 1971): *AAS* 63 (1971), pp. 401–441; John Paul II, Encyclical *Laborem Exercens* (September 14, 1981): *AAS* 73 (1981), pp. 577–647. Also Pius XII delivered a radio message (June 1, 1941) for the fiftieth anniversary of the Encyclical of Leo XIII: *AAS* 33 (1941), pp. 195–205.

3. Cf. Second Vatican Ecumenical Council, Dogmatic Constitution on Divine Revelation, *Dei Verbum*, n. 4.

4. Paul VI, Encyclical *Populorum Progressio* (March 26, 1967): *AAS* 59 (1967), pp. 257–299.

5. Cf. *L'Osservatore Romano*, May 25, 1987.

6. Cf. Congregation for the Doctrine of the Faith, Instruction on Christian Freedom and Liberation, *Libertatis Conscientia* (March 22, 1986), 72: *AAS* 79 (1987), p. 586; Paul VI, Apostolic Letter *Octogesima Adveniens* (May 14, 1971), n. 4: *AAS* 63 (1971), pp. 403f.

7. Cf. Encyclical *Redemptoris Mater* (March 25, 1987), n. 3: *AAS* 79 (1987), pp. 363f.; Homily at the Mass of January 1, 1987: *L'Osservatore Romano*, January 2, 1987.

8. The Encyclical *Populorum Progressio* cites the documents of the Second Vatican Ecumenical Council nineteen times, and sixteen of the references are to the Pastoral Constitution on the Church in the Modern World, *Gaudium et Spes*.

9. *Gaudium et Spes*, n. 1.

10. *Ibid.*, n. 4; cf. *Populorum Progressio*, n. 13: *loc. cit.*, pp. 263, 264.

11. Cf. *Gaudium et Spes*, n. 3; *Populorum Progressio*, n. 13: *loc. cit.*, p. 264.

12. Cf. *Gaudium et Spes*, n. 63; *Populorum Progressio*, n. 9: *loc. cit.*, p. 269.

13. Cf. *Gaudium et Spes*, n. 69; *Populorum Progressio*, n. 22: *loc. cit.*, p. 269.

14. Cf. *Gaudium et Spes*, n. 57; *Populorum Progressio*, n. 41: *loc. cit.*, p. 277.

15. Cf. *Gaudium et Spes*, n. 19; *Populorum Progressio*, n. 41: *loc. cit.*, pp. 277f.

16. Cf. *Gaudium et Spes*, n. 86; *Populorum Progressio*, n. 48: *loc. cit.*, p. 281.

17. Cf. *Gaudium et Spes*, n. 69; *Populorum Progressio*, nn. 14–21: *loc. cit.*, pp. 264–268.

18. Cf. the *Inscriptio* of the Encylical *Populorum Progressio*: *loc. cit.*, p. 257.

19. The Encyclical *Rerum Novarum* of Leo XIII has as its principal subject "the condition of the workers," *Leonis XIII P. M. Acta*, XI, Romae 1892, p. 97.

20. Cf. Congregation for the Doctrine of the Faith, Instruction on Christian Freedom and Liberation, *Libertatis Conscientia* (March 22, 1986), n. 72: *AAS* 79 (1987), p. 586; Paul VI, Apostolic Letter *Octogesima Adveniens* (May 14, 1971); n. 4: *AAS* 63 (1971), pp. 403f.

21. Cf. Encyclical *Mater et Magistra* (May 15, 1961): *AAS* 53 (1961), p. 440.

22. *Gaudium et Spes*, n. 63.

23. Cf. Encyclical *Populorum Progressio*, n. 3: *loc. cit.*, p. 258; cf. also *ibid.*, n. 9: *loc. cit.*, p. 261.

24. Cf. *ibid.*, n. 3: *loc. cit.*, p. 258.

25. *Ibid.*, n. 48: *loc. cit.,* p. 281.

26. Cf. *ibid.*, n. 14: *loc. cit.*, p. 264: "Development cannot be limited to mere economic growth. In order to be authentic, it must be complete: integral, that is, it has to promote the good of every man and of the whole man."

27. *Ibid.*, n. 87: *loc. cit.*, p. 299.

28. Cf. *ibid.*, n. 53: *loc. cit.*, p. 283.

29. Cf. *ibid.*, n. 76: *loc. cit.*, p. 295.

30. The decades referred to are the years 1960–1970 and 1970–1980; the present decade is the third (1980–1990).

31. The expression "Fourth World" is used not just occasionally for the so-called *less advanced* countries, but also and especially for the bands of great or extreme poverty in countries of medium and high income.

32. Second Vatican Ecumenical Council, Dogmatic Constitution on the Church, *Lumen Gentium*, n. 1.

33. Encyclical *Populorum Progressio*, n. 33: *loc. cit.*, p. 273.

34. It should be noted that the Holy See associated itself with the celebration of this International Year with a special Document issued by the Pontifical Commission *Iustitia et Pax* entitled: "What Have You Done to Your Homeless Brother?" *The Church and the Housing Problem* (December 27, 1987).

35. Cf. Paul VI, Apostolic Letter *Octogesima Adveniens* (May 14, 1971), nn. 8–9: *AAS* 63 (1971), pp. 406–408.

36. A recent United Nations publication entitled *World Economic Survey 1987* provides the most recent data (cf. pp. 8–9). The percentage of unemployed in the developed countries with a market economy jumped fromn 3% of the work force in 1970 to 8% in 1986. It now amounts to 29 million people.

37. Encyclical Letter *Laborem Exercens* (September 14, 1981), n. 18: *AAS* 73 (1981), pp. 624–625.

38. *At the Service of the Human Community: An Ethical Approach to the International Debt Question* (December 27, 1986).

39. Encyclical Letter *Populorum Progressio*, n. 54: *loc. cit.*, pp. 283f.: "Developing countries will thus no longer risk being overwhelmed by debts whose repayment swallows up the greater part of their gains. Rates of interest and time for repayment of the loan could be so arranged as not to be too great a burden on either party, taking into account free gifts, interest-free or low-interest loans, and the time needed for liquidating the debts."

40. Cf. "Presentation" of the document *At the Service of the Human Community: An Ethical Approach to the International Debt Question* (December 27, 1986).

41. Cf. Encyclical Letter *Populorum Progressio*, n. 53: *loc. cit.*, p. 283.

42. *At the Service of the Human Community: An Ethical Approach to the International Debt Question* (December 27, 1986), III, 2, 1.

43. Cf. Encyclical Letter *Populorum Progressio*, nn. 20–21: *loc cit.*, pp. 267f.

44. Address at Drogheda, Ireland (September 29, 1979), n. 5: *AAS* 71 (1979), II, p. 1079.

45. Cf. Encyclical Letter *Populorum Progressio*, n. 37: *loc. cit.*, pp. 275f.

46. Cf. Apostolic Exhortation *Familiaris Consortio* (November 22, 1981), especially in n. 30: *AAS* 74 (1982), pp. 115–117.

47. Cf. Human Rights: Collection of International Instruments, United Nations, New York, 1983; John Paul II, Encyclical Letter *Re-*

demptor Hominis (March 4, 1979), n. 17: *AAS* 71 (1979), p. 296.

48. Cf. Second Vatican Ecumenical Council, Pastoral Constitution on the Church in the Modern World, *Gaudium et Spes*, n. 78; Paul VI, Encyclical Letter *Populorum Progressio*, n. 76: *loc. cit.*, pp. 294f.: "To wage war on misery and to struggle against injustice is to promote, along with improved conditions, the human and spiritual progress of all men, and therefore the common good of humanity ... peace is something that is built up day after day, in the pursuit of an order intended by God, which implies a more perfect form of justice among men."

49. Cf. Apostolic Exhortation *Familiaris Consortio* (November 22, 1981), n. 6: *AAS* 74 (1982), p. 88: "... history is not simply a fixed progression toward what is better, but rather an event of freedom, and even a struggle between freedoms. ..."

50. For this reason the word "development" was used in the Encyclical rather than the word "progress," but with an attempt to give the word "development" its fullest meaning.

51. Encyclical Letter *Populorum Progressio*, n. 19: *loc. cit.*, pp. 266f.: "Increased possession is not the ultimate goal of nations or of individuals. All growth is ambivalent. ... The exclusive pursuit of possessions thus becomes an obstacle to individual fulfillment and to man's true greatness ... both for nations and for individual men, avarice is the most evident form of moral underdevelopment"; cf. also Paul VI, Apostolic Letter *Octogesima Adveniens* (May 14, 1971), n. 9: *AAS* 63 (1971), pp. 407f.

52. Cf. Pastoral Constitution on the Church in the Modern World, *Gaudium et Spes*, n. 35: Paul VI, Address to the Diplomatic Corps (January 7, 1965): *AAS* 57 (1965), p. 232.

53. Cf. Encyclical Letter *Populorum Progressio*, nn. 20–21: *loc. cit.*, pp. 267f.

54. Cf. Encyclical Letter *Laborem Exercens* (September 14, 1981), n. 4: *AAS* 73 (1981), pp. 584f.: Paul VI; Encyclical Letter *Populorum Progressio*, n. 15: *loc. cit.*, p. 265.

55. Encyclical Letter *Populorum Progressio*, n. 42: *loc. cit.*, p. 278.

56. Cf. *Praeconium Paschale, Missale Romanum*, ed. typ. altera, 1975, p. 272: "O certe necessarium Adae peccatum, quod Christi morte deletum est! O felix culpa, quae talem ac tantum meruit habere Redemptorem!"

57. Second Vatican Ecumenical Council, Dogmatic Constitution on the Church, *Lumen Gentium*, n. 1.

58. Cf. for example, St. Basil the Great, *Regulae Fusius Tractatae, Interrogatio* XXXVII, nn. 1–2: PG 31, 1009–1012; Thedoret of Cyr, *De*

Providentia, Oratio VII: *PG* 83, 665–686; St. Augustine, *De Civitate Dei*, XIX, n. 17: *CCL* 48, 683–685.

59. Cf. for example, St. John Chrysostom, *In Evang. S. Matthaei, Hom.* 50, 3–4: *PG* 58, 508–510; St. Ambrose, *De Officiis Ministrorum*, lib. II, XXVIII, 136–140: *PL* 16, 139–141; St. Possidius, *Vita S. Augustini Episcopi*, XXIV: *PL* 32, 53f.

60. Encyclical Letter *Populorum Progressio*, n. 23: *loc. cit.*, p. 268: " 'If someone who has the riches of this world sees his brother in need and closes his heart to him, how does the love of God abide in him?' (1 Jn 3:17). It is well known how strong were the words used by the Fathers of the Church to describe the proper attitude of persons who possess anything toward persons in need." In the previous number, the Pope had cited n. 69 of the Pastoral Constitution, *Gaudium et Spes*, of the Second Vatican Ecumenical Council.

61. Cf. Encyclical Letter *Populorum Progressio*, n. 47: ". . . a world where freedom is not an empty word and where the poor man Lazarus can sit down at the same table with the rich man."

62. Cf. *ibid.*, n. 47: "It is a question, rather, of building a world where every man, no matter what his race, religion or nationality, can live a fully human life, freed from servitude imposed on him by other men. . . ;" cf. also Second Vatican Ecumenical Council, Pastoral Constitution on the Church in the Modern World, *Gaudium et Spes*, n. 29. Such *fundamental equality* is one of the basic reasons why the Church has always been opposed to every form of racism.

63. Cf. Homily at Val Visdende (July 12, 1987), n. 5: *L'Osservatore Romano*, July 13–14, 1987; Paul VI, Apostolic Letter *Octogesima Adveniens* (May 14, 1971), n. 21: *AAS* 63 (1971), pp. 416f.

64. Cf. Second Vatican Ecumenical Council, Pastoral Constitution on the Church in the Modern World, *Gaudium et Spes*, n. 25.

65. Apostolic Exhortation *Reconciliatio et Paenitentia* (December 2, 1984), n. 16: "Whenever the Church speaks of *situations* of sin, or when she condemns as *social sins* certain situations or the collective behavior of certain social groups, big or small, or even of whole nations and blocs of nations, she knows and she proclaims that such cases of *social sin* are the result of the accumulation and concentration of many *personal sins*. It is a case of the very personal sins of those who cause or support evil or who exploit it; of those who are in a position to avoid, eliminate or at least limit certain social evils but who fail to do so out of laziness, fear or the conspiracy of silence, through secret complicity or indifference; of those who take refuge in the supposed impossibility of changing the world, and also of those who sidestep the effort and sacrifice required, producing specious reasons of a higher order. The

real responsibility, then, lies with individuals. A situation — or likewise an institution, a structure, society itself — is not in itself the subject of moral acts. Hence a situation cannot in itself be good or bad": *AAS* 77 (1985), p. 217.

66. Encyclical Letter *Populorum Progressio*, n. 42: *loc. cit.*, p. 278.

67. Cf. *Liturgia Horarum*, Feria III Hebdomadae III^{ae} Temporis per annum, Preces ad Vesperas.

68. Encyclical Letter *Populorum Progressio*, n. 87: *loc. cit.*, p. 299.

69. Cf. *ibid.*, n. 13: *loc. cit.*, pp. 263f., 296f.

70. Cf. *ibid.*, n. 13: *loc. cit.*, p. 263.

71. Cf. Address at the Opening of the Third General Conference of the Latin American Bishops (January 28, 1979): *AAS* 71 (1979), pp. 189–196.

72. Congregation for the Doctrine of the Faith, Instruction on Christian Freedom and Liberation, *Libertatis Conscientia* (March 22, 1986), n. 72: *AAS* 79 (1987), p. 586; Paul VI, Apostolic Letter *Octogesima Adveniens* (May 14, 1971), n. 4: *AAS* 63 (1971), pp. 403f.

73. Cf. Pastoral Constitution on the Church in the Modern World, *Gaudium et Spes,* Part II, Ch. V, Section 2: "Building Up the International Community," nn. 83–90.

74. Cf. John XXIII, Encyclical Letter *Mater et Magistra* (May 15, 1961): *AAS* 53 (1961), p. 440; Encyclical Letter *Pacem in Terris* (April 11, 1963), Part IV: *AAS* 55 (1963), pp. 291–296; Paul VI, Apostolic Letter *Octogesima Adveniens* (May 14, 1971), nn. 2–4: *AAS* 63 (1971), pp. 402–404.

75. Cf. Encyclical Letter *Populorum Progressio*, nn. 3, 9: *loc. cit.*, pp. 258, 261.

76. *Ibid.* n. 3: *loc. cit.*, p. 258.

77. Encyclical Letter *Populorum Progressio*, n. 47: *loc. cit.*, p. 280; Congregation for the Doctrine of the Faith, Instruction on Christian Freedom and Liberation, *Libertatis Conscientia* (March 22, 1986), n. 68: *AAS* 79 (1987), pp. 583f.

78. Cf. Second Vatican Ecumenical Council, Pastoral Constitution on the Church in the Modern World. *Gaudium et Spes*, n. 69; Paul VI, Encyclical Letter *Populorum Progressio*, n. 22: *loc. cit.*, p. 268; Congregation for the Doctrine of the Faith, Instruction on Christian Freedom and Liberation, *Libertatis Conscientia* (March 22, 1986), n. 90: *AAS* 79 (1987), p. 594; St. Thomas Aquinas, *Summa Theol.* II^a II^{ae}, q. 66, art. 2.

79. Cf. Address at the Opening of the Third General Conference of the Latin American Bishops (January 28, 1979: *AAS* 71 (1979), pp. 189–196; *Ad Limina Address* to a group of Polish Bishops (December 17, 1987), n. 6: *L'Osservatore Romano*, December 18, 1987.

80. Because the Lord wished to identify himself with them (Mt 25:31–46) and takes special care of them (cf. Ps 12[11]:6; Lk 1–52f.).

81. Encyclical Letter *Populorum Progressio*, n. 55: *loc. cit.*, p. 284: "These are the men and women that need to be helped, that need to be convinced to take into their own hands their development, gradually acquiring the means"; cf. Pastoral Constitution on the Church in the Modern World, *Gaudium et Spes*, n. 86.

82. Encyclical Letter *Populorum Progressio*, n. 35: *loc. cit*, p. 274: "Basic education is the first objective of a plan of development."

83. Cf. Congregation for the Doctrine of the Faith, Instruction on Certain Aspects of the "Theology of Liberation," *Libertatis Nuntius* (August 6, 1984), Introduction: *AAS* 76 (1984), pp. 876f.

84. Cf. Apostolic Exhortation *Reconciliatio et Paenitentia* (December 2, 1984), n. 16: *AAS* 77 (1985), pp. 213–217; Congregation for the Doctrine of the Faith, Instruction on Christian Freedom and Liberation, *Libertatis Conscientia* (March 22, 1986), nn. 38, 42: *AAS* 79 (1987), pp. 569, 571.

85. Congregation for the Doctrine of the Faith, Instruction on Christian Freedom and Liberation, *Libertatis Conscientia* (March 22, 1986), n. 24: *AAS* 79 (1987), p. 564.

86. Cf. Pastoral Constitution on the Church in the Modern World, *Gaudium et Spes*, n. 22; John Paul II, Encyclical Letter *Redemptor Hominis* (March 4, 1979), n. 8: *AAS* 71 (1979), p. 272.

87. Encyclical Letter *Populorum Progressio*, n. 5: *loc. cit.*, p. 259: "We believe that all men of good will, together with our Catholic sons and daughters and our Christian brethren, can and should agree on this program"; cf. also nn. 81–83, 87: *loc. cit.*, pp. 296–298, 299.

88. Cf. Second Vatican Ecumenical Council, Declaration on the Relationship of the Church to Non-Christian Religions, *Nostra Aetate*, n. 4.

89. *Gaudium et Spes*, n. 39.

90. Cf. Second Vatican Ecumenical Council, Dogmatic Constitution on The Church, *Lumen Gentium*, n. 58: John Paul II, Encyclical Letter *Redemptoris Mater* (March 25, 1987), nn. 5–6: *AAS* 79 (1987), pp. 365–367.

91. Cf. Paul VI, Apostolic Exhortation *Marialis Cultus* (February 2, 1974), n. 37: *AAS* 66 (1974), pp. 148f.; John Paul II, Homily at the Shrine of Our Lady of Zapopan, Mexico (January 30, 1979), n. 4: *AAS* 71 (1979), p. 230.

92. Collect of the Mass "For the Development of Peoples": *Missale Romanum*, ed. typ. altera, 1975, p. 820.

COMMENTARIES

1

Toward a New Methodology in Catholic Social Teaching

Philip S. Land, S.J.,
and Peter J. Henriot, S.J.

In 1991 the one hundredth anniversary of papal-guided social teaching will be commemorated. Since Leo XIII's *The Condition of Labor (Rerum Novarum)*, there have been over a dozen major documents from popes, a council, and synods, and countless statements from bishops at the regional, national, and local levels. The 1988 encyclical of John Paul II, *On Social Concern (Sollicitudo Rei Socialis)*, is the latest in a developed body of teaching on social, economic, political, and cultural matters. This body of "social wisdom" is based on biblical insights, the tradition of early church writers, scholastic philosophy, contemporary theological reflection, and the lived experience of the people of God struggling to be faithful to the religious call for justice and peace.

John Paul in *Sollicitudo* writes within this evolving tradition of Catholic social thought. He makes his own significant contributions to that evolution. The evolution or aggiornamento, begun a few decades before Vatican II, was greatly advanced during the course of Vatican II. It was further enhanced by the deliberation of the 1971 synod, to which theologians as *periti* made enormous contributions. This aggiornamento can be described in a variety of ways. It can be called a shift from a more deductive to a more inductive or historical approach. It can be viewed as the newness of "reading the signs of the times." The shift can also be understood as one emphasizing less orthodoxy and more orthopraxy—that is, a praxis methodology.

This trend toward the historical and toward reading the signs of the times is manifestly present in John Paul's statement of the church's social concerns. In a number of places it is an explicitly stated methodology. It is equally evident in the use the pope makes of this innovative methodology as he addresses particular questions.

This chapter confines itself to exploring the more explicitly methodological issues. We leave to other chapters to introduce, in probing particular questions, methodological observations pertinent to the topics under consideration.

But before discussing the methodology of social teaching demonstrated in *Sollicitudo*, it will be helpful to clarify how we are using the terms "social teaching" and "social thought." We explicitly prefer these terms to "social doctrine." Doctrine for many connotes a maximum or very high degree of authoritativeness. It also suggests systematization, organicity, completeness. On both grounds, but especially on the former, it is widely rejected. The eminent French Dominican theologian, M.D. Chenu, exemplifies this rejection in the title to his important book, *La "Doctrine Sociale" de l'Eglise comme Idéologie*.[1] Chenu dismisses the emphasis on doctrine as mere ideology.

Latin American theologians have also widely joined Chenu in rejecting the use of the term "doctrine" to describe the social teaching of the church. They believe that, far from being either authoritative or organic, the social teaching is in many instances irrelevant. Indeed, many of them dismiss it completely.

John Paul has not been unaware of this challenge to the teaching of the church. His reaction would appear to be twofold. First, he has not wanted to exacerbate the dispute by insisting too absolutely on doctrine. He has in the course of many presentations, written and oral, used the expression "social teaching" and other phrases alongside "social doctrine." Still, because of the challenge coming from liberation theologians especially, he has been much more likely in speaking to Latin

Americans—as at Puebla in 1979, for example—to insist on "doctrine."

What about *Sollicitudo*? In the passages that discuss Catholic ideas about society, the pope shifts freely from "doctrine" to "teaching." Thus, he speaks of "an updated doctrinal corpus" (no. 1), but also of a "large body of social teaching" (no. 2). In the following section, he reverts to using "social doctrine" but in the context of its need for continual renewal, and then speaks of "teaching in the social sphere" (no. 3). "Social teaching" appears again in section 6, only to be followed by "social doctrine" in section 8. In this latter section, he goes on to describe the character of the social doctrine of the church as being "an application of the word of God to people's lives and the life of society, as well as to the earthly realities connected with them, offering 'principles for reflection,' 'criteria of judgment,' and 'directives for action' " (no. 8). The three elements he names come from Paul VI's highly important 1971 statement, *A Call to Action (Octogesima Adveniens)* (no. 4).

Clearly and significantly, John Paul, in this highly authoritative medium of an encyclical, has not wanted to decide the debate over the use of the terms "social doctrine" and "social teaching." In any case, he is not prepared to abandon what appears to be his favorite, "doctrine." But whatever word is used, he wants the church to respect and profit from the social wisdom that is part of our heritage. The more substantive questions to ask about *Sollicitudo* are whether there is a social message, how it is constructed, and what it holds. This chapter addresses the key question of how it is constructed—that is, its methodology.

METHODOLOGICAL APPROACH OF JOHN PAUL II

Readers will have some familiarity with what has been called the "pastoral circle." In its more simple form it relates the experiential to the reflective in a dialogical fashion. A more elaborate form, described by Holland and Henriot in *Social Analysis: Linking Faith and Justice*, has four components: (1) *insertion*, (2) *social analysis*, (3) *theological reflection*, and (4) *pastoral planning*.

We believe that this pastoral circle can serve as a very helpful

Diagram 1

Social Analysis

Theological Reflection

EXPERIENCE

Insertion

Pastoral Planning

From Joe Holland and Peter Henriot, *Social Analysis: Linking Faith and Justice* (revised and enlarged ed.: Maryknoll, N.Y.: Orbis Books, and Washington, D.C.: Center for Concern, 1983), p. 8.

framework within which to examine John Paul's methodological approach. A brief overview shows these stages. (1) Replacing an earlier heavy reliance on speculation and deduction, we now proceed more inductively, more experientially—out of an insertion into living history. (2) This experience, in order to become the matrix of reflection, must be subjected to an analysis that defines and clarifies the experience. Only with such analysis can we adequately comprehend the full meaning of experience. (3) On reality thus analyzed, we proceed to reflect in the light of a Christian anthropology and cosmology. This reflection draws on reason and natural law, on scripture, and on theological tradition. (4) Action options can now be made, through pastoral planning, in light of this reflection on socially analyzed experience. This circle is an operation of practical reason coupled with imagination, both operating under the virtues of faith, hope, and love.

Depicted as a circular flow, the pastoral circle in fact contains these four moments in a crisscross and dialogical fashion. For instance, my Christian anthropology may well guide me to see some facts as more relevant than others. It may help me to be open to facts that I had been blind to before. I may now see that housing the poor is a serious human problem that cries out for effective response. Similarly, my reflection on scripture may help me shape my options for action. Without the Jesus story, could I easily make an option for the poor? It should also be added that the pastoral *circle* turns out to be a pastoral *spiral*, as action once taken or vision affirmed becomes the object of further reflection in the light of subsequent experience. The circle goes deeper and deeper and wider and wider into the reality of experience.

Let us now examine John Paul's methodology in terms of each of the four stages of the pastoral circle. In allotting different sections of the encyclical to different stages, we run the risk, of course, of fragmenting the pope's unified study. But we think that there is significant gain in linking to the pastoral circle the many things said in the document about the topic of Catholic social teaching. It serves to lay bare the methodological approach of John Paul.

First Stage: Insertion into the Experiential

It is in the name of being historically relevant that we are called to embrace the experiential. In the very opening section of *Sollicitudo*, the pope lays down his fundamental principle as he notes that the church "reads events as they unfold in the course of history" (no. 1). Two sections later he states that the church's "teaching in the social sphere . . . is ever new because it is subject to the necessary and opportune adaptations suggested by the changes in historical conditions and by the unceasing flow of the events which are the setting of the life of people and society" (no. 3). This "unceasing flow" that requires rethinking is reaffirmed in the next section: "the configuration of the world in the course of the past twenty years, while preserving fundamental constants, has undergone notable changes and presents some totally new aspects" (no. 4).

This seems to be a clear recognition that reality has forced the social thinkers of the Catholic Church to abandon the rigid application of natural law to the social order, as if all possible concrete situations were already envisioned by that law of nature.

It is highly significant that John Paul draws our attention to the approach of "reading the signs of the times" as it appeared in *Peace on Earth (Pacem in Terris)*, the great 1963 social encyclical of John XXIII. There the signs of the times are treated as means of discernment of evangelical values in the interior of the great social and political transformations of humanity. John Paul also explicitly links his emphasis on the experiential, the historical, to another announcement of a sea change in the approach to Catholic social teaching. This is Paul VI's 1971 *Call to Action (Octogesima Adveniens)*. That announcement deserves ample quotation:

> In the face of so many new questions the church makes an effort to reflect in order to give an answer. . . . If today the problems are original in their breadth and their urgency, are men and women without the means for solving them? It is with all its dynamism that the church accompanies persons in their search. If it does not intervene to authenticate a given structure or to propose a ready-made model, it does not thereby limit itself to recalling general principles. It develops through reflection applied to the changing situations of the world, under the driving force of the gospel as the source of renewal when its message is accepted in its totality and with all its demands. . . . It draws upon its rich experience of many centuries, which enables it . . . to undertake the daring and creative innovations that the present state of the world requires [no. 42].

This paragraph only restates and amplifies the much better known statement in paragraph 4 of *Call to Action*: "It is up to the Christian communities to analyze with objectivity the situation proper to their own country, to shed on it the light of the gospel's unalterable words, and to draw principles of reflection, norms of judgment and directions for actions from the social teaching of the church."

John Paul repeatedly turns to Vatican II to validate his ideas. This is particularly true regarding the reading of the signs of the times. One prominent commentator, Chenu, confirms from his own experience as a *peritus* at the council how much importance the bishops attached to reading the signs. He affirms that the changing situations in which persons find themselves have become a theological source (*locus theologicus*) for a reading of the signs of the times. "One knows that the council ... . recognized in the reading of the signs of the times the most typical act of a Christian engaged in the construction of the world." He adds in explanation: "The seemingly adventitious (*apparement occasionelle*) thus becomes structural, not just as a way of acting socially but as a definition of the presence of the Christian in the world."[2]

It is true that John Paul does not always follow the methodology of experience in his teaching on development. At least this would seem to be the explanation for his surprising lack of attention to some major issues in development today—for example, the central role of women in agricultural work in the Third World.

Second Stage: Social Analysis

In *Sollicitudo* John Paul shows that he has abandoned social doctrine's reliance on moralizing. An example of this tendency to moral reformism is given by Chenu, pointing to Leo XIII's *The Condition of Labor*. According to Chenu, Leo's evangelical distress over the condition of the working class did not lead the pope to a serious structural analysis of the causes of that distress.[3]

This moralizing—sentiment without analysis—can also be seen in the first draft of the U.S. Catholic bishops' pastoral letter on women's concerns, *Partners in the Mystery of Redemption*. There the bishops openly acknowledged the sinfulness of certain attitudes and actions prejudicial to women. But they failed completely to analyze what is behind these attitudes and actions—to provide any structural analysis. Were they to do so they would discover that the sinfulness in the attitudes and actions stems from structures of dominant and dominative male patriarchy. These are in large measure those structures that constitute "orders"—"holy orders"—in the Catholic Church.

By contrast, John Paul, with respect to world injustice, goes to the heart of the matter. It is structures — "sinful structures" — that are behind the injustice in the relationships of interdependence/dependency that bind the poor nations of the South to the rich nations of the North (nos. 36–37). In an early part of *Sollicitudo*, John Paul first surveys the contemporary world (nos. 11–18). He concludes that "modern underdevelopment is not only economic, but also cultural, political, and simply human" (no. 15). This underdevelopment is then subjected to a social analysis of "the economic, financial, and social mechanisms that . . . often function almost automatically, thus accentuating the situation of wealth for some and poverty for the rest" (no. 16).

These mechanisms "are maneuvered directly or indirectly by the more developed nations" (no. 16). They operate against the poor in a disastrous fashion, affecting the poor in the First World as well as in the Third World (no. 17). The pope then turns to the ruinous impact on the development of the poor countries of their enormous debts. Specifically referring to international credit — supposedly an instrument for contributing to the poor nations' progress — John Paul rightly diagnoses interest payments, under present circumstances, as a flow of capital from poor nations to rich ones (no. 19).

What is new in the analysis of *Sollicitudo* is the pope's shift from a fairly traditional view of the world to one that had received very little attention in previous official studies on development. He offers an important analysis of the consequences on the Third World of the existence of two powerful contending blocs: the West represented by "liberal capitalism" and the East by "Marxist collectivism" (no. 20). Rooted in ideological conflict and resting on the power of their respective armaments, these two "imperialist" and "colonial powers" force the developing countries to become parts of their respective machines, "cogs in a wheel" (no. 22). In our opinion, this analytical emphasis on the existence and consequences of the East/West blocs is an important example of the methodological contribution of John Paul to overall Catholic social teaching.

Third Stage: Theological Reflection

We have seen that reading the signs of the times has become a *locus theologicus*. But one approaches such a reading from a tradition of reflection. John Paul, while affirming historicity, remains faithful to traditional principles. Historicity for the pope does not preclude continuity with reflection on the sources of Christian anthropology to be found in the scriptures and in natural law. One example of the latter is the extensive use he makes in *Sollicitudo* of the analysis of human development found in Paul VI's encyclical, *The Development of Peoples* (1966). This is based largely on an understanding of the human as it manifests itself to men and women everywhere — which is natural law. But there is also heavy reliance placed upon scripture. For instance, John Paul's careful reading of Genesis leads him to add another key dimension to an understanding of integral human development. This is human responsibility for the earth and for the protection of the environment (no. 34).

A sign of John Paul's fidelity to tradition, even while espousing openness to the historical, is the great use he makes of two official church sources. We saw how much he drew for his own philosophizing from *The Development of Peoples*. But he also draws heavily upon Vatican II for his theology. This is especially true for the decree on *The Church in the Modern World (Gaudium et Spes)*, to which he repeatedly appeals.

John Paul's theological reflection in *Sollicitudo* can also be seen in what he does with his understanding of the structural character of underdevelopment. We saw earlier that he is very explicit in going behind attitudes and actions to their embodiment in structures. But he goes further to name these destructive realities as *sin*. Throughout sections 35–37, he repeatedly uses the phrase "structures of sin." Though he repeats cautions he has made elsewhere about structural sin, he still emphasizes how important this theological category is to fully understand and respond to the reality that faces us.

Fourth Stage: Pastoral Planning

In our discussion of the first stage of the pastoral circle, we saw how clearly John Paul stands in the line of legitimate pluralism in respect to actions to be taken, options to be explored. Thus he argues, "In order to take this path [toward true development] the nations themselves will have to identify their own priorities and clearly recognize their own needs according to the particular conditions of their people, their geographical setting and their cultural traditions" (no. 44). And, in the line of Paul VI's statement in *A Call to Action*, "It is not for us to give solutions" (no. 4), John Paul says, "the church does not have technical solutions to offer for the problem of underdevelopment as such" (no. 41).

In lieu of *specific directives* to be implemented—directives that in times past were frequently said to be applications deriving from natural law—the pope offers several *basic guidelines* for action. Some of these are suggested by way of his critique of their opposites. To cite only a few of these guidelines: the right of economic initiative, for the service of the common good, must be recognized (no. 15); interdependence cannot be separated from ethical considerations (no. 17); demographic problems must be met with respect for persons (no. 25); ecological respect must grow (no. 26); "having" should not distract from "being" (no. 28); solidarity must be promoted (no. 39); the "option for the poor" affects individual actions and social responsibilities (no. 42); international economic structures should be reformed (no. 43); there is an intimate connection between liberation and development (no. 46). There are of course many other suggested guidelines and specific recommendations. But these we have cited are enough to show the approach of John Paul's methodology of taking action steps.

We believe that, in fact, a major contribution of *Sollicitudo* to the development of Catholic social teaching is, precisely, its methodology. Experientially in touch with today's reality through a reading of the signs of the times, analytically focused on the global structures of underdevelopment, theologically sensitive to both tradition and scripture, and pastorally open to whatever system respects authentic human development, the encyclical demonstrates an approach to social teaching that will have long-term consequences.

NOTES

1. M. D. Chenu, *La "Doctrine Sociale" de l'Eglise comme Idéologie* (Paris: Cerf, 1979).
2. Ibid., p. 65.
3. Ibid., p. 25.

2

Liberal Capitalism

Gregory Baum

Many Catholics in North America were surprised by the severe criticism of "liberal capitalism" contained in John Paul II's encyclical *Sollicitudo Rei Socialis*. His critical remarks deserve explanation. They are, as we shall see, in continuity with the church's social teaching.

Let us first look at some of the controversial texts of the recent encyclical. John Paul II laments the division of the Northern part of the world into two blocs, organized around two superpowers, in political opposition and competition with one another:

This political opposition takes its origin from a deeper opposition which is ideological in nature. In the West there exists a system which is historically inspired by the principles of liberal capitalism which developed with industrialization during the last century. In the East there exists a system inspired by Marxist collectivism which sprang from an interpretation of the condition of the proletarian classes made in the light of a particular reading of history. ... It was inevitable that developing antagonistic systems and centers of power, each with its own form of propaganda and indoctrination, the ideological opposition should evolve into a growing military opposition and give rise to two blocs of armed forces, each suspicious and fearful of the other's domination [no. 20].

The logic of the two blocs, the encyclical continues, generates a dynamics of hostility that creates the "cold war," in some regions "wars by proxy," and even preparation for "open and total war." The encyclical argues that the logic of the two blocs also has devastating consequences on the Third World. If the nations of the South wish to develop their own resources, they are forced to choose between the two blocs and thus to endorse one or other of the two ideologies, liberal capitalism or Marxist collectivism, both of which are false, in need of correction, and essentially harmful to the developing nations (no. 21).

The church's opposition to orthodox Marxism has been constant. Communism in particular has been condemned many times. There is no need to deal with this at length in the present article. What requires explanation in North America is the encyclical's critique of liberal capitalism. What is this "liberal capitalism"?

LIBERAL THEORY

Liberal capitalism, according to ecclesiastical teaching, refers to a particular economic system as well as to the theory or ideology that stands behind it and justifies it. An economic system is called liberal capitalism when the free market is the one essential mechanism for regulating the production and distribution of goods. Of course, markets have existed for a long time. Catholic teaching, echoed in *Rerum Novarum* (1891) and *Quadragesimo Anno* (1931), has always appreciated the market as an enormously useful mechanism, but the same teaching also demanded that the market be (1) embedded in a culture of generosity and self-limitation, opposed to greed and the excessive desire for profit, and (2) regulated by public norms specifying what could be bought and sold and where and when these exchanges could take place.

The inventors of liberal capitalism at the end of the eighteenth century, protesting against the control of economic activity by the kings, argued that the freedom of the market would greatly increase economic development, generate enormous wealth, and eventually raise the material well-being of the entire society.[1]

Why would the free market be helpful to all, rich and poor alike? To answer this question these inventors developed a theory to justify their economic system. They argued that the market, ruled by supply and demand, made persons give their very best and at the same time limited the profit they could make. If merchants asked too much for their merchandise, customers would not buy it; they would turn instead to the competition that offered a lower price. The free market, the liberals argued, was the wonderful regulating device that transformed desire for gain into socially useful activity. The market liberated persons from the restraints of the past. Persons could dispense with virtue; all they needed was enlightened self-interest. While players reached for the best deal they could get, the market mechanism, ruled simply by supply and demand, would regulate the economic activity—like a hidden hand—so that it benefited society as a whole.

The liberal ideology believed that it was in the nature of human beings to strive to improve their material condition. This is often called an "economistic" view of humankind. The same ideology looked upon the free market as the marvelous institution that made the self-concern of each into a contribution to the material well-being of all. Interference in the market mechanism by the government or other authorities, even when inspired by the best of intentions, would only upset the careful balance and have negative results in the long run.

This ideology, I note, made economics into an exact science: for if persons were essentially oriented toward increasing profit and comfort, in other words if they were utility-maximizers, then their economic behavior would be predictable and scientists would be able to discover the laws operative in the economic life of society.

The theory of liberal capitalism was thought out in reference to the commodity market. In fact, the theory was also applied to labor, land, and money, which were not at all the work of human hands: they were commodities in a purely fictitious sense.

Has this liberal capitalism ever existed? The answer is no. For most persons economic activity remained embedded in the ethical culture they had inherited. And there continued to exist certain laws limiting the market. According to Karl Polanyi's famous book, *The Great Transformation*,[2] reaction against liberal theory and practice began to take place in England already in the second half of the nineteenth century, especially in regard to the fictitious commodities of labor, land, and money.

But it was only during the great depression in the 1930s that capitalism underwent a significant transformation. Relying on the economic theory of John Maynard Keynes, governments began to assume greater responsibility for the national economy. They helped the industries during periods of slowdown, they protected the unionization of labor and defined rules for collective bargaining, and they introduced welfare legislation to help the unemployed and the poor. What emerged, as we shall see further on, were forms of modern welfare capitalism.

LIBERAL DEMOCRACY

Having dealt with the theory of liberal capitalism, it may be interesting to look at its affinity with the ideals of liberal democracy. Allan Bloom's recent, best-selling *The Closing of the American Mind*[3] has again expounded and defended the political philosophy of John Locke, which, according to Bloom, was the theoretical foundation of the democractic state. According to Locke, human beings were by nature aggressive competitors, each one a threat to all neighbors. By nature, human beings were afraid of one another: they lived in mortal fear that they would be attacked and robbed of their property. Their overriding passion was to survive, keep their property, and pursue their own interests.

In the past, Locke argued, persons believed in all sorts of fairy tales pretending that human beings were good, that they constituted a family of brothers and sisters, that they were destined to solidarity, or even that a benevolent divinity watched over them. But believing these legends did not change the cruel reality: it made things worse because persons did not take adequate care to protect themselves. War followed upon war.

If only persons allowed themselves to be guided by enlightened self-interest, they would recognize that the only rational way to overcome their fears and assure their safety was to create, by means of a contract, a democratic state that would protect the human rights of all, including their property. This was the great discovery of the Enlightenment. Here people were delivered from exhortations to virtue and solidarity, and freed from the guilt feelings that their selfishness neglected concern for the common good. It was precisely their individual self-interest, guided by reason, that prompted them to constitute the democratic state, affirm the rights to life and property, and create a political space of freedom where they could peacefully increase their property and pursue their happiness.

The democratic state, then, was the marvelous invention that transformed the enlightened self-interest of all into protection for society as a whole. Allan Bloom recognized the affinity between democracy thus conceived and liberal capitalism. Enlightened political reason, he writes, "wipes the slate clean of all the inherited theories and inscribes on this slate contracts calmly made in expectation of profit, involving the kind of relations involved in business."[4]

Catholic social teaching criticized these liberal theories of capitalism and democracy. As mentioned earlier, Catholic social teaching appreciated the institution of the market and along with it, profit and competition, but it demanded nonetheless that the desire for material success be restrained by virtue and that authorities responsible for the common good limit the market in its exercise. Commerce and industry must make a reasonable profit, but the maximization of profit was reprehensible. The popes believed that the free market allowed the rich, the powerful, and the clever to triumph over ordinary persons and that good goverment had to intervene to protect the poor from exploitation. While Catholic social teaching strongly defended private property of productive goods against Marxist theory, Catholic teaching on private property differed considerably from the liberal theory inasmuch as the Catholic viewpoint associated ownership with social obligations. Property was indeed private, but its use was to serve the whole society.

During the depression, in *Quadragesimo Anno*, Pius XI even

recognized that in certain situations the state was ethically entitled to nationalize privately owned corporations: such situations occurred, according to Pius XI, when corporations had become so powerful that they prevented the government from protecting the common good of society.[5]

Still, Catholic social teaching continued to warn against excessive power attributed to the state. One argument against Marxist theory and practice was precisely that the state as the sole owner of property would end up as totalitarian master. Catholic social teaching sought a balance between the freedom of small enterprises and the government's responsibility for the well-being of all. The principle of "subsidiarity" protected smaller groups, capable of taking care of their own concerns, from interference by a higher authority, while the balancing principle of "socialization" demanded that higher authorities coordinate help from above whenever smaller groups were in fact unable to take care of themselves.

Catholic social teaching thus tended to favor a mixed economy. When liberal capitalism moved in the direction of welfare capitalism—the impact of Keynesian economics was mentioned above—Catholic social teaching looked with greater favor on the economic system of the West.[6] In the early 1960s the Vatican Council expressed a certain hopefulness with regard to the humanizing possibilities of welfare capitalism.

AN ALTERNATIVE DEFINITION

Before we come to John Paul II's evaluation of liberal capitalism, let me say a few words about Catholic social teaching on democracy. The liberal theory, derived from John Locke and still passionately defended by Allan Bloom, was unacceptable to Catholics. They rejected the idea that human beings came into the world alone and unprotected, and were by nature hostile to one another; they defended instead the traditional view that persons were born into communities and had a natural inclination toward solidarity. Catholics also repudiated the view that an institution, moved simply by enlightened self-interest without commitment to virtue, would be of benefit to the wider community. Catholic social teaching repudiated liberal democracy defined in terms of maximizing personal freedom.

However, in dialogue with a wider range of political thought, Catholic social teaching eventually developed an alternative concept of democracy. Here a regime is democratic when it allows the participation of all in the important decisions that affect their lives. This idea was explored in the encyclicals of John Paul II, especially *Laborem Exercens* and the recent *Sollicitudo* (nos. 15, 25, 44). Human beings, created in God's image, are meant to be "subjects"—that is, responsible agents—of the institutions to which they belong. If they are not allowed to share in the important decisions that affect their lives, they are reduced to mere "objects" and deprived of their human rights. Even when governments protect the common good and legislate in its favor, their measures are ethically acceptable only if they respect what the pope calls "the subjectivity" of the people (no. 15)—that is, their human right to share in the decision-making process. Democracy is here defined as maximizing participation, not as maximizing freedom—the liberal theory.

John Paul's theory of "subjectivity" has important consequences even for his perception of economics. He argues that the dignity of workers is such that they are meant to be "subjects," not "objects," of production.[7] Workers are destined to participate in the decisions that affect the work process and the use of the goods they produce. If workers are excluded from these decisions, they become "objects" of production and victims of injustice. We note that this radical teaching, expounded at length in *Laborem Exercens*,[8] is critical of capitalism and communism. For in capitalism decisions regarding the work process and the use of profit lie in the hands of owners, directors, or managers, and in communism the corresponding decisions are made by the government bureaucracy. According to John Paul II, social ethics calls for the extension of democracy (defined as maximizing participation) into the economy. Ultimately workers are to become the co-owners of the giant workbench at which they labor.[9] This radical critique calls for the reconstruction of Western and Eastern economic institutions.

WELFARE CAPITALISM

Under the impact of the labor movement and progressive political parties, from the second half of the nineteenth century on, capitalism slowly evolved. I have mentioned the influence of Keynes's economic theories during the great depression. After World War II the economic system in the West moved in the direction of welfare capitalism. Governments regarded themselves increasingly as responsible for the well-being of the national economy, for improving the distribution of income, and for creating the conditions of full employment.

Welfare capitalism can be conceived in two ways. According to a later "liberal theory," the arguments in favor of the welfare system are drawn simply from enlightened self-interest. These liberals argue that a commercial civilization can thrive only if there is social peace: it is thus important to avoid an excessive gap between rich and poor. Poverty among the masses creates unrest. It is, moreover, economically useful to allow workers to organize and fight for higher wages because then they will be able to buy more goods, become devoted customers and consumers, and invigorate the market.

There are also theoretical defenses of welfare capitalism that—beyond enlightened self-interest—rely on ethical principles such as the common good, justice, and solidarity. Such theories also lead to different practices. "Social-democratic theory," for instance, flows from an ethical vision of a just society. Improved income distribution and greater material equality are here seen as a requirement of justice. The greater participation of workers, the majority of the population, on all levels of political and economic life, is an ideal derived from the vision of an egalitarian, democratic society. Social-democratic theory relies on an ethical tradition and calls for ethical commitment.

After World War II, Catholic social teaching also recommended the creation of a just society, a form of welfare capitalism—even though the word was never used. Catholic social teaching proposed that strong government should contain and steer the capitalist economy so that it would serve the well-being of the entire nation. Government should also make laws to assist the poor and protect labor from exploitation. This Catholic social theory, based on an ethical tradition and calling for commitment, was adopted by the so-called Christian Democratic parties of Italy and several other European and Latin American countries. Christian Democracy sometimes presented itself as "a third way" between liberal capitalism and Marxist socialism.[10] Christian Democratic governments favored welfare capitalism in one form or another, even if at certain times they became the defenders of capitalism *tout court* against the socialist parties.

In the late 1970s and 80s, or possibly already before that, welfare capitalism, based on Keynesian economic principles, seemed unable to cope with the economic problems of Western society. The reasons for this are disputed by economists. In any case, the group of economists who became influential at that time, Milton Friedman among them, argued against Keynesian economics and welfare capitalism in favor of a return to the principles of liberal capitalism—that is, the reliance of the economy on the market forces alone. Their theory, called "monetarism," has been adopted with greater or lesser consistency by the British and the United States governments, and following them by an increasing number of Western nations.

Reacting to this momentous transformation, the defenders of welfare capitalism, especially those who vindicated it on ethical grounds, have pointed to the tragic human consequences of monetarist economics. As a result Catholic social teaching has become more critical. In *Laborem Exercens* John Paul II claims that contemporary capitalism has entered a new phase after the more benign Keynesian period, a new phase guided by the principles of "liberal capitalism," a new phase that will be marked by dislocation and widespread human suffering.[11]

Following the lead of this encyclical, the pastoral letters of American and Canadian bishops have offered an extended critique of the new direction of the economy: substantial structural unemployment, spreading pockets of poverty, growing insecurity of employment, increasing economic inequality, dramatic housing shortage, marginalization of persons of color and women in particular, and the return to a split-level or class-divided society.

The Canadian bishops have lamented the change in the structure of capital.[12] The free-market philosophy and the corresponding public policies have encouraged the reorganization of the economy around privately owned, internally diversified, giant corporations, operating on the global level without ties of loyalty to the societies to which they belonged. What is now taking place is the widening of the gap between rich and poor nations, and between rich and poor within these nations, and the surrender of decision-making power affecting the well-being of society, to an ever-shrinking economic elite. Governments help this process through privatization and deregulation, and by removing institutions designed to constrain the market to protect the common welfare. Relying heavily on *Laborem Exercens* and its principle, "the priority of labor over capital,"[13] the Canadian bishops have raised serious ethical questions regarding the very foundation of capitalism.

The bishops of the United States did not question the capitalist system as such. They did not deal with the foundational issues raised in *Laborem Exercens*. The American pastoral simply criticized free-market, monetarist economics (liberal capitalism) in the name of a Catholic commitment to an ethical form of welfare capitalism. It was not surprising that the bishops were vehemently attacked by the defenders of the economic policies adopted by the Reagan administration.

To defend this "neoconservative" economic orientation on ethical grounds, some authors have introduced the term, "democratic capitalism." What does this term mean? Democratic capitalism does not refer to any particular quality of the capitalist economy. It does not designate, for instance, the entry of democracy into the organization of the economy—John Paul II's proposal mentioned above. Nor does democratic capitalism refer to a capitalist economy constrained by government to serve the common welfare. Democratic capitalism refers to any form of capitalism as long as it is located in a democratic society. The term, therefore, allows one to praise capitalism in Western democracies without having to ask any question about its impact on society, such as income distribution, rate of unemployment, spread of chronic poverty, and so forth.

SOLLICITUDO REI SOCIALIS

This is the background that helps us understand the critical remarks of the encyclical linking "liberal capitalism" and "Marxist collectivism."

It was well-known that Catholic social teaching has always repudiated Soviet bloc communism, here called "Marxist collectivism." There is no need to document this. But according to *Sollicitudo*, strange as it may sound at first, certain faults of the Marxist theory are shared by the theory of liberal capitalism: both theories rely exclusively on enlightened self-interest, in liberal capitalism on personal self-interest of the individual and in Marxism on the collective self-interest of the working class. Both theories entertain an "economistic" view of human beings, both look upon economic behavior as following certain laws and hence as determined, both regard economics as an exact science, and both reject the entry of traditional values, such as justice and solidarity, into the logic of the economy.

At the same time, the encyclical recognizes that the two systems and their ideologies have defined themselves against one another:

> Each of the two ideologies, on the basis of two very different visions of man and of his freedom and social role, has proposed and still promotes, on the economic level, antithetical forms of the organization of labor and of the structures of ownership, especially with regard to the so-called means of production [no. 20].

I note that the interest of the encyclical in these two systems is quite limited. The pope's reflections concentrate on the negative impact of the North, divided as it is into an Eastern and Western bloc, on the less developed nations of the South. The logic of the two opposing blocs — this is the term used in the encyclical — creates a climate of suspicion and hostility that prompts the two superpowers to look upon the Third World not in terms of its needs and aspirations, but rather in terms of their own geopolitical strategies. The poor countries seeking development are forced to choose between one of the two blocs.

This is a tragic dilemma for them. For as they choose one side, they generate unrest among their own people, some of whom would have preferred the other side, unrest that often leads to internal division and sometimes even to armed struggles. Or again a country having opted for one side may discover that the adjacent country has opted for the other. Here too conflicts emerge that in some cases lead to war. The poor countries then become obliged to spend their limited resources on weapons and the military.

More than that, according to the encyclical, a country that has opted for one of the two blocs is then obliged to accept the ideology of this bloc, "liberal capitalism" or "Marxist collectivism," and organize its own economic development accordingly. But since both of these ideologies are false, both based on an "economistic" understanding of human beings, and both generating economic projects on a purely scientific basis, they will promote forms of economic development that disregard the cultural and religious values of the people. These alienating economic projects are bound to fail. Theories of development, the encyclical insists, must be based on an appropriate understanding of the human being, including the cultural-spiritual dimension.

The poorer nations of the South find it hard to escape from their economic underdevelopment because the international trade agreements and the world monetary and financial systems have been put into place by the powerful in the North to the detriment of the Third World. "These mechanisms, maneuvered directly or indirectly by the more developed countries, favor by their very function the people manipulating them" (no. 16). "Through these mechanisms, the means intended to assist the development of peoples has turned into a brake upon development, and in some cases has even aggravated underdevelopment" (no. 19).

The logic of the two competing blocs, the encyclical argues, tends to make both sides cling to their ideology in an inflexible manner. Indoctrination prevents persons on both sides from discovering that the system they praise does not work so well in their own countries. Persons caught in these ideologies do not recognize the danger in which they live: the endless production and sale of arms, the relentless preparation for nuclear war, and the ongoing race to increase production regardless of the damaging impact on the environment. The ills produced by the logic of the competing blocs are thus not confined to the Third World. According to John Paul II, they threaten the entire world community. We have become a civilization "oriented toward death rather than life" (no. 24).

At the same time, John Paul II believes that both the Western and the Eastern economic system can be reformed and reconstructed. He argues that economic systems are never subject to a strict internal logic, even though this is what the ideologues claim. Economic systems always operate through concrete mechanisms and institutions that have been designed by individuals and that could be changed. What is needed first, therefore, is a new spirit, the virtue of solidarity.

Guided by the logic of solidarity, the Western system could be made to serve the well-being of all the people—some form or other of ethically-steered, mixed economy welfare capitalism—and the East European system could become more responsive to the economic initiative of individuals, or—to use the pope's terminology—more respectful of the subjectivity of the people.

Respect for the subjectivity of the people is demanded in a paragraph of the encyclical addressed to Poland, the pope's homeland, and the other Eastern bloc countries (no. 15). This paragraph criticizes the total control exercised by government and party, and strongly vindicates the right of the people to economic initiative. The paragraph analyzes the paralyzing and alienating effect produced by the bureaucratization of Marxist economies and in fact by any "bureaucratic apparatus that wants to be the only ordering and decision-making body . . . thus putting everyone in a position of almost absolute dependence" (no. 15). Such bureaucratization kills the spirit of economic initiative and "the creative subjectivity of the citizens" (no. 15).

Some North American readers have suggested that this spirited defense of the human right to economic initiative constitutes a vindication of the free enterprise system. A more careful reading reveals that the text is addressed to the Eastern bloc countries and that in addressing himself to the Western bloc countries the pope offers his critique of "liberal capitalism." The Toronto-based, Jesuit-sponsored review *Compass* asked several Canadians to respond to *Sollicitudo*, among them—tongue in cheek—Mr. Bill Vander Zalm, the premier of British Columbia, a church-going Catholic and an ardent advocate of monetarist economics, deregulation, and privatization. In his response, he regaled the readers of the review with the confession that the encyclical had greatly encouraged him, because in the paragraph on economic initiative, the pope was recommending what he had always believed in—namely, the free-enterprise system.[14]

Laborem Exercens and *Sollicitudo* make it clear that the Catholic critique of "liberal capitalism" is not a call to revolution, but rather to reform and reconstruction. John Paul II here seems to believe that it is possible to create an ethically guided, mixed economy, solidary welfare capitalism—a capitalism with a human face. At the same time, some theoretical issues raised in *Laborem Exercens* suggest that it may be necessary to move beyond capitalism. I have briefly mentioned "the priority of labor over capital" and the human right of workers to be "subjects of production" and therefore ultimately co-owners of industries. In these times of world hunger, preparation for war, and ecological devastation, the important ethical debate about the economy continues.

NOTES

1. A popular introduction to Western economic history is John K. Galbraith's excellent *The Age of Uncertainty* (Boston: Houghton Mifflin, 1977). For a more thorough look at this history and the contemporary economic debate, see Charles Wilber and Kenneth Jameson, *The Poverty of Economics* (Notre Dame: University of Notre Dame Press, 1983), which follows a perspective largely defined by Catholic social values.

2. Karl Polanyi, *The Great Transformation* (Boston: Beacon, 1957).

3. Allan Bloom, *The Closing of the American Mind* (New York: Simon & Schuster, 1987). See G. Baum, "The Theoretical Life of Allan Bloom," *The Ecumenist* 27 (July/August 1989):65–70.

4. Bloom, *Closing*, p. 167.

5. *Quadragesimo Anno*, no. 114.

6. Joseph Gremillion, *The Gospel of Peace and Justice* (Maryknoll, N.Y.: Orbis Books, 1976), pp. 15–37.

7. *Laborem Exercens*, no. 7.

8. Ibid., nos. 9, 14.

9. Ibid., no. 14.

10. See G. Baum and J. Coleman, eds., *The Church and Christian Democracy* (*Concilium* no. 193, Edinburgh: T. & T. Clark, 1987).

11. *Laborem Exercens*, no. 1.

12. G. Baum, "Toward a Canadian Catholic Social Theory," *Theology and Society* (New York: Paulist Press, 1987), pp 66–87.

13. *Laborem Exercens*, no. 12.

14. *Compass*, 6 (Nov. 1988), pp. 21–22.

3

The Culture of Death

John A. Coleman, S.J.

Many commentators on *Sollicitudo Rei Socialis*, especially conservative or right-wing voices in the United States, seem genuinely irked or painfully puzzled by what they regard as a papal doctrine of "moral equivalence" in comparing state socialism in the eastern bloc (the Second World) with advanced capitalism in the West (the First World). They argue that the Western constitutional guarantee of civil freedoms places any of its moral failings on an entirely different ethical footing from totalitarian abuses of human rights.

Did the pope indulge in a total "moral equivalence" in his judgment of his two ideal typifications of these political systems? Should knowledgeable commentators have been surprised at the apparent evenhandedness of this pope from the East? What moral imperatives can Christians in the West derive from the pope's analysis of their so-called civilization of consumption?

WAS IT TOTAL MORAL EQUIVALENCE?

Note that *Sollicitudo Rei Socialis* addresses itself primarily to the *external* impact of the First and Second World on Third World development. Civil liberties or standards of living honored in the home country may not be exported. Notoriously, domestic and foreign policy do not always mesh. In this regard, the encyclical decries, in both the First and Second Worlds, variant forms of new imperialism by which "the unity of the human race is seriously compromised" (no. 12).[1]

The pope notes that in both variants of neocolonialism, "it often happens that a nation is deprived of its subjectivity, that is to say, the 'sovereignty' which is its right, in its economic, politico-social, and in a certain way cultural significance" (no. 15). Presumably, Hungary or Angola feel this burden of neo-colonialism as much as El Salvador and Guatemala! "Each of the two blocs harbors, in its own way, a tendency toward imperialism, as it is usually called, or toward forms of neocolonialism" (no. 22).

John Paul II ties neocolonialism to the East-West bloc formation itself. "It was inevitable that by developing antagonistic centers of power, each with its own forms of propaganda and indoctrination, the ideological formation should evolve into a growing military opposition and give rise to two blocs of armed forces, each suspicious and fearful of the other's domination" (no. 20). In each bloc, "an unacceptably exaggerated concern for security" (no. 22) means that "investments and aid for development are often diverted from their proper purpose and used to sustain conflicts, apart from and in opposition to the interests of the countries that ought to benefit from them" (no. 21).

When the Third World's development is caught up in exaggerated bloc formation, the arms trade—"a trade without frontiers, capable of crossing even the barriers of the blocs" (no. 24)—eats into and sabotages rightful economic development. "Everyone knows that in certain cases the capital lent by the developed world has been used in the underdeveloped world to buy weapons" (no. 24). Thus, in a bitingly ironic remark, John Paul contends: "We are confronted with a strange phenomenon: while the economic aid and development plans meet with the obstacle of insuperable ideological barriers, arms of whatever origin circulate with almost total freedom all over the world" (no. 24).

John Paul II sounds a final evenhanded indictment of both East and West:

When the West gives the impression of abandoning itself
to forms of growing and selfish isolation, and the East, in
its turn, seems to ignore, for questionable reasons, its duty
to cooperate in the task of alleviating human misery, then
we are up against not only a betrayal of humanity's legitimate expectations—a betrayal that is a harbinger of unforeseeable consequences—but also a real desertion of a
moral obligation [no. 23].

In what specific ways, then, does the pope engage in moral
equivalence in judging the East and West blocs? Basically he
poses a poised moral blame toward the two for (1) culpability
in fostering ideological bloc formation itself, with its negative
consequences for development; (2) the arms race; (3) lack of a
realistic sense of a "radical interdependence and consequently
of the need for a solidarity that will take up interdependence
and transfer it to a moral plane" (no. 26) and (4) in exporting
to the Third World two different concepts of "the development
of individuals and peoples, both concepts being imperfect and
in need of radical correction" (no. 21).

But the moral equivalence is not total. The pope nuances his
judgment and his blame. In a clear condemnation of most socialist models of development he notes:

It should be noted that in today's world, among other
rights, the right of economic initiative is often suppressed.
Yet it is a right which is important not only for the individual but also for the common good. Experience shows
us that the denial of this right or its limitation in the name
of an alleged "equality" of everyone in society diminishes
or in practice absolutely destroys the spirit of initiative,
that is to say, the creative subjectivity of the citizen. As a
consequence, there arises not so much a true equality as
a "leveling down." In the place of creative initiative there
appears passivity, dependence, and submission to the bureaucratic apparatus which, as the only "ordering" and
"decision-making" body—if not absolute owner—of the
entire totality of goods and the means of production, puts
everyone in a position of almost absolute dependence. . . .

This provokes a sense of frustration or desperation and predisposes persons to opt out of national life, impelling many to emigrate and also favoring a form of "psychological" emigration [no. 15].

Clearly, in this passage, the pope has his own Polish homeland in mind.

In the above passage and in others where the pope explicitly points to signs of hope in the contemporary world, such as "the more lively concern that human rights should be respected" (no. 26) and growing ecological concern, the encyclical does not accord total moral equivalence to East and West. In their own societies, the pope yields implicitly, the West respects economic initiative and other human rights, although they are not always exported in its dealings with the Third World. Assuredly, concern for fostering human rights and an ecological sense — although they are not totally absent as movements in the Eastern bloc — flourish better on Western soil. But, as we will see, the West's notion of freedom is often empty, purely procedural, or materialistic — a pseudo freedom which "easily makes persons slaves of 'possession' and of immediate gratification with no other horizon than the multiplication or continual replacement of things already owned with others still better" (no. 28).

Many of the critics of the papal doctrine of "moral equivalence" are intent on keeping alive an ideological grounding for a continued and strongly etched bloc formation: the "free world" vs. a totalitarian "evil empire." The pope not only unmasks the failures of the free societies to export freedom to the Third World, he clearly points to the disastrous effects of bloc formation for Third World development. Against those who want to see all global conflicts in East-West security terms, he insists on the integrity of the North-South debates on aid, trade, debt, and development as issues in their own right. Insisting on an *absolute* imbalance between East and West, in this context, skirts the papal admonition: "In order to be genuine, development must be achieved within the framework of solidarity and freedom without ever sacrificing either of them under whatever pretext" (no. 36). To the critics of "moral equivalence" the pope is saying: "You want to sacrifice solidarity in the putative name of freedom!"

THIS POPE FROM THE EAST

John Paul II is a sophisticated philosopher from Poland, critically knowledgeable of Marxist writings. Indeed, he does not hesitate to borrow, very selectively and with his own reinterpretations, from socialist ideas to mount a critique of the West. His earlier writings as Professor Karol Wojtyla of Lubin and later cardinal-archbishop of Krakow should have alerted readers to a different voice in Catholic social teaching. As George Huntston Williams has noted, "in all the discourses and writings of John Paul II, prepapal and papal, something new and distinctive is happening to the categories and terms so basic to understanding church-state relations."[2] In particular, Wojtyla takes his point of reference—as do most Polish Catholic intellectuals—with culture rather than the state as such. Without doubt, a serious and sustained critique of both liberalism and socialism can be found in the prepapal writings of John Paul II.

This pope from the East is both a socio-cultural and economic pluralist. He is also a personalist in the mold of the French Catholic thinker Emmanuel Mounier.[3] One should be no more surprised at John Paul's trenchant critique of Western materialism and consumerism than at Lech Walesa's remark, upon visiting Paris during 1988, that he found the West materialistic, superficial, and without a deep soul.

Wojtyla had especially studied Max Scheler's writings, which are replete with a theory of social togetherness. He found notabley congenial Scheler's formulations of *Gesellschaft* (society), *Gemeinschaft* (community), and *Genossenschaft* (fellowship). Permutations of these themes, modified to fit Polish society, appear in Wojtyla's prepapal writings. He had written about society in its many forms: (1) capitalistic, individualistic society (characterized by him with three terms: individualism, utilitarianism, social egoism); (2) Marxist collectivism (captured by two terms: totalitarianism and totalism); and (3) ideal community and intimate communities (these latter characterized as

I-Thou communities moving into we communities.[4]
Williams comments:

> Although in his prepapal writings, Wojtyla was well on his
> way to giving a distinctive meaning to these terms [of
> Scheler's] in sociology and sociology of religions, of which
> states or various ideologies and confessions of faith are
> reflections, he had shown the most analytical and then
> constructive interest in that kind of togetherness in which
> the sovereign person emerges, is sustained and, by per-
> sonal intention, freely transcends himself for the common
> good, namely within the *gemeinschaft/communio*, this last
> term in the sense both of sacramental communion and an
> I-Thou-we-you intimacy and mutual concern.[5]

In many ways, this pope, unlike his recent predecessors who
enjoyed a rich experience in the Vatican diplomatic corps, is
much more fuzzy and less focused in defining his notions of
either state or economy. Critics have claimed that in both *Sollicitudo Rei Socialis* and *Laborem Exercens*, John Paul II carica-
tures modern welfare capitalism, equating it with the rigid
capitalism and doctrinaire laissez-faire liberalism of the early
nineteenth century which, these critics claim, no longer exists
except in peripheral groups. They counterpose their arguments
for the superior economic productivity (even when it touches
the issue of caring for the poor) and the superior justice of
Western liberal democracies over every existent Marxist economy and state.[6] Although there is some merit to their claims for
the superiority of advanced capitalism and the liberal state,
when these claims are based on recourse to economic productivity or political science, these critics frequently simply bypass
the impact of the papal critique, which is primarily cultural and
moral rather than economic or political in the narrow sense.
For, surely, neither Marxist nor Western liberal states and economies successfully educate for "that form of togetherness in
which sovereign persons emerge, are sustained and, by personal
intention, freely transcend themselves for the common good."
From this vantage point, a certain moral equivalence of the ideological blocs seems in order.

A hint of this sort of principally *cultural* analysis of the two blocs can be found in the announcement for the first issue of the journal *Il Nuovo Areopago*, edited by Professor Stanislaw Grygiel of Krakow, a close friend and ally of the pope. The pope called Grygiel to Rome to become the founding director of the new Institute of Polish Christian Culture, which publishes *Il Nuovo Areopago*. Grygiel points out in the announcement for the journal that "in the Europe of today, whether democratic or totalitarian, there still prevails the same 'iron law of slavery imposed by the materialism of civilization, which excludes the liberty of the Resurrection,' and which upholds, like the Epicureanism of the Areopagus, 'the wisdom of death with limits on human possibilities' and 'the totalary culture of death.' "[7] The culture of both blocs is seen as a culture of death. There can be little doubt that Grygiel's formulation reflects the pope's own deep concern for the essential unity of Europe, a Europe of Christendom, a unity that must be fostered culturally and ecumenically and, eventually, must take on ecclesiastical and political form.

In both *Laborem Exercens* and *Sollicitudo Rei Socialis* the pope's main intention is to commend his practical proposals to responsible persons in *any* system (East or West, North or South), to ease tensions between the blocs and within societies and industries in any and every society, to restrain the exploitation of the underdeveloped nations by supranational, multinational, or ideological combinations, indeed by any inordinate corporate economic power that lies outside appropriate national and international regulations.[8] No one who knows the *oeuvre* of Karol Wojtyla, papal or prepapal, should have been surprised by the apparent evenhandedness of this pope from the East. For had he not declared in his address to the Union of European Broadcasters on April 3, 1981, in a commemoration of the fiftieth anniversary of Radio Vatican:

> The Apostolic See places itself above all the diversity of ideology but at the same time it nourishes, as it has always done, a profound respect for the grand variety of cultures in which the evangelical message incarnates itself among diverse peoples and it is open to every form of fruitful

collaboration with Christians of other confessions, with the believers of other great religions, and with persons of good-will.[9]

THE WESTERN CIVILIZATION OF CONSUMPTION

The pope especially accentuates in *Sollicitudo Rei Socialis* the civilization of consumption, which fosters "artificial needs" (no. 29). He explains:

> In fact there is a better understanding today that the mere accumulation of goods and services, even for the benefit of the majority, is not enough for the realization of human happiness. . . . Side by side with the miseries of underdevelopment, themselves unacceptable, we find ourselves up against a form of superdevelopment, equally inadmissible, because, like the former, it is contrary to what is good and makes for true happiness. This superdevelopment, which consists of an excessive availability of every kind of material goods, easily makes people slaves of "possession" and of immediate gratification with no other horizon than the multiplication or continual replacement of things already owned with others still better. This is the so-called civilization of consumption or consumerism, which involves so much throwing away and waste. An object already owned but now superceded by something better is discarded with no thought of its possible lasting value in itself nor of some other human being who is poorer.
>
> All of us experience firsthand the sad effects of this blind submission to pure consumerism: in the first place a crass materialism and at the same time a radical dissatisfaction because one quickly learns—unless one is shielded from the flood of publicity and ceaseless and tempting offers of the products—that the more one possesses the more one wants, while deeper aspirations remain unsatisfied and perhaps even stifled. . . . The evil does not consist in "having" as such, but in possessing without regard for the quality and the ordered hierarchy of the goods one has [no. 28].

Elsewhere, John Paul also speaks of real forms of idolatry, hidden behind certain decisions, apparently inspired only by economics or politics: the idolatries of money, ideology, class, technology (no. 37).

In the rest of this chapter, I want to expand on the rather consistent papal decrying of individualism (as opposed to the moral virtue of solidarity; see no. 35), consumerism, and the idolatry of technology and, secondly, suggest what moral imperatives we Christians in the West can derive from the papal encyclical's analysis of the so-called civilization of consumption. I will argue that in the West, and especially in the United States, consumerism, the idolatry of the technological paradigm and the technical "fix" and individualism are both very deeply rooted in culture and intertwined. The task, then, will be to attain a certain level of cultural literacy (to become both aware and on guard about the deformations and power of these three) and to seek elements of culture that counteract them. Finally, following the papal exhortation at the end of this encyclical, I will suggest that we need to seek out (discern and unite with) both movements of liberation for the poor in our own settings and movements that promote greater communal solidarity.

CONSUMERISM

What is a culture of consumerism? On what structural elements does it rest (this pope is not too strong on structural as opposed to cultural analysis)? What are its main cultural themes? How pervasive are these in America? Are there alternative cultural currents in American life to restrain the culture of consumerism?

Consumer culture represents a highly complex social construction. It is not well understood by the tendency among many commentators to moralize about it from an elitist perspective. We wrongly perceive the relationship of consumers to producers if we assume that consumers have no control or are passive victims. Involvement in a consumer culture results from active choices and a "buying into the project" by consumers. A consumer culture is neither imposed by conspiracy from above nor acquiesced in passively from below.[10]

Persons also draw from it selectively. They accept some aspects of it and reject others. As an analytic element, consumer culture remains partially autonomous: it possesses its own themes, materials, and mechanisms. We cannot totally reduce it to some other factor, even to corporate capitalism as such.

British sociologist John Hargreaves articulates the major themes of a culture of capitalism:

It is the way other discourses and practices are articulated around features of a consumer culture, and the way the whole complex is orchestrated by certain key themes, that gives it its coherence and power. The orchestrating themes of this culture are directed at selling a specifically modern pagan version of the good life. The dominant discourse/practice is of youth, beauty, romance, sexual attraction, energy, fitness, health, movement, excitement, adventure, freedom, exotica, luxury, enjoyment, entertainment, fun. Above all, this culture valorizes "self-expression." A truly astonishing variety of goods and services—from washing powder, cars, and foreign holidays, to cosmetics, fashionwear, eating, and aerobics circulate on this basis; and concomitantly, major segments of social life are organized around consumer culture.[11]

To nurture and sustain it, consumer culture relies on important structural elements in advanced capitalist society: the growing centralization of economic power among producers; the extended scale of bureaucratic control and market operations; the growing remoteness of controllers and decision-makers from local sites of decision; the packaging of family entertainment and sport and leisure time.

Consumerism reinforces excessive individualism:

What we encounter especially is a meticulous attention to those aspects of their lives that are deeply personal to people. The close attention to what is personally important can be seen in the way, for example, one's appearance (how one dresses, what cosmetics to use, whether one is too fat, how good one's teeth are), how one feels (headache? confident? happy?) and even how one smells are given priority. The discourse selects, from the range of experience, certain ways in which we are affected personally and offers personal solutions. Collective concerns and collective, as opposed to individual, forms of consumption as a solution to problems are largely absent from this discourse. The collective is displaced to the level of personal reality and the individual is made solely responsible for doing something about it. The priority given to individual autonomy and responsibility and the ideal of a private existence shows consumer culture drawing strongly on bourgeois tradition.[12]

That consumer culture has become pervasive in America is, perhaps, best caught in Daniel Boorstin's remark, "it would not be an overstatement to describe advertising as the characteristic rhetoric of democracy."[13] Moreover, we now speak of "selling" candidates for public office. Consumer culture reinforces the priority of things over persons, indeed, the thingification of persons. This is what Marx meant when he evoked the phrase "commodity fetishism."

The dangers in this consumer culture—dangers both to the Christian faith and to our humanity—are evoked for us by John Kavanaugh: "We are only as we possess. We are what we possess. We are, consequently, possessed by our possessions, produced by our products."[14] Yet Hargreaves reminds us wisely:

It is not that this kind of systematically produced imbalance displaces what is important with what is trivial; it is that this culture is hegemonized through the thematization of concerns which are, indeed, absolutely central to people's sense of identity, on the one hand, and the suppression of the relationship between these and other equally important public issues or collective concerns, on the other. For example, the discourse of diet gives priority to personal care of one's body but diet is not unrelated to the problem of food production, world prices, and food shortages. Rather than express concern about the latter, consumer culture articulates diet with the issue of convenience foods and family life or *haute cuisine* and bourgeois sociability.[15]

Consumer culture's strength derives from its ability to channel and harness deep bodily needs and desires—for youth, health, longevity, beauty, sexual fulfillment, achievement, self-expression, enjoyment, excitement—to the necessities of production and economic growth. These are all true human goods. The problem lies in the hiddenness of a pervasive sense of commodity fetishism and a systematically produced imbalance lacking restraints. So long as something like the institutions of a free market and corporate capitalism remain in America—as they surely will—the only moral strategy that promises any hope remains one of recognition and restraining, tilting imbalances, correcting systematically produced distortions.

There exists an alternative American vision, against the grain of consumerism, documented for us in David Shi's intellectual history, *The Simple Life*. Shi tells the tale of the subversion, yet continual reemergence, of the American ideal of plain living in American culture from the Puritan ethic, through the simplicity of Jeffersonian classicism, down to the transcendental plain living of Thoreau and later in Whitman.

After an eclipse during the gilded age, the quest for a simple life reemerged in what Shi calls "progressive simplicity" during the Progressive movement, with its characteristic practices, which right the imbalance in consumerism: "discriminating consumption, uncluttered living, personal contentment, aesthetic simplicity in art and architecture, civic virtue, social service, renewed contact with nature."[16] After another eclipse in the post-World War I era of prosperity, the ideal reemerged again with the early New Deal vision of a cooperative commonwealth and the simple life embodied in the youth of the Civilian Conservation Corps.

In our own time, environmentalists and others tap into this persistent minority strand in American culture inimical to a consumerism run riot. After surveying the vast expanse of American intellectual history, Shi concludes:

Though a failure as a societal ethic, simplicity has nevertheless exercised a powerful influence on the complex pattern of American culture. As a myth of national purpose and as a program for individual conduct, the simple life has been a perennial dream and a rhetorical challenge, displaying an indestructible vitality even in the face of repeated defeats. It has, in a sense, served as the nation's conscience, reminding Americans of what the founders had hoped they would be and thereby providing a vivifying counterpoint to the excesses of materialist individualism.[17]

As it turns out, sociological evidence exists to suggest that there is, in fact, a substantial popular tendency to endorse simplicity as a value (to act on it is quite another question!). Simplicity as a value is endorsed in this country by a majority of two-thirds of the respondents of a recent poll. The ones who actually try to practice simplicity may cover a third of the population.[18] Luckily, then, Catholics do not have to invent, whole cloth, cultural alternatives to a culture of consumerism. There already exist movements for simple living, an ecological movement, and desires to replace quality for quantity. But we do need to educate in our church in ways that will give our congregants a literacy to recognize the rootedness, pervasiveness, and hidden agenda of consumerism (reaching even to how many Americans conceive of love and human relationships—e.g., something they want to consume) and to elicit the moral resolve to restrain its imperialistic tendencies to hegemony.

One of the truly unique features of *Sollicitudo Rei Socialis* is its recognition, for the first time in papal teaching, of the ecological crisis:

> Among today's positive signs we must also mention a greater realization of the limits of available resources and of the need to respect the integrity and the cycles of nature and to take them into account when planning for development, rather than sacrificing them to certain demagogic ideas about the latter. Today this is called ecological concern [no. 26].

The pope does not give us a developed theological vision or ethical judgment about ecological concerns. He does note, however:

The appropriateness of acquiring a growing awareness of the fact that one cannot use with impunity the different category of beings, whether living or inanimate — animals, plants, the natural elements — simply as one wishes, according to one's economic needs. . . . The second consideration is based on the realization — which is perhaps more urgent — that natural resources are limited: some of them are not, as it is said, renewable. . . . The third consideration refers directly to the consequences of a certain type of development on the quality of life in the industrialized zones. We all know that the direct or indirect result of industrialization is, ever more frequently, the pollution of the environment, with serious consequences for the health of the population [no. 34].

THE IDOLATRY OF TECHNOLOGY

In taking up the papal indications that there can be an idolatry of technology, I want to indicate my distance from anti-technological polemics such as those of Jacques Ellul or from the, perhaps, utopian schemes of someone such as Ivan Illich.[19]

We need to recognize both the promise and limits of technology. The original promise of technology was increase in productive abundance and wealth, the reduction of dehumanizing labor, and its replacement by work worthy of human skills and the harnessing of nature and matter toward human goals and for the removal of human ills. No one need subscribe to some Luddite desire to destroy the machines or engage in simple fear of them. But no one should be lured to a view that sees the deeply rooted American romance with the machine as simply innocent, value-neutral. Technical rationality and the technical paradigm can take on a life of its own and become a sort of idolatry.

There are decisive dangers to our common life in extending the technological paradigm into many or all domains. It has its appropriate, delimited sphere, but rarely remains contained there. Langdon Winner notes the tendency to expansion implicit in the technological paradigm: "The original ends have atrophied: society has accepted the power of technique in all areas of life; social decisions are now based upon the validity of instrumental modes of evaluation; the ends are restricted to suit the requirements of techniques of performance and measurement."[20]

When we make technology center rather than servant of human purposes, we eschew all notion of *telos* or purpose, for technology—pure means—knows no ends. "Neither science nor technology has a theory of what is worthy and in need of explanation or transformation. Given an *explanandum* and *transformandum*, they will explain and transform the problematic phenomenon: neither has a principled way of problem stating." For "modern science cannot embody a substantive worldview of a scientifically authenticated sort."[21] Technological progress, at its best, can only be a liberation *from*. It can never provide us with a liberation *for*.

Technology is linked to consumerism since, in its foreground, the ends of technology foresee commodities and consumption as one of its liberating promises. As the old slogan had it, "better products through chemistry." The miracle and promise of technology can yield to the skewed abundance the pope speaks of. John Kenneth Galbraith caught this skewing when he spoke of "private luxury and public poverty."[22]

Survey data points to considerable ambiguity by Americans concerning the machine in their garden. On balance, the attitude seems favorable but there lurks hidden—because unasked—in most survey questions an assumption that technology is the comprehensive and dominant way in which reality should be shaped today.[23] Technology in our society is rarely offered as something we choose—as a way of life we are asked to prefer over others—but, rather, is promoted as the indispensable basis for choices. The technological paradigm reinforces both consumerism and individualism.

The corrective balance to the deformation of modern culture through the technical-rational paradigm lies in embracing what Albert Borgmann has called focal practice.[24] Focal practices envision established cooperative human action that can conceive of "internal goods," standards of excellence of a human activity or practice inherent in the activity itself, which entail the good of the individuals as well as the good of the whole community.

Characteristically, in modern societies only "external goods"—that is, money, status, welfare, power, external success judged by technical standards—count as goods to be distributed and accounted for by a theory of justice. Focal practice focuses on excellence, intrinsic enjoyment, even play—the skill of craft rather than the mastery of technique.

Speaking of the technological paradigm, Borgmann notes:

> If there is a way of recovering the promise of technology, it must be one of disentangling the promise from the dominant way in which we have taken up with the world for two centuries now. It must be a way of finding counter-forces to technology that are guided by a clear and incisive view of technology and will not be deflected or coopted by technology. At the same time such counter-forces must be able to respect the legitimacy of the promise and to guard the indispensable and admirable accomplishments of technology.[25]

Borgmann continues: "A reform of the cultural paradigm is even less, of course, a dismantling of technology or of the technological universe. It is rather the recognition and restraint of the paradigm. To restrain the paradigm is to restrict it to its proper sphere."[26] The proper sphere of technology serves as a useful context for, but not the rule of and center of, life. For technology is blind to *telos*, the proper end of human action. When it becomes the center of life it necessarily, then, subverts the proper ends of humanity. It becomes in John Paul II's words, an idolatry.

INDIVIDUALISM

The third in our triad is individualism, a term the pope uses to describe Western capitalistic societies. Robert Bellah et al., in their *Habits of the Heart*, take up in a more straightforward sociological fashion, through interviews, the question of how Americans see the nature of successful life and society, and the meaning for them of freedom and the requirements of justice in the modern, postindustrial world. Utilitarian and expressive individualism, these authors argue, are the dominant sociological moral logic in modern America. For the first, moral judgment of alternative actions consists in cost-benefit analysis of competing actions judged by a criterion of external, technical success. There are no "internal goods" in any social practices as such.

For the expressive individualist, moral judgment lodges in an intuition of feeling inwardly more or less free, comfortable, authentic. Following the logic of modern liberalism, selves are defined by their self-chosen life-projects, which lie beyond the realm of rational adjudication. The consequences for public discourse and democratic political policy are disastrous. "Now if selves are defined by their preference but these preferences are arbitrary, then each self constitutes its own moral universe and there is finally no way to reconcile conflicting claims about what is good in itself."[27]

Instead of the virtuous self defined by moral commitments and practices, entailed in free allegiance to a community of memory and a tradition of humane freedom, Bellah et al. find in modern America the socially unsituated self. Instead of work and careers as intrinsically meaningful, a locus for the practice of "internal goods," they discover "mere work" as a source of external livelihood and status. But "the absence of a sense of calling in work means an absence of a sense of moral meaning."[28] Neither utilitarian nor therapeutic individualism can carry the weight of sustained and enduring commitments.

Once again sociological research shows a reaction by Americans to the culture of individualism. A Roper poll found that 76 percent of those sampled thought business executives in large corporations acted mostly in their self-interest, in disregard of the public interest. The same survey showed that 50 percent of the public regarded "selfishness," persons not thinking of others, as one of the major problems facing the United States.[29] Once again, Catholics do not have to invent, whole cloth, a constituency open to countervailing the power of individualism.

CONCLUSION

In a recent very thoughtful book on American culture and religion, Princeton sociologist Robert Wuthnow argues to the interconnection of individualism, consumerism, and technology as a myth.[30] The deeply rooted American success ethic and the equally pervasive idea of freedom, he argues, all too easily degenerate into mere "freedom of choice" (which validates both consumerism and individualism). Wuthnow quotes, with approval, the remark of Richard Neuhaus: "Much of the course of public reasoning in America can be read from the fact that our highest appeal is no longer to Providence but to privacy.[31]

Speaking of the technological myth, sociologist Robert Nisbet has written: "Technology for many Americans is not simply a good thing; it is in its own way millennialist, offering happiness beyond earlier dreams to the world and with America leading the way."[32]

Unfortunately, argues Wuthnow, American faith in technology is virtually immune to the criticism or doubts that might arise from the risks (e.g., of radiation pollution or environmental damage) accompanying the growth of technology. Thus, too, "the mythologization of technology . . . comes at the point when a full range of public values cannot be seriously debated because technical considerations have already ruled some of them out."[33] Wuthnow deplores the craving for the technological fix:

> In a subtle, but perhaps important, way technology has, therefore, become linked with that most fundamental value — freedom — on which Americans rely to legitimate their way of life. If the marketplace gradually redefined freedom to mean freedom of choice, technology now begins to replace the marketplace as the main source of that kind of freedom. Not simply the modern supermarket, with its panoply of choices, but the Electronic Candy Store, filled with word processors and software, becomes the symbol of our expanded freedom to choose.[34]

The cultural task, then, of Western Christians when faced with the civilization of consumption, Western individualism, which subverts solidarity, and the idolatry of technology is threefold: (1) to acknowledge and face up to the deformations of these three values that embody — culturally — deeper desires for self-expression, freedom, material security, and knowledge.

(2) To seek out alternative strands, already available in our wider culture, which might counteract these deformations. (3) To seek out and join social and cultural movements that struggle for restraining or counteracting these three cultural tendencies.

In the very last section of the papal encyclical, the pope proposes two main criteria for Catholic discernment and alliance with movements of cultural, political liberation: solidarity and love of preference for the poor (no. 47). Both values (and the movements in the West that promote them, whether of Catholic origin or not) will keep our civilization of consumption from degenerating even further into becoming a civilization of death.

NOTES

1. Citations from *Sollicitudo Rei Socialis* are by paragraph number in the translation found in *Origins*, vol. 17, no. 38 (March 3, 1988), pp. 641–60.

2. George Huntston Williams, "John Paul II's Concepts of Church, State, and Society," *Journal of Church and State*, vol. 24 (Autumn 1982), p. 464.

3. Mounier, who flourished in the 1930s and 40s, held a critical but open view of Marxist movements. The writings of Mounier, the editor of *Esprit*, have been very influential for Polish personalism of the Lublin school. See the 4-volume Emmanuel Mounier *Oeuvres* (Paris: Seuil, 1962).

4. See Williams, "John Paul II's Concepts," and Williams's book-length study of Wojtyla's prepapal writings, *The Mind of John Paul: Origins of His Thought and Action* (New York: Seabury, 1981).

5. Williams, "John Paul II's Concepts," p. 472.

6. For this case of capitalism and the liberal state, see Michael Novak's two books, *The Spirit of Democratic Capitalism* (New York: Simon and Schuster, 1982) and *Will It Liberate?* (Mahwah, N.J.: Paulist Press, 1986).

7. Cited in Williams, "John Paul II's Relations with Non-Catholic States and Current Political Movements," *Journal of Church and State*, vol. 25 (Spring 1983), p. 29.

8. See Williams, "John Paul II's Concepts," pp. 477–78. The masterful commentary in English on *Laborem Exercens* is that of Gregory Baum, *The Priority of Labor* (New York: Paulist Press, 1982).

9. *L'Osservatore Romano*, April 4, 1981, p. 2.

10. See Richard Fox and Jackson Learns, eds., *The Culture of Con-*

sumption (New York: Basic Books, 1983). In the following pages I draw on my paper, "American Culture as a Challenge to Catholic Intellectuals," which will appear in a forthcoming book edited by Cassian Yuhaus for Duquesne University Press.

11. John Hargreaves, *Sport, Power, and Culture* (New York: St. Martin's Press, 1975), p. 131.

12. Ibid., p. 133.

13. Daniel Boorstin, *Democracy and Its Discontents* (New York: Basic Books, 1975), p. 28.

14. John Kavanaugh, *Following Christ in a Consumer Society* (Maryknoll, N.Y.: Orbis Books, 1981), p. 26.

15. Hargreaves, *Sport*, p. 133.

16. David Shi, *The Simple Life: Plain Living and High Thinking in American Culture* (New York: Oxford University Press, 1985), p. 176.

17. Ibid., p. 278.

18. For this sociological evidence, see Duane Elgin, *Voluntary Simplicity* (New York: Harper and Row, 1981), pp. 129–31.

19. See Jacques Ellul, *The Technological Society* (New York: Vintage, 1964), and Ivan Illich, *Tools for Conviviality* (New York: Harper & Row, 1973).

20. Langdon Winner, *Autonomous Technology* (Cambridge: Harvard University Press, 1977), p. 235.

21. Albert Borgmann, *Technology and the Character of Everyday Life* (Chicago: University of Chicago Press, 1984), pp. 27–29.

22. John K. Galbraith, *The New Industrial State* (Boston: Little, Brown, 1972), p. 8.

23. See Daniel Yankelovich, *New Rules* (New York: Harper and Row, 1982).

24. For focal practice, see Borgmann, *Technology*, pp. 196–210.

25. Ibid., p. 153.

26. Ibid., p. 220.

27. Robert Bellah et al., *Habits of the Heart* (Berkeley: University of California Press, 1985), p. 76.

28. Ibid., p. 71.

29. Published in *Public Opinion*, Aug.-Sept. 1982, p. 5.

30. Robert Wuthnow, *The Restructuring of American Religion* (Princeton: Princeton University Press, 1988).

31. Cited in Wuthnow, *Restructuring*, p. 282.

32. Robert Nisbet, "Utopia's Mores: Has the American Vision Dimmed?," *Public Opinion*, April-May 1983, p. 9.

33. Wuthnow, *Restructuring*, p. 290.

34. Ibid., p. 293.

4

Structures of Sin

Gregory Baum

It is always surprising to me how quickly certain new theological concepts enter into the church's official social teaching, even though they raise difficult ecclesiological questions for which there are as yet no answers. The radical understanding of social justice and the ethical critique of institutions found in recent papal and episcopal documents make Catholics ask questions about the justice of ecclesiastical institutions. The 1971 Synod of Bishops clearly recognized that when the church gives public witness to social justice, it will be heard only if it appears just in the eyes of the faithful.[1] That is why the synod summoned the church to an institutional self-examination.

DISCOVERY OF THE SOCIAL DIMENSION

In this article I wish to deal with the theological concept of "social sin" or "structures of sin," set forth in *Sollicitudo Rei Socialis*, a concept that represents a recent doctrinal development.

In the past, Christian preaching emphasized personal sin, the sin of individual persons. Even the church's social teaching, following a corporatist understanding of society, proposed that violations of social justice were due to human greed and selfishness and that the right order could be reestablished in society if persons, rich and poor, owners and workers, underwent a moral conversion to greater love, accepted the norms of justice, and saw themselves as serving the common good.

In the face of human exploitation, the church at that time appeared to "moralize"—that is, to call persons individually to moral conversion. This tied in well with the main trend of Christian preaching, which emphasized the need for personal conversion. Confronted with social evil of various forms, Christian preaching created the impression that if each person became more loving and more generous, the problems of society would straighten themselves out.

In the 1960s Latin American liberation theology and German political theology criticized the "moralizing" of Christian preaching. Liberation theology embraced the notion of "conscientization," a notion eventually confirmed by the Latin American Bishops' Conference at Medellín (1968).[2] It demanded that in the face of exploitation and oppression the people become aware of the institutions that account for marginalization. Part of the church's pastoral mission, according to Medellín, was the raising of personal consciousness with regard to the institutional obstacles that prevented persons from assuming responsibility for their lives. The necessary moral conversion was therefore not simply to private virtue but to a new way of seeing social reality and a new way of acting.

German political theology adopted as its program the "deprivatization" of the Christian message. J. B. Metz argued that the good news was addressed simultaneously to individuals and to society as a whole. Inasmuch as Christian preaching had advocated a highly private understanding of sin, conversion, and newness of life, political theology set itself the task of recovering the social dimension of the Christian message.[3] Sin, therefore, was not simply private malice; it also had a social dimension. Sin also referred to structural realities, produced by human beings, that inflicted exploitation and oppression on sectors of the population.

The social dimension of sin was acknowledged by several ecclesiastical documents. At Medellín (1968) the Latin American bishops spoke of situations that were so massively unjust, exploitive, and repressive that they had to be called "institution-alized violence."[4] The 1971 Synod of Bishops recognized sin "in its individual and social manifestation,"[5] spoke of the gospel as freeing persons "from sin and from its consequences in social life,"[6] and recognized "the network of domination, oppression, and abuses,"[7] built around the world, that kept the greater part of humanity excluded from power and resources. The Canadian bishops, following John Paul II, spoke of the plague of unem-ployment as a "moral evil" and as "symptomatic of a basic moral disorder."[8] In their economic pastoral, the American bishops defined injustice as the structured exclusion of persons from political, economic, and cultural participation, and acknowl-edged that since these structures were created by free human beings, "they can be called forms of social sin."[9] And the Vatican Instruction on Christian Freedom and Liberation (1986) also recognized that while sin in the primary sense referred to vol-untary acts, it was possible to speak of "social sin" and "sinful structures" in a secondary and derived sense, for unjust struc-tures were created by sinful human beings.[10]

In chapter 5 of *Sollicitudo Rei Socialis*, entitled "A Theolog-ical Reading of Modern Problems," John Paul II argues that it is impossible to understand the troubled world of today without the theological category of structural sin. "A world which is divided into blocs, sustained by rigid ideologies, and in which instead of interdependence and solidarity different forms of im-perialism hold sway, can only be a world subject to structures of sin" (no. 36). In the previous chapters John Paul had ex-plained in detail how the increasing impoverishment of the Third World, the growing gap between rich and poor in the developed countries, and the death-dealing militarization of so-ciety were largely caused by the hostile logic of the two blocs, the false human self-understanding created by the two compet-ing ideologies, and the global economic mechanisms set up by the powerful to the detriment of the poor.

Structural sins, then, are institutional realities, such as colon-ialism and imperialism, that create an unjust distribution of wealth, power, and recognition, and thus push a section of the population to the margin of society where their well-being or even their life is in danger. Inasmuch as structures and institutions have no consciousness and hence no conscience, how can they be called sinful? The encyclical gives a brief answer to this, an answer that deserves careful analysis.

Sinful structures are "rooted in personal sin, and thus always linked to the concrete acts of individuals who introduce these structures, consolidate them and make them difficult to remove" (no. 36). In a footnote, the text refers to a previous papal document, *Reconciliatio et Paenitentia* (1984), which recognized social sin and amplified on the manifold ways in which it is related to personal sin:

[There are] the personal sins of those who cause and support social evil or who exploit it, of those who are in a position to avoid, eliminate, or at least limit certain social evils but who fail to do so out of laziness, fear, or the conspiracy of silence, through secret complicity or indifference, of those who take refuge in the supposed impossibility of changing the world, and also of those who sidestep the effort and sacrifice required, producing specious reasons of a higher order.

These sentences emphasize personal responsibility in the construction and reform of institutions. If structures generate injustices—that is, reveal themselves as sinful—personal sin is committed by persons who refuse to listen to the critics, who resist social change, or who take measures to forestall it.

We note that the papal sentences cited above are not as sensitive as the teaching of Medellín to the unconscious, nonvoluntary dimension of social sin—to the blindness produced in persons by the dominant culture, blindness that prevents them from recognizing the evil dimension of their social reality. Exploitive institutions are successfully maintained because they are made to appear legitimate to their participants. Even the oppressed learn to look at their social situation through the cultural symbols supplied by the dominant classes. Sinful economic and political structures tend to create a culture of conformity and passivity. What is required before persons can be mobilized for social action is their "conscientization"—that is, the raising of consciousness so that the structure of society can be recognized for what it is. As long as there is ignorance or nonrecognition, as long as human minds — on any level of an institution — are caught in ideological prisons, there is no critical freedom and hence no personal sin in the strict sense.

John Paul II recognizes this blinding caused by ideology. He suggests that the dominant ideologies of West and East, "liberal capitalism" and "Marxist collectivism," actually blind citizens in the two blocs from seeing that their system does not work very well, even in their own country. And he acknowledges that economic and political institutions, following a logic of their own, function "almost automatically" (no. 16), so that responsible decision making requires an antecedent socio-ethical analysis.

It would be an error to think that all institutions of society were created with the sinful intention to exploit and dominate the population. On the contrary, many institutions were created with the best of intentions to supply a service to the community. But good institutions can become bad. In a new historical situation, an institution that has served the common good in the past may become a source of injustice and hence a structure of sin. What happens is that the hidden contradictions implicit in the institutional structure become visible under new circumstances and produce irrational, wholly unintended, consequences.

In his first encyclical, *Redemptor Hominis* (1979), John Paul II offers an interesting example of such an institutional dialectic.[11] The pope warns us of the ambiguity of modern instrumental rationality. We create technologies and bureaucracies as instruments intended to help us serve the rational interests of society, yet after a certain period of time, under new circumstances, the situation seems to be reversed. While we still think of ourselves as masters of these instruments, they have actually escaped our control. Following a logic of their own, the instruments have become our masters and despite our good intention, produce effects in society that harm the common good and undermine ethical consensus. We are then tempted to cling to the illusion that we are still in charge; we rely on our good intentions, and we attribute to other causes the evil results that follow. I note in passing that this process of inversion, dramatized in the story of the Sorcerer's Apprentice, has been recognized by sociologists such as Max Weber and the social thinkers of the Frankfurt school.

I conclude that John Paul II is aware of the unconscious, nonvoluntary, quasi-automatic dimension of social sin. The pope recognizes the power of ideology. At the same time, the greater emphasis in his analysis of social sin lies on personal responsibility. In his two social encyclicals, *Laborem Exercens* and *Sollicitudo Rei Socialis*, the pope wrestles against the "economism" or "sociologism" on the left and on the right. He repudiates "positivism" as the dominant scientific approach in Eastern Marxism and Western social science. He opposes all forms of determinism and all ideologies that deny human freedom. Although in contemporary megainstitutions the space left to human freedom is indeed small, we must not allow deterministic social theories to deny this remnant of freedom and in doing so promote resignation and political passivity. Here again the teaching of John Paul II has a certain affinity with the emphasis on personal agency in the sociology of Max Weber and the contemporary thinker, Anthony Giddens.

The stress on personal agency affects the pope's understanding of capitalism and communism in his two social encyclicals. He argues that an economic system always operates through certain concrete institutions—banks, trade agreements, exchange rates, and so forth—and that the effects of an economic system, therefore, do not simply flow from its inner logic in a deterministic way, but depend also on the institutions that individuals have set up and for which they are personally responsible. It follows that an economic system does not operate in accordance with fixed laws. Human decisions and human responsibility are never totally excluded. According to the pope, capitalism and communism can be looked at as "ideologies" and as "economic systems." As "ideologies" liberal capitalism and Marxist collectivism are fixed, internally defined systems, both of which deserve repudiation (no. 21). But the "economic systems" that call themselves capitalist and communist operate through institutions that are set up more or less arbitrarily and therefore could undergo transformation.

According to John Paul II, then, as economic systems both capitalism and communism are open to reforms that could in-

troduce qualitative changes. How can this be done? The important change that must take place in these economic systems is
the increase of responsible participation on the part of the workers. This is not the place to review the pope's theory of labor,
set out in his *Laborem Exercens*.[12] His repeated emphasis in that
encyclical and in *Sollicitudo Rei Socialis* is on the human vocation
to be a responsible agent or "subject" of society and of all the
institutions belonging to it. Thus workers are meant to be the
"subject," not the "object," of industrial production. Persons are
destined to be the actors responsible for their social existence.
This ethical concept is so dear to the pope that he invents a
special term for it. He speaks of human "subjectivity" and argues
that society and its institutions are unethical if they do not respect the "subjectivity" of the people (no. 15). Both capitalism
and communism violate the "subjectivity" of workers.[13] In *Sollicitudo Rei Socialis* we are told that all rigid, centrally-controlled
bureaucratic regimes are unethical because they do not honor
"the subjectivity" of the citizens (no. 15). (I shall investigate
further on whether the same principle also holds for the church.
Must the ecclesiastical regime respect the subjectivity of the
faithful?)

Social sin, then, has a voluntary and a nonvoluntary dimension. The papal encyclicals emphasize the voluntary aspect. According to *Sollicitudo Rei Socialis*, the economic and political
structures of sin that cause the present poverty-producing and
death-dealing orientation of the world are driven by special attitudes and choices that include "the all-consuming desire for
profit" and "the thirst for power with the intention of imposing
one's will upon others":

Better to characterize each of these attitudes — *indissolubly
united* in today's world — one can add the expression "at
any price." We are faced here with the *absolutizing* of human attitudes with all its possible consequences. . . . Obviously, not only individuals fall victim to this double
attitude of sin; nations and blocs can do so too. . . . If
certain forms of modern "imperialism" were considered in
the light of these moral criteria, we would see that hidden
behind certain attitudes, apparently inspired by economics

or politics, are real forms of idolatry: of money, ideology, class, technology [no. 37].

These remarkable sentences reveal that the voluntary aspect of social sin lies not only in the choice of the concrete institutions through which the system operates but also and more especially in the attitude or disposition of the heart that drives the entire system forward. From liberation theology and the Latin American bishops, the pope takes the idea that in today's world this attitude includes an absolutizing trend and thus represents in the strict theological sense a form of idolatry. The idolatrous attitude exists most prominently in the decision-making elite, but it is shared by vast numbers of persons who without fully realizing it are brainwashed by the dominant ideology.

What follows from this reflection on social sin is that hunger, poverty, misery, and unemployment are not simply economic problems, nor are other forms of oppression simply political problems for which technical solutions may be found. For John Paul II, economic and political marginalization is a moral evil, a social sin. Today's social crisis is a crisis of values. And because our civilization has fallen into idolatry, the crisis is in the last analysis a theological crisis regarding the identity of the true God.

CONVERSION AND SOLIDARITY

How does the true God deliver us from this social sin? What are we to do, under the impact of God's grace, to overcome and transform the structures of sin, in which we are caught?

In *Laborem Exercens*, published in 1981, John Paul II gave a reply to this question that had an immediate political relevance. The encyclical named the principal social actor destined to push through the urgently needed reforms. The pope argued that because workers were deprived of their subjectivity in capitalism and in communism, the labor movement should become the collective agent of social transformation in the societies of West and East—the labor movement fully aware of its historical vocation, backed up and supported by all in society who love justice, including the church. The great ethico-political imperative of *Laborem Exercens* was "the solidarity of labor and with labor."[14]

The main concern of *Sollicitudo Rei Socialis* is the future of the Third World. Because the pope thinks that the main obstacle to the human development of the South lies in the wealthy nations of the North, it is to them mainly that he addresses his encyclical. What can and must we in the North do to overcome the structures of sin that devastate the world at this time? The answer given by this encyclical is not as clear as in *Laborem Exercens*. We are told that "the path is long and complex" (no. 38). The pope constructs his reply to this ethico-political question around two theological concepts, "conversion" and "solidarity." Let us examine these two imperatives.

The encyclical recalls that the biblical understanding of conversion refers to a change of heart and mind, and a new way of existing in the world (no. 38). Confronted with present social evil and the orientation-toward-death of our civilization, the required conversion is not simply a turning to greater love and generosity but also an entry into a new awareness. The papal text does not use the expression "conscientization," introduced into the church's official teaching by the Latin American bishops. Instead the encyclical includes in the process of conversion "growing awareness" (no. 38) — that is, a new, critical awareness of the interdependence of a people, groups of persons, nations and continents. We are all interdependent, we are told in a previous section (no. 17), a fact we only too often forget. What counts in the present context is to recognize the nature of this interdependence. Is it just? Is it based on reciprocity? Or is it exploitive? Does it have disastrous consequences for poor countries and the poor everywhere? Does it trigger negative effects even in the wealthy countries? Conversion to the biblical message, then, includes the raising of awareness with regard to the structures of sin in which, like it or not, we live. Thus conversion cannot take place without a certain social analysis.

We notice how far this teaching has moved from the customary "moralizing" of traditional Christian preaching. In the face of these grave social injustices, we are indeed in need of moral conversion, but the process of conversion, as we have seen, also has an intellectual dimension: it includes a raising of awareness, an entry into a critical perception of society, a growing recognition of the structures of sin.

The encyclical does not offer a more detailed analysis of the needed conversion. Does the social sin in which we live implicate us in guilt and culpability? And correspondingly, must the conversion of which we speak include repentance? The text does not reply to this difficult question. Following traditional theological principles, we have to say that we are guilty to the extent that we knowingly support and defend the structures of evil, and we are not guilty to the extent we are blinded by ideology and unaware of what is going on, except possibly for having been unmoved by the misery of others and for not having tried harder to get a better grasp of the situation. Guilt increases, I suppose, in proportion to one's closeness to the decision-making elite.

It is my opinion, however, that guilt is not a useful theological concept for understanding the situation of the great majority of persons, caught as they are in the inherited structures and in the corresponding legitimating ideologies. It is, I believe, more appropriate to say that for vast numbers of persons the proper spiritual response to their entrapment in structures of sin is mourning. Mourning unites those in the middle classes with the victims of society who also mourn, even if for different reasons.

Mourning is part of the process of conversion. In a remarkable sentence of their peace pastoral, the American bishops commission the members of their church to influence public opinion in the United States so that all Americans, the bishops included, "sorrow" over the dropping of the atomic bomb in 1945.[15] Without such sorrowing or mourning, the pastoral continues, Americans will not acquire the consciousness required for solving the political problems of the present without recourse to nuclear arms. The process of conversion in the face of social sin includes mourning. The Bible speaks of lamentation. We lament before God over the great suffering inflicted upon us, and more especially upon those with whom we are in solidarity. We sorrow over our deafness that prevents us from hearing God's word; we grieve over our blindness that prevents us from recognizing the structural sin in which we live; and we lament the disaster that has befallen us.

Only the victims, discarded and despised by society, can lament before God over their suffering without any sense of guilt. But this is not the historical situation of the great majority of North Americans. There are of course many oppressed groups among us; there are also women, half the population, who suffer discrimination. Yet, to quote a well-known Christian feminist, it is dangerous for women to define themselves simply as victims, for then they do not discover the extent to which they participate in privilege. What we need for our spiritual life and our political practice, whether we belong to the middle class or to a marginalized sector, is a critical social analysis of the structures in which we live. The needed conversion includes the raising of consciousness.

In the face of the contemporary crisis, the second imperative is solidarity. The encyclical devotes several pages to what it calls "the virtue of solidarity" (no. 38). Solidarity should generate a logic of action on every level that could overcome the destructive logics operative in contemporary society. The logic of solidarity has to replace the "logic of the two blocs" (no. 20) in the political order and the logic of maximizing profit and power in the economic order. The virtue of solidarity, uniting love and justice, binds us to those who are close to us, to society as a whole, and to the world community. This solidarity, the encyclical notes, is "not a feeling of vague compassion or shallow distress at the misfortune of so many people . . . ; on the contrary, it is a firm and persevering determination to commit oneself to the common good" (no. 38). As the ultimate expression of the love of neighbor, solidarity cannot be achieved without God's hidden presence in the heart.

Despite the lengthy treatment, the concept of solidarity proposed by the encyclical is not free of ambiguity. Solidarity always expresses a commitment to a joint social project. But who defines this social project? If we look at society from a functionalist perspective, solidarity must be extended to all the members of society, rich and poor, laborers and economic elite, in the hope that working together we can free society from its idolatry and reform the social and economic institutions so that they promote the well-being of all. Here solidarity serves the common good.

But if we look at society from a critical, conflictive perspective, if—in other words—we recognize society as divided by structures of oppression, then we must extend solidarity preferentially to the poor, the unemployed, the workers, all those who are disadvantaged by society, so that struggling together in the same movement they succeed in transforming the social order. Inasmuch as the overcoming of unjust structures produces a qualitative change in the social order, preferential solidarity also serves the common good.

I conclude that the call to solidarity remains unclear unless one specifies whose social project is to be sustained.

In *Laborem Exercens*, as we saw above, John Paul II summoned persons to preferential solidarity with the labor movement. He called for "the solidarity of labor and with labor." In a brief reference to the Third World, the pope even advocated "the solidarity of the poor and with the poor."[16]

Yet in *Sollicitudo Rei Socialis*, the call to solidarity is not so clear. There are passages that seem to recommend greater solidarity among all members of society in the hope that then the powerful will take better care of the weak:

> The exercise of solidarity within each society is valid when its members recognize one another as persons. Those who are more influential, because they have a greater share of goods and common services, should feel responsible for the weaker and be ready to share with them all they possess [no. 39].

At the same time there are other passages that seem to return to the preferential solidarity of *Laborem Exercens*.

> Positive signs in the contemporary world are the growing awareness of solidarity of the poor among themselves, their efforts to support one another, and their public demonstrations on the social scene which, without recourse to violence, present their own needs and rights in the face of the inefficiency or corruption of the public authorities [no. 39].

Again we are told that the church must take its stand beside the poor. Yet a close look at this passage reveals that what is being challenged by the oppressed are simply abuses of the social order, not the structures themselves.

After the radical analysis offered by *Sollicitudo Rei Socialis* of the economic and political causes of Third World misery and of the orientation-toward-death inscribed in the wealthy cultures of the North, the encyclical's call to action seems rather weak. The strong imperatives of *Laborem Exercens*, published in 1981, are not repeated.

What is the reason for this shift of emphasis? In 1981 the preferential solidarity urged in *Laborem Exercens* greatly encouraged liberation movements in Latin America. It is my opinion that since that time, the Vatican has decided to discourage these liberation movements. The attempt to question the orthodoxy of liberation theology has not been successful. In a letter addressed to the Brazilian bishops in March 1986, the pope in fact acknowledges the importance of liberation theology for the church.[17] What is taking place, instead, is an administrative effort to weaken the Christian base communities and the liberation theology associated with them. The Vatican has tried to control the Brazilian bishops who have committed themselves collectively to preferential solidarity. The Vatican has harassed individual theologians, especially Leonardo Boff and to a lesser extent Gustavo Gutiérrez, and sharply criticized individual bishops who have given courageous witness to their option for the poor. Although *Sollicitudo Rei Socialis* confirms growing Third World misery as a crime and a scandal that cries to God, the encyclical locates the principal causes for this misery in the economic and political institutions built by the industrialized countries of the North. The encyclical calls for conversion and political reconstruction in the North, yet is almost completely silent about what the impoverished peoples of the South should do.

Can one divine the reasons for this shift? Has the Vatican sided with the U.S. government intent on defending U.S. economic hegemony in Latin America and preventing another Nicaragua? Does the Vatican want the church in Latin America to support the national security states that brutally crush critical and opposing forces? I do not think so. The Latin American bishops have repeatedly repudiated the national security state.

It seems more likely to me that the Vatican shares a view held by some political observers that the present historical situation in Latin America eliminates any hope for the success of liberation movements. If there was a *kairos*, a propitious moment, during the 1960s and 70s, it certainly no longer exists. What is important today, according to these observers, is that the Latin American left moderate its aims and work together with the progressive sector of the bourgeoisie to stabilize civilian, democratic rule and assure the protection of civil liberties. This raises a political question that merits debate.

STRUCTURES OF THE CHURCH

The last issue that deserves brief mention in this article is the question whether the concept of "structures of sin" applies to the Catholic Church as a social organization. There is no mention of this in the papal encyclical. The issue is a delicate one. While official Catholic teaching always recognized that the church was a community of sinners, it always denied that the church itself was sinful. Thanks to the special presence of the Holy Spirit, the church as such was believed to remain holy. For this reason, the church as such was not in need of repentance.

The recognition of sinful structures throws new light on this important ecclesiological issue. Catholic teaching regarding justice in society and its institutions also applies to the Catholic Church. The church as an organization ruled by human beings and made up of men and women who must live up to the principles of justice applicable to all social institutions. One could not argue that the church is exempt from these norms because it was set up for a supernatural end, an end that transcended the dimensions of this world. This is not a valid argument because the Catholic Church regards itself as "the sign and sacrament of the unity of the human race"[18] and hence as the earthly community that has overcome the divisions impairing human unity in the world. As sacramental sign, the church must be the visible embodiment of what it means to be a just society.

We saw that in his encyclicals Pope John Paul II greatly emphasized that human beings are meant to be "subjects," responsible agents, and that society and its institutions are just only if those in authority respect the "subjectivity" of their members. The pope has never applied this principle to the church. And yet there is no reason why this principle should not apply to the church. The papal-collegial structure of ecclesiastical government, which the Catholic Church regards as of divine origin, is no obstacle to the subjectivity of its members. All depends on the manner in which ecclesiastical authority is exercised. The papal-collegial structure can give rise to autocratic rule and bureaucratic centralization, but the same structure could also be open to dialogue, consultation, and cooperation, and thus generate a truly participatory ecclesiastical organization. *Sollicitudo Rei Socialis* draws attention to bureaucratic oppression as a sinful structure diminishing the subjectivity of the people. Addressing himself to the East European situation, the pope laments the suppression of the right of economic initiative and the rigid control of all economic activity by the state bureaucracy:

> Experience shows us that the denial of this right ... diminishes, or in practice absolutely destroys, the spirit of initiative, that is to say the subjectivity of the citizens. ... In the place of creative initiative there appears passivity, dependence, and submission to the bureaucratic apparatus which, as the only "ordering" and "decision-making" body ... of the totality of goods and means of production, puts everyone in a position of absolute dependence, which is similar to the traditional dependence of the proletariat in capitalism. This provokes a sense of frustration or desperation and predisposes people to opt out of national life, impelling many to emigrate and also favoring forms of "psychological" emigration [no. 15].

A little further on, the encyclical defines a system that destroys the subjectivity of society as "totalitarian": "In this situation the individual and the people become 'objects,' in spite of all verbal assurances and declarations to the contrary."

It is impossible to avoid the question to what extent the religious, pastoral, and theological initiatives of the Catholic people are diminished and controlled by a bureaucratic apparatus that regards itself as the only ordering and decision-making body in the church, and to what extent the passivity, dependence, and submission consequent upon this provokes a sense of frustration or desperation, and predisposes many Catholics to opt out of ecclesiastical life, impelling them to leave altogether or turn to psychological withdrawal, despite all verbal assurances and declarations to the contrary offered by the bureaucratic apparatus.

There has emerged in the Catholic Church a sense that the recent social teaching, with its ethical critique of institutional life and the denunciation of "structural sin," questions and challenges the church's own self-organization. An autocratic exercise of papal or episcopal authority introduces a contradition in the church's life between its official social teaching and its actual practice. The 1971 Synod of Bishops was very conscious of this.[19] If the church wants to summon society to social justice, the church must appear just itself. The synod called upon the church to make a critical analysis of its own institutional life. In composing their pastoral letter on economic justice, the American bishops were also conscious of a possible contradiction between their social teaching and their institutional behavior. This is their text: "As we have proposed a new experiment in collaboration and participation in decision making by all those affected on all levels of U.S. society, so we also commit the church to become a model of collaboration and participation."[20]

Despite a certain vagueness and some as yet unresolved questions, the concept of structural sin introduced in *Sollicitudo Rei Socialis* represents a significant development in the church's official teaching. In my opinion it is an important breakthrough. One wonders how, after this doctrinal development, treatments of moral theology that do not take sinful structures into consideration can present themselves as trustworthy. For it is now recognized that human behavior, however virtuous, must still be evaluated according to its structural implications. Do personal attitudes and actions, consciously or unconsciously, serve the stability of unjust institutions, or do they serve the social forces that seek to overcome the structure of sin? Echoing the challenge of liberation theology, John Paul II has initiated a serious rethinking of moral theology.

NOTES

1. *Justitia in Mundo*, 1971, no. 40.
2. Medellín Documents, "Justice," nos. 17, 23; "Peace," no. 18.

3. J. B. Metz, *Theology of the World* (New York: Seabury, 1973), pp. 107–24.

4. "Peace," no. 15.

5. *Justitia in Mundo*, no. 51.

6. Ibid., no. 5.

7. Ibid., no. 3.

8. "Ethical Reflections on the Economic Crisis," G. Baum and D. Cameron, *Ethics and Economics: Canada's Bishops on the Economic Crisis* (Toronto: Lorimer, 1984), p. 3. See John Paul II, *Redemptor Hominis* (1979), no. 52.

9. "Economic Justice for All" (1986), no. 77.

10. Instruction on Christian Freedom and Liberation (1986), no. 75.

11. *Redemptor Hominis*, no. 15.

12. See G. Baum, *The Priority of Labor* (New York: Paulist Press, 1982).

13. See *Laborem Exercens*, nos. 6, 7. "Converting the means of production into state property in the collectivist systems is by no means equivalent to 'socializing' that property. We can speak of socializing only when the subjectivity of society is ensured, that is to say, when on the basis of his work each person is fully entitled to consider himself a part owner of the great workbench at which he is working with everyone else" (no. 14).

14. *Laborem Exercens*, no. 8.

15. "The Challenge of Peace" (1983), no. 302.

16. *Laborem Exercens*, no. 8.

17. G. Baum, *Theology and Society* (New York: Paulist Press, 1987), p. 104.

18. Vatican Council II, *Lumen Gentium*, no. 1.

19. See note 1, above.

20. "Economic Justice for All" (1986), no. 358.

5

The Search for Authentic Development

Denis Goulet

Development, both as idea and as project, has served as the governing myth of the post–World War II age. Nowadays, however, a growing chorus of voices condemns development as the instrument used by rapacious industrialized Western nations to destroy the cultures and the autonomy of societies throughout Africa, Asia, and Latin America. For many, development has become a dirty word.

The noted French agronomist, René Dumont, sees the performance of the last forty years as a dangerous epidemic of misdevelopment.[1] In Africa, he argues, development has simply not occurred. And in Latin America much new wealth has been created, ranging from sophisticated nuclear and electronic industries to vast skyscraper cities, but growth has been won at the price of massive pollution, urban congestion, and monumental resource waste. What is worse, the majority of the Latin American population has not benefited from this new wealth. Dumont concludes that misdevelopment, or the mismanagement of resources in both the socialist and capitalist worlds, is the main cause of world hunger.[2] And it afflicts "developed" countries as severely as it does Third World nations.

Other writers strike the same theme — namely, that economic growth is often inequitable, destructive, and worsens the lot of the poor. Among these are the late Swiss anthropologist Roy Preiswerk, the African civil servant Albert Tévoédjrè, and the Haitian geographer Georges Anglade.[3] The most categorical attack, however, comes from the pen of those who totally repudiate development, both as concept and as project. Prominent among these are the French economist Serge Latouche,[4] and the Montreal-based Monchanin Intercultural Centre; both tirelessly promote the thesis that development must be rejected because it destroys native political, juridical, and economic institutions, while demolishing precious symbolic meaning systems.[5] Similarly, the Cultural Survival Movement headquartered at Harvard University has struggled, since its creation in 1972, to prevent "development" from destroying indigenous peoples and their cultures. Its founder, anthropologist David Maybury-Lewis, maintains:

> Violence done to indigenous peoples is largely based on prejudices and discrimination that must be exposed and combated. These prejudices are backed up by widely held misconceptions, which presume that traditional societies are inherently obstacles to development or that the recognition of their rights would subvert the nation state. Our research shows that this is untrue.[6]

Notwithstanding the attacks made upon it, however, development continues to be the dominant concept shaping social policy throughout the world. Indeed most national governments and international financial agencies still take development to mean maximum economic growth and a concerted drive toward industrialization and mass consumption. The success stories praised worldwide are Korea and Taiwan, twin paragons of capital-intensive and high-technology economic growth, allied to competitive international trading.[7] Most development reports remain discreetly silent, however, as to the costs in political repression attendant upon these economic successes![8]

Conventional growth models still enjoy a practical hegemony in macro arenas of policy setting. Nevertheless, a new development paradigm is now in gestation in micro, or small-scale, arenas of strategy innovation. A twofold search—conceptual and practical—is on for what John Paul II, in his encyclical letter *On Social Concern*, calls "an authentic development of man and society which would respect and promote all the dimensions of the human person."[9]

This encyclical takes its place in a growing normative stream of development writings that center attention on ethical value questions posed by development decisions and actions.[10] Until recent years such normative writings on development were readily dismissed as the work of a minority of writers, who remained largely "outsiders" to the self-confident universe managed by expert development professionals. Certain dissident authors, most notably Mahatma Gandhi,[11] worked as utopian social activists, preaching and experimenting with the merits of small-scale village development, the slow progression from artisanal to technological skills, and simple modes of living so that persons might free themselves from the thraldom of escalating desires for more material goods.

Other critics, like L. J. Lebret and Erich Fromm,[12] after systematically evaluating competing visions of the good life and the just society, opted for a model of development that promotes community, spiritual fulfillment, and the enhancement of creative freedom over mere material abundance, technological prowess, or functionally efficient institutions. Others still, notably E. F. Schumacher,[13] pleaded for an economics that gives primacy to people, and for soft technologies that protect local cultures and environments. Finally, alternative paradigm-setters, like Ivan Illich and J. P. Naik,[14] called for the recapture by ordinary people of the monopoly on problem solving appropriated, under the banner of modernization, by expert specialists of all kinds: educational, medical, and economic.

The value themes and action priorities advocated by these dissident strategists have now made their way into the general lexicon of mainstream development planners and policymakers. Participation of nonelites, self-reliant local initiatives, the primacy of basic needs, a regard for ecological sanity, equity in the distribution of the fruits of economic growth, and respect for traditional cultures—all these have now become indispensable agenda items in all development debates. Even large impersonal financial organizations that promote structural adjustment—the "rationalization" of finances around market forces, the orientation of production toward export trade, and the privatization of enterprises—look for ways of putting a "human face" onto their policy.[15] Although development thinking and action is still dominated by a concern with the adjustment crisis in the Third World,[16] macroplanners and policy analysts nonetheless search for means of strengthening the poor[17] and for social policies that work in the fight against poverty.[18] In typical fashion, a recent World Bank technical report on public finance expresses its concern lest "careless fiscal austerity . . . lead to prolonged recession . . . and can place a disproportionately heavy burden on the poor. For this reason the structural aspects of public finance policy— how spending is allocated and revenue raised—matters as much as the overall macroeconomic balance."[19]

Although, as just noted, John Paul's encyclical takes its place in the body of normative writings on development, the methodology it employs differs sharply from that found in other works located in this stream. *On Social Concern* is evidently not an exercise in social analysis, but a sermon, an "appeal to conscience."[20] The Catholic Church aims at promoting the moral and spiritual welfare of humankind; consequently, when it speaks of development, it does so in order "to lead people to respond, with the support also of rational reflection and of the human sciences, to their vocation as responsible builders of earthly society."[21] The papal document, accordingly, draws the value content it places on "authentic development" from the religious doctrine of the church on the purposes of human life and history as revealed in its scriptures and traditions.

This approach differentiates it from other advocates of normative development who derive their conclusions from quite different sources. Gandhi gets his theory and vision of a developed society from what he calls his experiments with truth, endless trial-and-error probes into new patterns of work, social organization, and living style. Lebret, the national planner and strategist, derives his norms from a pluridisciplinary scientific study of economic and social reality, of resources and needs, of benefits and costs attaching to alternative policies. Dumont,

Latouche, and other radical critics of development obtain their values from a critique of mainstream development and its disastrous results. All critical strategists have this trait in common, however: they search for ways of broadening a purely economic or technical analysis of development so as to make economics serve larger human needs. Or, alternatively, they draw out in explicit terms what are the ethical requirements of conducting economic analysis and prescription in a realistic and socially responsible mode.[22]

Beyond the criticism of mainstream paradigms of development, however, one needs to ask what precise *value content* is to be given to diverse models of authentic development? Answers given to this question constitute the burden of the pages that follow.

AUTHENTIC DEVELOPMENT: ITS COMPONENTS

Normative Definitions of Development

A weeklong seminar, "Ethical Issues in Development," held in September 1986 at the Marga Institute in Colombo, Sri Lanka,[23] reached consensus that any adequate definition of development must include five dimensions:

1. an economic component dealing with the creation of wealth and improved conditions of material life;

2. a social ingredient measured as well-being in health, education, housing, and employment;

3. a political dimension pointing to such values as human rights, political freedom, enfranchisement, and some form of democracy;

4. a cultural element in recognition of the fact that cultures confer identity and self-worth to persons; and

5. a fifth register called the full-life paradigm, encompassing symbols and beliefs as to the ultimate meaning of life and of history.

Integral human development is all these things, according to Marga.

An almost identical definition of authentic development had emerged some years earlier from a Latin American seminar held in Ottawa, Canada. The definition of authentic development given by participants of that seminar embraced four pairs of words: economic growth, distributional equity, participation/vulnerability, and transcendental values.[24] The two final sets of words require explanation. "Participation" is a decisive voice exercised by those directly affected by policy decisions, whereas vulnerability is the obverse side of the participation coin: poor people, regions, and nations must be rendered less vulnerable to decisions that produce external shocks upon them.[25] The reference to "transcendental values" raises a vital question: "Does humankind live by GNP alone?" As David Pollock puts it:

> Let us assume that a country's economic pie increases. Let us further assume that there is a heightened degree of equity in the way the fruits of that economic pie are distributed. Let us, finally, assume that decisions affecting production and consumption of the economic pie — internationally and nationally — involve the full participation of all affected parties. Is that the end of the matter? Does man live by GNP alone? Perhaps the latter has been the prevailing line of thought throughout the postwar period since, in the short-run, policy-makers must focus primarily upon the pressing issue of increased incomes for the masses; particularly for those below the poverty line. But, despite the obvious importance of such short-run objectives, we should also be asking ourselves other, more uplifting, questions. Should we not take advantage of our longer-term vision and ask what kind of person Latin America may wish to evolve by the end of this century. What are the transcendental values — cultural, ethical, artistic, religious, moral — that extend beyond the current workings of the purely economic and social system? How to appeal to youth, who so often seek nourishment in dreams, as well as in bread? What, in short, should be the new face of the Latin American society in the future, and what human values should lie behind the new countenance?[26]

Human progress is not the fruit of some inevitable historical necessity: it is always the achievement of human wills struggling to master the determinisms they face from nature, from the social systems they have forged, and from their own technological and cultural artifacts. Progress or "development" takes place, therefore, when expanding freedoms find their expression in institutions, norms of exchange, patterns of social organization, educational efforts, relations of production, and political choices that enhance the human potential.

Because the human potential thrusts the human species forward into transcendence, no truncated model of humanism that neglects spiritual fulfillment or imprisons human destiny within the confines of an immanentist view of history is acceptable. Such a form of humanism closes the door to genuine transcendence and diminishes the stature of human beings.[27]

In the setting of development efforts, transcendence refers to the ability of all human beings to go beyond, or transcend, their own limitations and reach levels of achievement higher than those presently enjoyed. Champions of transcendence reject any mass-consumer model of development or any form of social utopia that unilaterally defines egalitarianism in reductionist terms of mere consumption or production. On the contrary, the opening toward metahistorical transcendence is a requisite of the full blooming of development potentialities.

One explicit and detailed formulation of the requirements of authentic development has been made by the French planner and philosopher, L. J. Lebret. Lebret is that rare development expert cited by name in the 1967 encyclical *On the Development of Peoples*, the text that is commemorated and amplified in the 1987 papal document *On Social Concern*. In the 1967 encyclical Paul VI recalls what "an eminent specialist has very rightly and emphatically declared: 'We do not believe in separating the economic from the human, nor development from the civilizations in which it exists. What we hold important is man, each man and each group of men, and we even include the whole of humanity.' "[28] Lebret served as the major expert advisor to Paul VI in drafting *On the Development of Peoples*. Accordingly, to analyze the formal requirements of authentic development as he defines them is to find the key to understanding the normative vision put forth by the two papal authors, Paul VI and John Paul II.

Lebret defines development as:

the series of transitions, for a given population and all the subpopulation units which comprise it, from a less human to a more human phase of existence, at the speediest rhythm possible, at the lowest possible cost, while taking into account all the bonds of solidarity that exist (or ought to exist) among these populations and subpopulation groups.[29]

It logically follows from this definition that the discipline of development is the study of how to achieve a more human economy.[30] The normative expressions "more human" and "less human" need to be understood in the light of a distinction Lebret considered vital: the difference between *plus avoir* ("to have more") and *plus être* ("to be more"). A society, Lebret contends, is more human or more developed not when men and women "have more," but when all its citizens are enabled "to be more."[31] The main criterion of value is not the production or possession of goods, but the totality of qualitative human enrichment. Some material growth and quantitative increases are doubtless needed for genuine development, but not any kind of growth or increase at any price. The world as a whole will remain underdeveloped or will fall prey to an illusory antidevelopment so long as a small number of nations or privileged groups remain alienated in an abundance of luxurious (facility) goods at the expense of the many who are thereby deprived of their essential (subsistence) goods. When such situations prevail, both rich and poor suffer from insufficient satisfaction of their "enhancement" needs.

The scope of Lebret's concept of development can be grasped by examining the attributes he deems essential to it. If development is to be genuine, he asserts, it must be:

1) *Finalized.* It must serve the basic ends—that is, to build a human economy and to satisfy all human needs in an equitable order of urgency and importance.

2) *Coherent.* All major problem sectors must be addressed in coordinated fashion. Agriculture must not be sacrificed to industry, or one segment of the population to another. (This injunction does not, however, rule out a strategy of deliberately

unbalanced growth, provided it is judiciously pursued and continually rectified.)

3) *Homogeneous.* Even when revolutionary innovations are introduced, these must respect a people's past history and present capacities. No elitist imposition from above, in total rupture with a people's cultural heritage and absorptive capacity, is justified.

4) *Self-propelling.* Unless development heightens a society's capacity to direct itself autonomously, it is invalid. This demands a battle against dependency, parasitism, passivity, and inertia.

5) *Indivisible.* There is no genuine development unless all the people benefit from it, unless the common good is achieved. Privilege systems, excessive gaps between the city and the countryside, alienating divisions of labor are all ruled out.

The policy implications of these attributes are as far-reaching as Lebret's analytical concept of development.[32]

Sound development policies ought to adopt as their first priority the production of goods of essential necessities for all, those goods that satisfy the basic human needs. A second priority is to produce goods and services that enhance the quality of life: amenities, comforts, esthetically, culturally, and spiritually ennobling goods. Only as a last instance can one justify devoting any significant resources to the production of luxury goods. Luxuries undoubtedly have some value and contribute to civilization, if only because they reveal the glittering esthetic possibilities latent in human imagination and creativity. To allocate significant resources to the production of luxuries for a few beneficiaries, however, whereas the more fundamental needs of the masses remain unmet, represents a gross structural distortion, at once irrational and immoral.[33]

The key moral element in Lebret's concept of development is solidarity, that perceptual and behavioral disposition that binds together the destinies of all human persons, societies, and nations. Solidarity places on the "haves" a moral claim, a veritable duty in justice, to assure that the "have nots" of the world come to *have* that minimum supply of essential goods without which they cannot *be* fully human. If there exists some threshold point *below which* human beings cannot be integrally human or live a truly human life, there also exists a ceiling *above which* the pursuit of further possessions that one desires to *have* interferes with the quality of one's *being*. In the words of the psychologist Erich Fromm, "affluent alienation" is no less dehumanizing than "impoverished alienation."[34] According to Lebret, it is the selfishness, avarice, and fear of the rich and powerful that undermine solidarity.[35] Many contemporary development writers blame the persistence of poverty on "a failure of political will" on the part of human societies to endow themselves with economic systems, social structures, and political institutions that could abolish massive underdevelopment. All acknowledge that sufficient material and technological resources to eliminate misery exist in the world. For Lebret, however, the major obstacle lies not in deficient *political* will, but in the *moral* blindness of the rich and the selfish in the defense of their privileges.[36] The Independent Commission on International Development Issues chaired by Willy Brandt likewise bases its appeals to solidarity on an ethical, or moral, value. In its report, *North-South, a Programme for Survival*, the commissioners write:

> History has taught us that wars produce hunger, but we are less aware that mass poverty can lead to war or end in chaos. While hunger rules, peace cannot prevail. He who wants to ban war must also ban mass poverty. Morally it makes no difference whether a human being is killed in war or is condemned to starve to death because of the indifference of others.
>
> Mankind has never before had such ample technical and financial resources for coping with hunger and poverty. The immense task can be tackled once the necessary collective will is mobilized. What is necessary can be done, and must be done, in order to provide the conditions by which the poor can be saved from starvation as well as destructive confrontation.
>
> Solidarity among men must go beyond national boundaries: we cannot allow it to be reduced to a meaningless phrase. International solidarity must stem both from strong mutual interests in cooperation *and* from compassion for the hungry.[37]

In no domain is solidarity more urgently needed than in ecology. Unless the human race extends its effective solidarity to the biosphere and to all life within it, it will itself perish. The ecological imperative is at once clear and absolute: nature must be saved or we humans will die. And the single greatest threat to nature – menacing irreversible destruction of its regenerative powers – comes from "development." This same "development" is also the culprit that perpetuates the underdevelopment of hundreds of millions of persons. Therefore, the task of eliminating dehumanizing underdevelopment imposes itself with the same urgency as the safeguard of nature. A comprehensive ethic of authentic development will, of necessity, look to the sustainability of economic growth and resource use as well as to the equitable distribution of its fruits. What Ignacy Sachs calls "Ecodevelopment" relies on an anthropological economics which simultaneously serves human needs and manages nature with wisdom.[38]

ECOLOGY: ON SEEING THE WHOLE PICTURE

Ecology has now become a *household* word. There is illuminating symbolism here for, in its Greek etymology, "ecology" designates the science of the larger household, the total environment in which living organisms exist. Indeed, whenever it is faithful to its origins and inner spirit, ecology is holistic: it looks to the whole picture, the totality of relations. As a recently certified pluridisciplinary field of study, ecology embraces four distinct, interrelated, subjects: environment, demography, resource systems, and technology. Its special contribution to human knowledge is to draw a coherent portrait of how these four realms interact in patterns of vital interdependence.

Ecological wisdom is the search for optimal modes and scales in which human populations may apply technology to resource use within their environments. Both as an intellectual discipline and as a practical concern, ecology *presupposes some philosophy of nature.* Traditional human wisdoms long ago parted ways, however, in their fundamental conceptions of nature and their views as to how human beings should relate to it. All wisdoms acknowledge humans to be part of nature and subject to its laws and constraints. The common destiny of all natural beings, humans included, is generation and corruption: they are born, grow, get old, and die. But certain worldviews more than others have elevated humans above their encompassing nature and assigned them a cosmic role of domination over that very nature of which they are a part. In the interrogatory words that aptly serve as the title of a recent publication in Sri Lanka, *Man in Nature, Guest or Engineer?*[39]

Nature and human liberty have, therefore, come to be perceived as opposing poles in a dichotomy. Are humans *free* to treat nature as they would? Or must humans, like all other animals, submit to nature's laws or at least to its penalties? The paradox lies in this: that human beings are not physically compelled to respect nature but they need to do so *if* they are to survive and preserve the very existential ground they need to assert their freedom. Because this is so, there can be no ultimate or radical incompatibility between the demands of nature and the exigencies of human freedom, those of environmental sanity, of wise resource stewardship, and of technology. Theoretical and practical problems arise because ecologists, betraying their very nature, have not looked at the whole picture. Looking at the whole picture also enables one to transcend numerous other apparent antinomies, chief among which is the alleged contradiction between anthropocentric and cosmocentric views of the universe.

CONCLUSION

The encyclical *On Social Concern* endorses the multi-dimensional, humanistic, ecologically wise, and culturally nurturing view of development advocated by alternative development strategists. John Paul II considers that "modern underdevelopment is not only economic but also cultural, political, and simply human. ... We have to ask ourselves if the sad reality of today might not be, at least in part, the result of a *too narrow idea* of development, that is, a mainly economic one."[40] The encyclical issues its summons to solidarity in universal terms:

It should be obvious that development either becomes shared in *common* by every part of the world or it undergoes a *process of regression* even in zones marked by constant progress. This tells us a great deal about the nature of *authentic* development: either *all* the nations of the world participate, or it will not be true "development."[41]

On Social Concern denounces the selfishness of both blocs — the capitalist West and the socialist East alike. Both are guilty of "a betrayal of humanity's legitimate expectations — a betrayal that is a harbinger of unforeseeable consequences — but also a real desertion of a moral obligation."[42] The twin elements of a comprehensive development ethic, namely, a regard for social justice and a call for ecological responsibility, are evoked by the encyclical, which calls for "an ever greater degree of rigorous respect for *justice* and consequently a fair distribution of the results of true development," along with "the need to respect the integrity and the cycles of nature and to take them into account when planning for development, rather than sacrificing them to certain demagogic ideas about the latter."[43]

For John Paul, the struggle to achieve authentic development is "an essential dimension of man's vocation."[44] The human race, he adds, is called by God to be a co-creator and co-manager of the whole creation. "When man disobeys God and refuses to submit to his rule, nature rebels against him and no longer recognizes him as its 'master.' "[45]

Development in the mode of solidarity, binding all human persons and communities to each other, and to the planet they inhabit, is the only authentic form. If humans persist in promoting antidevelopment, they will perish. In Barbara Ward's cryptic phrase: "We are either going to become a community, or we are going to die."[46]

NOTES

1. René Dumont and M. F. Mottin, *Le mal-développement en Amérique latine* (Paris: Seuil, 1981).

2. See Bob Bergmann, "René Dumont on Misdevelopment in the Third World: A 42-Year Perspective," in *Camel Breeders News* (Ithaca: Cornell University, Spring 1987), p. 19.

3. See Albert Tévoédjrè, *La pauvreté, richesse des peuples* (Paris:

Economie et Humanisme, 1978); and Georges Anglade, *Eloge de la pauvreté* (Montreal: ERCE, 1983).

4. Serge Latouche, *Faut-il refuser le développement?* (Paris: Presses Universitaires de France, 1986).

5. "No to Development?," *Inter-Culture* (Spring-Fall 1987), p. 95.

6. David Maybury-Lewis, editorial letter "Dear Reader" in *Cultural Survival Quarterly*, vol. 11, no. 1 (1987), p. 1.

7. See, e.g., Lawrence J. Lau, ed., *Models of Development. A Comparative Study of Economic Growth in South Korea and Taiwan* (San Francisco: Institute for Contemporary Studies, 1986); Arnold C. Harberger, ed., *World Economic Growth. Case Studies of Developed and Developing Nations* (San Francisco: Institute for Contemporary Studies, 1984).

8. Selig S. Harrison, "Dateline South Korea: A Divided Seoul," *Foreign Policy*, no. 67 (Summer 1987), pp. 154–75. Yu-ming Shaw and Guo-cang Huan, "The Future of Taiwan," *Foreign Affairs*, vol. 63, no. 5 (Summer 1985), pp. 1050–80.

9. John Paul II, *On Social Concern* (Washington, D.C.: United States Catholic Conference, 1987), p. 3.

10. On this see Denis Goulet, "An Ethical Model for the Study of Values," *Harvard Educational Review*, vol. 41, no. 2 (May 1971), pp. 205–27.

11. On this see J. P. Naik, "Gandhi and Development Theory," *Review of Politics*, vol. 45, no. 3 (July 1983), pp. 345–65.

12. L. J. Lebret, *Montée Humaine* (Paris: Ouvrières, 1958); Erich Fromm, *To Have or To Be?* (New York: Harper & Row, 1976).

13. E. F. Schumacher, *Small is Beautiful* (London: Blond & Briggs, 1973).

14. Ivan D. Illich, *Toward a History of Needs* (New York: Pantheon, 1977); and J. P. Naik, *An Alternative System of Health Care Services in India — Some Proposals and Some Perspectives on Non-Formal Education* (New Delhi: Allied Publishers Private Limited, 1977).

15. G. A. Cornia, R. Jolly, and F. Stewart, *Adjustment with a Human Face* (Oxford: Clarendon Press, 1987); see World Bank pamphlet, The Alleviation of Poverty.

16. See R. Feinberg and V. Kallab, eds., *Adjustment Crisis in the Third World* (New Brunswick, N.J.: Transaction Books, 1984).

17. John P. Lewis et al., *Strengthening the Poor: What Have We Learned?* (New Brunswick, N.J.: Transaction Books, 1988).

18. S. Danzinger and D. Weinberg, *Fighting Poverty. What Works and What Doesn't* (Cambridge: Harvard University Press, 1986).

19. *World Development Report 1988* (Washington, D.C.: World Bank, 1988), p. 1.

20. John Paul II, *On Social Concern*, p. 6.

21. Ibid., p. 4.

22. On this see Amartya Sen, *On Ethics and Economics* (London: Basil Blackwell, 1987); Mark A. Lutz and Kenneth Lux, *Humanistic Economics* (New York: Bootstrap Press, 1988); Thomas Michael Power, *The Economic Pursuit of Quality* (Armonk, N.Y.: M. E. Sharpe, 1988); Paul Ekins, ed., *The Living Economy. A New Economics in the Making* (London: Routledge & Kegan Paul, 1986).

23. No documents have yet been issued from the seminar. I participated in it and here report from notes taken at the time.

24. David H. Pollock, "A Latin American Strategy to the Year 2000: Can the Past Serve as a Guide to the Future?," *Latin American Prospects for the 80's: What Kinds of Development?* (Ottawa: Norman Patterson School of International Affairs, Carleton University, Conference Proceedings, vol. 1, November 1980), pp. 1–37.

25. Denis Goulet, "Participation in Development: New Avenues," *World Development*, vol. 17, no. 2 (February 1989).

26. Pollock, "A Latin American Strategy," p. 9.

27. On this see Denis Goulet, "Development Experts: The One-Eyed Giants," *World Development*, vol. 8, no. 7/8 (July/August 1980), pp. 481–89. See H. W. Richardson and D. R. Cutter, *Transcendence* (Boston: Beacon Press, 1969).

28. Pope Paul VI, *Populorum Progressio*, March 26, 1967, no. 14, citing L. J. Lebret, *Dynamique Concrète du Développement*, (Paris: Ouvrières, 1961), p. 28.

29. L. J. Lebret, Editorial, *Développement et Civilisations*, no. 1 (March 1960), p. 3. See also Lebret, *Développement = Revolution Solidaire* (Paris: Ouvrières, 1967), p. 82.

30. See Denis A. Goulet, "Secular History and Teleology," *World Justice*, vol. 8, no. 1 (September 1966), pp. 5–18.

31. For more on this distinction, see Erich Fromm, *To Have or To Be?*.

32. Cited in Madeleine Barthélemy Madaule, "La Personne dans la Perspective Teilhardienne," *Essais sur Teilhard de Chardin* (Paris: Fayard, 1962), p. 76.

33. The hierarchy of needs—life-sustenance needs, enhancement needs, and luxury needs—as well as the policy measures that flow from them, are examined in detail in Denis Goulet, *The Cruel Choice* (New York: Atheneum, 1971), pp. 236–49.

34. Introduction to Erich Fromm, ed., *Socialist Humanism: An International Symposium* (New York: Anchor Books), p. ix.

35. Lebret, *Revolution Solidaire*, p. 49.

36. For more on obstacles to development, see Denis Goulet, "Obstacles to Development: An Ethical Reflection," *World Development*, vol. 11, no. 7 (July 1983), pp. 609–24.

37. Willy Brandt, *North-South: A Programme for Survival* (Cambridge: MIT Press, 1980), p. 16.

38. Ignacy Sachs, *Développer, les Champs de Planification* (Paris: Université Coopérative Internationale, 1984).

39. S. J. Samartha and Lynn de Silva, eds., *Man in Nature. Guest or Engineer?* (Columbo: Ecumenical Institute for Study and Dialogue, 1979).

40. John Paul II, *On Social Concern*, no. 15.

41. *Ibid.*, no. 17.

42. *Ibid.*, no. 23.

43. *Ibid.*, no. 26.

44. *Ibid.*, no. 30.

45. *Ibid.*, no. 30.

46. This phrase served as the theme of the 25th Anniversary World Conference of the Society for International Development, "The Emerging Global Village," held in Baltimore, Maryland, July 18–22, 1982.

6

Solidarity and Integral Human Development

Donal Dorr

> The social doctrine of the Church, ... beginning with the outstanding contribution of Leo XIII and enriched by the successive contributions of the Magisterium, has now become an updated doctrinal "corpus." ... I wish principally ... to reaffirm the *continuity* of the social doctrine as well as its constant *renewal*. ... The aim of the present reflection is to emphasize ... the need for a fuller and more nuanced concept of development.
>
> *Sollicitudo Rei Socialis*, nos. 1.2, 3.1, 4.4[1]

These excerpts from John Paul's encyclical provide a key to understanding what he has to say on the subject of "solidarity." His aim is to add a relatively small but important element to the corpus of social doctrine, which has been built up over the past hundred years. He maintains that the understanding of human development worked out by Paul VI in *Populorum Progressio* was a major contribution to that body of teaching—relevant not merely to the world of the 1960s but also to the world of the 1980s (SRS, no. 4.1). The treatment of solidarity in the present encyclical has to be interpreted as one element in John Paul's effort to ensure that Paul VI's teaching will have greater impact today. The pope sees himself as elaborating on the brief reference made by Paul VI in *Populorum Progressio* to "the duty of solidarity" (nos. 44, 48). In this short study I shall endeavor to situate John Paul's account of solidarity within the context of the treatment of development in *Populorum Progressio*.

A NEW APPROACH TO DEVELOPMENT

Populorum Progressio represents a remarkable advance on previous church teaching about human development. The advance was a conceptual one. By this I mean that what is radically new is the *framework of understanding* rather than some specific details. At the heart of *Populorum Progressio* lies a notion of integrated development, which Paul VI took from Père Lebret, the Dominican scholar and activist who died some time before the encyclical appeared.[2]

To explain the newness of the approach to development of *Populorum Progressio*, let me give an analogy. If you ask me to describe my ideal house, there are two ways in which I can answer. I may say, "My ideal house would be smaller than this house in which I am now living; it would have better insulation than this one; it would have solar panels on the roof instead of roof tiles, and so forth."

Alternatively, I may say, "My ideal house is one where a family can work, eat, sleep, and relax, with a maximum of ease at a minimum cost to themselves, to the community, and to the environment; and so forth."

In giving the first kind of answer, I start from a known existing reality (e.g., my present house) and list the *differences* between it and the ideal. In the second kind of answer I begin by laying down certain general *criteria* that the ideal house must live up to.

In regard to human development, the first of these approaches was adopted by the fathers of Vatican II in *Gaudium et Spes*. Their starting point and term of reference was the kind of economic development to which governments all over the world were committed. They set out to correct and expand this conception, to produce a more integral and balanced conception of human development.

In sharp contrast to this, Paul VI in *Populorum Progressio* adopted the kind of approach used in the second of the answers given above to the person who asks, what is an ideal house. He did not take the current conception of economic development as a starting point and then modify it. Instead, he laid down certain basic criteria by which we can measure to what extent any changes brought about in society deserve to be called authentic human development. In other words, what *Populorum Progressio* gives is a *heuristic* notion of development, a framework or anticipation of the "shape" of genuine development.

The fathers of Vatican II made a very valuable contribution to the church's body of social teaching. But anybody who starts, as they did, from the current concept of "development" used by economists and planners, is in danger of ending up with a notion of development that is quite inadequate. One great danger is that of assuming, consciously or unconsciously, that *economic* development is the hard core of any authentic human development. Those who start with this explicit or implicit assumption quickly find themselves trapped into an awkward conceptual framework. They find that they have to engage in a kind of trade-off between the hard economic core of development and the "soft" elements that surround it. By the "soft" elements I mean those that are not strictly economic—for instance, respect for culture, for the environment, for human rights, for the sense of community, and for the quality of human life. The hard economic core seems to be in competition with the surrounding "soft" elements. Too much insistence on the "soft" elements may so limit the hard core that the essential element of development is lost. It is as though one had killed the goose that lays the golden eggs!

Starting with a purely heuristic conception of development, *Populorum Progressio* avoids this trap. It does not give a privileged place to the economic dimension of human development, any more than to the cultural, psychological, political, ecological, or religious dimensions. Rather it challenges Christians to take full account of the noneconomic elements—to recognize, for instance, that the protection of the right to free speech may be at least as valuable a part of authentic development as an increase in disposable income. Of course there will be a lot of balancing to be done; but one is less tempted to take facile shortcuts—to say, for instance, that in the name of development we *must* sacrifice the environment, or give up some treasured cultural tradition or some fundamental human right.

John Paul II carries on in this tradition. He insists that human development is essentially a *moral* matter, not merely an economic one. Of course there is an economic component in development; but, says the pope, to limit development to its economic aspect leads to the subordination of the human person to "the demands of economic planning and selfish profit" (SRS, no. 33.2). He goes on immediately to emphasize the importance of human rights—rights of individuals and rights of whole peoples (no. 33.3-7). In order to be considered genuine, he maintains, development must be brought about within the framework of *solidarity* and *freedom* (no. 33.8). In using the word "solidarity" here, and linking it to the word "freedom," John Paul is stressing the paramount need for any project of human development to be built around *respect*. And this respect has to be exercised at two distinct levels:

1. There must be respect for the individual person; the person has needs and values that go beyond the purely economic sphere.

2. There must also be respect for the cultural identity of whole communities—each "people" as well as each person.

The concept of "solidarity" as developed by John Paul II plays a key role in each of these two levels of human development.

FROM THE INDIVIDUAL TO THE COMMUNITY

John Paul's teaching on solidarity is designed to plug a notable gap that often arises when personal development is put at the heart of a system of morality. This gap is the one between the individual and the others with whom that person is linked in any way. If "right" or "good" means what is good for *me*, how does that fit in with what is good for persons around me, whose needs often seem (at least at first sight) to be in competition with mine? That is the question the pope is seeking to answer when he develops his teaching on solidarity. Rather than discussing this issue in abstract philosophical terms, he situates what he has to say in the context of the distinctive contribution of *Populorum Progressio* to our understanding of human development.

As John Paul points out, the originality of *Populorum Progressio* "consists in the basic insight that the *very concept* of development, if considered in the perspective of universal interdependence, changes notably" (SRS, no. 9.9). He is referring here to the way in which Paul VI's encyclical challenged one of the hidden assumptions of the present Western conception of development — namely, that the nation as a *whole* becomes more "advanced" through the growth in wealth of a fairly large number of *individuals* within it. In recent years the fallacy in this is becoming more evident; for even in the so-called developed countries there are what John Paul calls "bands of great or extreme poverty" (SRS, no. 31). This gap between the enrichment of some and the development of society as a whole leaves the popular Western notion of development very threadbare. By contrast, the more heuristic concept of development proposed in *Populorum Progressio* offers a way out of the trap of individualism.

For Paul VI, genuine human development includes not only the good of the total person but also the good of all persons (PP, no. 14; see also no. 42). The link between the individual and the wider society is provided by him when he includes among the criteria of genuine development an increased concern for others and a desire to cooperate with others for the common good (PP, no. 21). Therefore, self-fulfillment is not opposed to the welfare of others. This involves a major challenge to the presupposition of Western-style planning that persons are motivated mainly by self-interest.

Reflecting on this approach of Paul VI, John Paul notes that what Paul VI did was to bring out the fact that intrinsic to genuine human development is a strong *moral dimension* (SRS, no. 9.8). In his teaching on solidarity, John Paul sees himself as articulating a moral sense or conviction that is growing in the world today. There is an awareness of a "radical *interdepend-*

ence," a realization that persons everywhere are "linked together by a common destiny"; and this awareness is convincing persons "of the need for a solidarity which will take up interdependence and transfer it to the moral plane" (SRS, no. 26.5). These words are a key to understanding the word "solidarity" in the specific technical meaning the pope is giving to it: solidarity is the correct *moral response* to the *fact* of interdependence.

A SYNTHESIS

Clearly, the pope sees himself as making a contribution to moral theology — extending the traditional categories to take account of the new factual situation and the new moral awareness that is developing among those who understand and respond to the new situation. It is worthwhile spelling out the different elements in the synthesis that John Paul seems to have in mind — and which he would, presumably, wish to have incorporated into future textbooks of moral theology.

First, there is the fact of *interdependence*. By this he means that we live within a system that determines how we relate to each other in the economic, cultural, political, and religious spheres (SRS, no. 38.6). (Two obvious examples: the livelihood of a coffee farmer in Brazil or Kenya depends on economic trends in North America and Europe; and the values of persons in remote parts of Africa or Asia are now being affected by the television "soap operas" made in the U.S.A.)

Secondly, this interdependence is not a purely neutral fact; it raises a serious moral challenge. The person who recognizes human interdependence and wants to act in an appropriate moral way is called to overcome distrust of others and to *collaborate* with them instead (SRS, no. 39.8).

Thirdly, such *acts* of collaboration spring from the *virtue of solidarity* (SRS, no. 39.8). As a virtue, solidarity is not just a feeling but "a firm and persevering determination to commit oneself to the common good" (SRS, no. 38.6). It is an *attitude* of commitment to the good of one's neighbor, coupled with a readiness to sacrifice oneself in the service of the other (SRS, no. 38.6). (I shall return at more length in the next section to the pope's account of solidarity as a virtue.)

Fourthly, within any particular country, the virtue of solidarity transforms the *interpersonal relationships* of individuals with the persons around them. It causes the more powerful to feel responsible for those who are weak and makes them ready to share what they have with them. It leads those who are weak or poor to reject destructive or passive attitudes; while claiming their own rights, they will work for the good of all. It enables those in an in-between position to respect the interests of others (SRS, no. 39.1). This account seems somewhat bland. It could have benefited from a social analysis that would take more seriously the causes of the class structure of society and an examination of ways in which tensions between the different classes can be lessened. Furthermore, the account given here seems to lack a certain theological dimension: there is no great emphasis on the special role that God has given to those who are weak and poor in bringing liberation to all. The pope does, however, point out that the church feels called by the gospel to take a stand alongside the poor in their public but nonviolent demands for justice (SRS, no. 39.2).

Fifthly, the virtue of solidarity is exercised also by whole *nations* in their relationship with other nations. Nations, like persons, are linked in a system that makes them dependent on each other. Within this international system, the powerful and wealthy nations are morally bound to resist the temptation to "imperialism" and "hegemony"; in other words, they must not dominate, oppress, or exploit the others (SRS, nos. 39.3, 39.4, 39.6). In addition to the kind of economic exploitation and political oppression that occurs so frequently, there is a less obvious form of cultural "imperialism" that Western nations exercise over other peoples. It arises from the very concept of "development." The economists and planners who draft "development plans" for First World, Second World, or Third World countries generally take for granted that the central elements include rapid "growth" of the economy, a high level of investment, increased productivity, a higher average per capita income, increased use of "high" technology rather than labor-intensive technology, and so forth. This conception of "development" is based very much on the experience of Western countries (even though it now operates in Japan, Korea, and elsewhere). More basically, it is a product of Western culture. Non-Western countries that adopt it are importing an idea (and ultimately a model of living) that did not grow out of their own traditional patterns of thought and action. To make this kind of development "work" in other cultures involves imposing, to a greater or lesser extent, a *Western* concept on other cultures. The conception of development proposed in *Populorum Progressio* and the understanding of international "solidarity" outlined in the present encyclical offer a strong challenge to this imposition. What the pope proposes here is a community of *peoples*, each with its own unique culture. "Solidarity" means taking seriously the different value systems of the various cultures (see SRS, no. 14), rather than the imposition of a Western model of development on other peoples.

Sixthly, by transforming both the relationship between individuals and that between nations, the virtue of solidarity brings about a radical change in society as a whole. It gives persons the ability to oppose diametrically the desire for profit and the thirst for power, as well as the "structures of sin," which are the fruit of the many sinful acts of choosing profit and power at any price (SRS, nos. 38.6 and 37). In this way it provides a foundation of a whole new set of *structures*, which can be called "the civilization of love" (SRS, no. 33.8).

Seventhly, there is a sense in which one might speak not merely of "human solidarity" but even of "ecological solidarity." The pope does not quite use this phrase, but it seems to sum up what he has in mind. For he speaks of "a greater realization of the limits of available resources and of the need to respect the integrity and the cycles of nature" (SRS, no. 26.7). He insists on the moral requirement that we have "respect for the beings which constitute the natural world, which the ancient Greeks called . . . the 'cosmos' "(SRS, no. 34.1) – and he goes on to write at some length about the moral obligations imposed on us by our ecological situation (SRS, no. 34). Later, he speaks of "the urgent need to change the spiritual attitudes which define each individual's relationship with self, with neighbor, with even the remotest human communities, and with nature itself " (SRS, no. 38.3). This indicates that the moral dimension of genuine human development involves a sense of responsibility for the whole cosmos; such moral responsibility is either a part of the virtue of solidarity itself or else it is a sister virtue that has very much in common with it.

Finally, there is the matter of what happens if persons refuse the challenge to be in solidarity with others—if they respond with disinterest instead of concern, if their attitude is one of "using" others rather than respecting them. Individuals or groups or nations that act in this way may grow more wealthy but they cannot be said to be truly "developed," for they are ignoring the crucial *moral* dimension of human development (SRS, no. 9.9). The pope notes that the lack of solidarity between the nations has "disastrous consequences" for the weaker ones; but it also has serious "negative effects even in the rich countries" (SRS, no. 17.1). These include negative economic effects such as inadequate housing and growing unemployment (SRS, nos. 17.2, 18.2). Even more serious are the moral and political effects. For instance, failure of the nations to overcome their distrust of each other leads to continued imperialism and a turning away from the path to peace (SRS, nos. 39.8, 22.3); and the so-called developed nations of East and West become locked into ideological and military opposition (SRS, no. 20.6), wasting on an arms race the resources needed for development (SRS, no. 22.5).

THE VIRTUE OF SOLIDARITY

Nearly twenty years ago the pope (then Cardinal Karol Wojtyla) was already writing about solidarity. He described it as an *attitude*, a commitment on the part of those who form a community, to participate in the life of that community in a way that promotes the common good.[3] He took up the topic again in his 1981 encyclical *Laborem Exercens* (*On Human Labor*). In that encyclical he did not go into a philosophical or theological analysis of solidarity, but concentrated on its practical aspects. He used the term as it is commonly used, to denote the kind of concrete activities of mutual support by which members of an oppressed group strengthen each other to resist injustice. For instance, he wrote about a "call to solidarity and common action addressed to the workers" (LE, no. 8).

In the present encyclical the pope puts forward a more the-

ological analysis of the virtue of solidarity. It is an enabling
power that gives us the capacity to respect others:

> Solidarity helps us to see the "other"—whether a person,
> people, or nation—not just as some kind of instrument
> with a work capacity and physical strength to be exploited
> at low cost and then discarded when no longer useful, but
> as our "neighbor," a "helper" (see Gn 2:18-20), to be made
> a sharer, on a par with ourselves, in the banquet of life to
> which all are equally invited by God [SRS, no. 39.5].

In this way the virtue of solidarity enables us to overcome distrust and to collaborate with others (SRS, no. 39.8). Consequently, the exercise of this virtue is the path to true peace (SRS,
no. 39.9).

Interestingly, the pope at this point notes that the achievement of peace involves not merely the putting into effect of
social and international *justice*, but also requires "the practice
of the virtues which favor togetherness, and which teach us to
live in unity, so as to build in unity, by giving and receiving, a
new society and a better world" (SRS, no. 39.10). This helps us
to understand the relationship between the virtue of justice and
the virtue of solidarity. Solidarity is not just a matter of fulfilling
the obligations of strict justice. It presupposes that but goes
beyond it by including generosity, care for others, even (perhaps) a warm friendliness (though the encyclical does not have
much to say about such "mere" feelings, as I shall point out
later).

The aspect of generous self-sacrifice is developed more fully
by the pope when he goes on to focus attention on the *Christian*
character of the virtue of solidarity. He suggests that "solidarity
seeks to go beyond itself, to take on the specifically Christian
dimensions of total gratuity, forgiveness, and reconciliation."
John Paul finds the basis for this selfless love in the fact that
each person is the living image of God (SRS, no. 40.2). He goes
on to say that, for the Christian, the ultimate inspiration for
solidarity comes from a unity that is even deeper than any unity
based on natural and human bonds; this is a *communion*, a re-

flection of the unity of the three Persons in one God (SRS, no. 40.3).

AFFECTIVE BASIS?

Pope John Paul's account of the virtue of solidarity is a valuable one. He has made a praiseworthy attempt to give solid theological content to a word that is widely used in the world today, a word that describes a feature of modern moral consciousness at its best. There can be no doubt that he has met a real need, since a moral account of human development that is confined to such traditional words as "charity" and "justice" can seem at times to lack the flavor of real life.

However, there is one point at which his account of the virtue of solidarity seems to be somewhat underdeveloped: it appears to lack an *affective* dimension. This is perhaps surprising, for one suspects that his account of solidarity owes a great deal to the strong affective bonds that link him so closely to his own people in their history and their struggles. In any case, I feel that what he has to say about solidarity could be enriched significantly by some account of the *experience* of solidarity and the strong *feelings* that are part of it.

By the "experience" of solidarity I mean the actual sharing of life with a group of persons. When one shares the living conditions of a community, one can begin to share their sufferings and joys, their fears and their hopes. Out of this lived solidarity grow the bonds of affection that make one feel part of this people and enable them to accept one as truly part of themselves. It is a kind of miracle of the human spirit, and of God's grace, that this can take place even across boundaries of class and race.

The bonds of shared life and feelings are the most effective way to evoke and nourish a strong sense of responsibility for the whole community and especially for its weaker members. This suggests that the virtue of solidarity should not be defined as purely an attitude of the *will* in contrast to "mere feelings": for the lived experience of solidarity and the feelings that go with it are the normal way in which commitment grows. Book study on its own is not very helpful in bridging the gap that often exists between the *fact* of interdependence and the undertaking of an appropriate *moral response*. Neither is prayer on its own. Study and prayer are certainly useful and even necessary. But they must be situated within the context of some degree of shared life with persons and the bonds of affectivity to which such sharing gives rise.

NOTES

1. I am using the English-language edition of the encyclical issued by the Vatican (Libreria Editrice Vaticana). Because the numbered sections are sometimes quite lengthy, I am using the following reference system to facilitate those who may wish to look up references to, or quotations from, the encyclical: SRS, no. 1.2, refers to the second paragraph of the first numbered section in the encyclical; SRS, no. 3.1, refers to the first paragraph of the third numbered section in the encyclical; and so on. (The paragraphs are not numbered in this way in the text, but they can easily be so counted.)

2. The inspiration of Lebret pervades *Populorum Progressio*, and some of the statements in the encyclical are taken almost word for word from Lebret's writings. See François Malley, *Le Père Lebret: l'économie au service des hommes* (Paris: Cerf, 1968), p. 99.

3. Karol Wojtyla (Pope John Paul II), *An Anthology*, Alfred Bloch and George T. Czuczka, eds. (New York: Crossroad, 1981), p. 47; the material in this part of the anthology is taken from a study entitled *Osoba i Czyn* (The self and the act) published by Karol Wojtyla in 1969.

7

John Paul II and Fidel Castro: Two Views of Development

William K. Tabb

In *Sollicitudo Rei Socialis* John Paul II commemorates the twentieth anniversary of Paul VI's *Populorum Progressio*. He proposes to extend the impact of that message "by bringing it to bear, with its possible applications, upon the present historical moment." The importance of this task, the characterization of the present configuration of relations between the rich and the poor of the world, the proper nuancing of the concept of development, and the ways of putting the social gospel into effect, are among the most crucial questions of our time. Hence the importance of this encyclical cannot be overestimated. The positive and very important contribution of John Paul II's encyclical is to offer a moral counter to the lack of solidarity that dominates the individualistic, selfish, neoconservative culture and public policy that have gained favor in our time. *Sollicitudo* offers spiritual legitimation to progressive Christians and other caring persons who struggle for a just society.

In evaluating the encyclical, the question from my perspective is whether this moral orientation is embedded in an economic and social analysis sufficient for effective translation of its principles into a praxis of meaningful social change?

I must say at the outset that my judgment (to be developed below) is that the imprecision of John Paul's formulations do not offer the best guidance to those working for social justice. He writes in general terms. He denounces the existence of "economic, financial, and social *mechanisms* which, although they are manipulated by people, often function almost automatically, thus accentuating the situation of wealth for some and poverty for the rest" (no. 16). He describes debt as a changed circumstance in which debtors find they must "export the capital needed for improving or at least maintaining their standard of living" (no. 19). John Paul quotes his predecessor's famous words, "development is the new name for peace" and asks, "How can one justify the fact that huge sums of money, which could and should be used for increasing the development of peoples, are instead utilized for the enrichment of individuals or groups or assigned to the increase of stockpiles of weapons, thereby upsetting the real priorities?" (no. 10). These are powerful statements.

Moral exhortation in this mode is badly needed but it is also insufficient. One is either preaching to the converted, who certainly would not want to justify the sinful priorities of this world, or ineffective in reaching those who might argue both that the communist threat requires such military spending and that capital accumulation, premised on savings and reward to economic activity, benefits rich and poor alike. Even for those prepared to accept the pope's message, the unanswered question is still, What is to be done?

There is an inadequacy in the pope's appeal to the rich to help the poor. The lack of social analysis leaves the pontiff's message resting on an appeal to the powerful to voluntarily redress the unfairness of the "unequal distribution of the means of subsistence originally meant for everybody, and thus also an unequal distribution of the benefits deriving from them" (no. 9). Extending Pope Paul's "duty of solidarity," John Paul writes:

> Political leaders and citizens of rich countries considered as individuals, especially if they are Christians, have the moral obligation, according to the degree of each one's responsibility, to take into consideration in personal de-

cisions and decisions of government this relationship of universality, this interdependence which exists between their conduct and the poverty and underdevelopment of so many millions of people [no. 9].

The pope sees the rich nation succumbing to the temptation to close in upon itself and failing "to meet the responsibility following from its superior position in the community of nations" (no. 23). It is certainly true that in a period of stagnant or declining living standards for most U.S. citizens, foreign aid is a low priority. In point of fact, existing foreign aid programs are hardly what the pope has in mind. They are close adjuncts to the projection of military policy, earmarked for regional allies, and based neither on the index of suffering nor on a strategy of autonomous development geared to meet basic needs.

At a more basic level, neither the United States, nor the international agencies it influences, like the International Monetary Fund, have turned their backs on the Third World.[1] Our government is busy attempting to force these nations to stop protecting their domestic producers, to buy more U.S. exports, and to pay debts owed U.S.-based banks at the expense of the hungry who badly need these resources to be allocated to domestic development. It is simply incorrect to see the rich nations as "growing in selfish isolation." The selfishness is there, but it exists in the context of immense transfers from the poor to the rich.

If as John Paul has written, "the social question has acquired a worldwide dimension, this is because the demand for justice can only be satisfied at that level" (no. 10). This does not mean that we should move quickly to propose solutions without first understanding the forces that have created and perpetuate injustice. This is an important necessary step. It is the task of social analysis. But it is for the most part omitted from *Sollicitudo Rei Socialis*.

Important as it is to state the reality of an innumerable multitude of unique human persons who are suffering under the intolerable burden of poverty, it is not sufficient. While we may be moved by concern for our brothers and sisters, how are we to be empowered to understand not just this suffering but the institutional impediments to social justice? The pope appears to suggest that knowledge of the existence of suffering, and of the abundance of goods and services available in the developed parts of the world, when combined with an appeal to conscience, will provide sufficient basis for a solution. The unity of the human race is the ultimate reality; indifference is a sin that cannot continue. This is a basic message of church social teachings, but it must be contextualized in an understanding of our present situation.

The pope states clearly that what is hindering full development is the "desire for profit and thirst for power." He is aware of the "structures of sin," but his appeal for change is directed to "those who are more influential because they have a greater share of goods and common services" and so "should feel responsible for the weaker and be ready to share with them all they possess" (no. 39). The weaker are called on to be neither passive nor destructive of the social fabric, but they are given little guidance as to how to claim what is their legitimate right except that they should do what they can for the good of all. This is so imprecise a formulation that it could be interpreted as condemning action to demand the very redistribution of wealth and power for which the situation of injustice would seem to cry out. Further, the church "feels called to stand beside the poor, to discern the justice of their requests, and to help satisfy them without losing sight of the good of groups in the context of the common good" (no. 39). These are not words to inspire those who would take risks in solidarity with the oppressed. It is a wish that change could come without struggle.

A prophetic statement that the rich should give to the poor as a matter of charity or justice must also explore the sources of their riches. How have they "built their upper stories"? If these are found to be in part or in full the result of unequal social relations, then they must be dismantled. The call for justice for the poor must include the structural inequalities that created and perpetuate both their poverty and the wealth enjoyed by the privileged. It is not only a matter of the responsible use of wealth but the investigation of where the wealth came from. If it came from the oppression of subject peoples, this is reason enough to build new institutions through which the development of each person is the goal and need of the whole population.

In treating the key relation as that between the rich countries, which should be more generous, and the poor nations which lack resources, the pope implicitly ignores the advantages gained by the core nations from low-cost commodities produced in the periphery. He also overlooks the natural political alliance based on economic interests between elites in these nations and the core economies. One could also note the extent to which these elites rule through coercion. The success of their export model thrives on low wages (enforced by repression) and this economic policy makes popular support difficult, if not impossible, to attain. The fact that wealthy nations, as a matter of policy, support these economic relations commits them to military aid and often direct involvement in suppressing dissent. Under conditions of extreme inequality of wealth and power, free trade and free markets require unfree societies.

The pope might also reflect on what has been called "development as a threatening myth." The very notion of development as it is projected by the experts seems to have an inherent bias against the poor. Gustavo Esteva has written:

> Most peasants were aware that development undermined their subsistence on centuries' old diversified crops. People in the barrios knew that development made their skills redundant and their education inadequate. When they succeeded in fostering community life in hand-made shanties or abandoned buildings, bulldozers and police—both in the service of development—deported them to "relocation sites."[2]

What does development mean? What does it cost? Whom does it benefit? How is it paid for? These are some of the questions that must inform a moral intervention on the issue of development. There are a number of topics that might be considered in this light.

Alternative development approaches, which stress land reform and grass-roots development, require the expropriation of land holdings from elites and a shift to production of food for local consumption to more profitable cash crops. Appropriate technologies using local resources and renewable labor-intensive methods that are not import-dependent fly in the face of existing patterns of profit making. A shift from encouraging giant transnational investment to small-scale local producers and other strategies that seek directly to raise living standards through self-development and participation are not welcomed by military-bureaucratic regimes nor by their foreign allies and local elite sponsors. How do we address this ongoing conflict between the vast majority of the poor and the few who now dominate them?

It would seem to me that raising such concerns would be appropriate. But even if the pontiff preferred to stay at the most general level, there are important points that could be made about the debt crisis and the misery it is causing. Such points have been made by many world leaders, especially from Latin America. If we believe that "what happens in Latin America will, humanly speaking, determine the fate of the church in the next century," as Pope John Paul II said to the Latin American bishops' meeting at Puebla in 1979, then the articulation of solidarity with such a position would seem a powerful and important step the pope might take.

In the remaining portion of this paper I will draw on such an articulation made by perhaps the most prominent spokesman for the Third World, Fidel Castro. Let me be clear that I am not proposing a debate between Catholic social teaching and Marxism. Rather I am contending that given the faith commitment to be in solidarity with the poor, the analysis presented by Fidel Castro deepens our understanding of the important insights of *Sollicitudo Rei Socialis*. If readers think even consideration of such a prospect is outrageous, they should clearly stop reading at this point. However, I would hope many will be interested in the essential compatibility I think can be demonstrated between the two documents, one the encyclical, the other the text of an extensive interview by Fidel Castro on debt and the development process.[3]

A system of privileged economic relations for the industrial countries (the phrase and the following analysis are Castro's) is one in which the Latin American countries are expected to develop and yet are paid less for their exports and charged more for their imports, in which their hard currency is drained away through capital flight, and their exports are restricted. They are subjected to devastating forms of unfair competition. They are forced to devalue their currencies and are charged arbitrarily high interest rates on the enormous debts that have been imposed on them.

This last point is of great significance because debt is strangling the Latin Americans (and others in the poorer nations). Much of the debt went to military armaments, luxury imports, corruption, and capital flight. The people got very little and now are told they must pay. Castro offers the analysis of a political economist, but his judgment belongs in the prophetic tradition:

> What is truly immoral, an act of bad faith, practically a betrayal of humankind, is to force the people to go hungry, to live in poverty; to live in the worst material, educational, cultural, and health conditions in order to spend a trillion dollars on weapons and military activities every year—for this is what is being spent on preparing the conditions for a catastrophe, to kill hundreds of millions of people and perhaps even to wipe out humankind.

The greater power of the richer nations makes it appear that it is the poor who most need trade, while for the rich it is somehow a matter of charity. Castro sees the matter differently:

> Can you imagine an industrialized society without chocolate? Can you imagine those countries without coffee, tea, or cashew nuts to go with their drinks? Can you imagine them without nutmeg, cloves, other spices, peanuts, sesame seeds, pineapples, coconut oil for their mild and fragrant soaps? Well, life would be very sad and unpleasant in the industrialized countries if the steel, copper, aluminum, chemical and power industries were also to stop. They cannot do without any of that.

From a moral perspective Castro questions the existing pattern of trade. He asks: What do we get for our products? And he answers: "Very low wages, no social security or unemployment compensation, no medical care, no education, no culture, no recreation, no hope of progress, premature aging and early death. And things are getting worse ... everyday there is more hunger for more people; everyday there is more poverty." There are not many Latin Americans who would disagree. The stance Castro takes is from the Third World and his advocacy of change starts from the viewpoint of those who have been brought into the world system by force and held in positions of subordination by structural relations of injustice.

Castro offers various mathematical calculations to show that the debt is also unpayable. No matter what the growth rate, even with optimistic forecasts and low interest, the debt could never be repaid. Here we would need to add that the banks would not want it repaid. They would then have to go through the trouble of finding someone else to lend to. What they want is dependable, uninterrupted, and perpetual interest payments. But, because this is currently not possible, some solution to the crisis of nonpayment of interest (the bank's problem) needs to be found without transferring the burden to the poorest of the poor. Castro's solution is simple and it would seem to me morally unobjectionable. If accepted, the debtor nations could again become customers for industrial products, putting workers back to work in the rich nations. He does not suggest that the banks lose their money or that taxpayers pay more taxes. He suggests something very simple:

> To use a small percent of military expenditures—which could not be more than 12 percent—so the creditor states can assume the debts of their own banks. This way, neither the banks nor the depositors would lose: on the contrary, the banks would have that money guaranteed.

Why could not the rich nations do this? If they consider themselves capable of dreaming up and waging "Star Wars" with barely a thought to the risks involved in a thermonuclear conflict that would in the first minute destroy a hundred times more than what is due the banks—in short, if the idea of universal suicide does not scare them, why should they be afraid of something as simple as cancelation of the Third World debt?

Castro notes: "I'm not advocating social revolution in those countries; I'm not advocating the nationalization of foreign enterprises; I'm not advocating any of those steps. I am proposing formulas in the financial sphere, which I feel, would benefit all the underdeveloped and even the developed countries." Castro asserts also that a different, more egalitarian and fraternal relation between superpowers and smaller, poorer states would or at least could include some of these mechanisms: long-term purchasing agreements, loans without interest, respect for basic needs before exports, and so on.

Castro says a socialist can better understand and is better prepared to understand from a theoretical point of view the folly of spending on weapons the resources needed to meet pressing human needs. Why not Christians? Do they not also believe "the arms race is a crime against humankind"? Is peacemaking the province solely of Marxists? It would seem that John Paul does not believe so. He makes the same connection in *Sollicitudo Rei Socialis* that Castro does between the cost of weapons of death and the needs of development. Is not Castro's proposal one logical extension of a shared understanding?

The pope speaks of the "unacceptable delay" in not sharing the wealth from the developed North with the poor of the South. "The pace of progress in the developing countries in recent years has differed, and thus serves to widen the distances." The pope's formulation contrasts with Castro's analysis of underdevelopment and his treatment of the mechanisms and relations of domination. But interestingly, with the pope, Castro believes that "all the countries that, in one way or another, have achieved the privilege of development have the elementary duty of expressing solidarity with this immense area of poverty and underdevelopment. This entails human and moral principles." This is not very different from John Paul's understanding.

Castro notes that some religions denounce interest and even assert that charging interest constitutes robbery. From such perspectives the current high interest rates demanded for refinancing when debtors cannot pay is robbery "in a way that is not permitted by any religion." Few contemporary religious leaders, and not the pope in this encyclical, have spoken out in such a direct moral condemnation of the debt relation as one of social bondage.

It is important to see that Castro's proposals, while dramatic, are not revolutionary in the way we have come to associate with his name. As he says:

> I'm not advocating social revolution in those countries; I'm not advocating the nationalization of foreign enterprises. ... I am proposing formulas in the financial sphere, which I feel, would benefit all the underdeveloped and even the developed countries. ... It would even help the foreign companies with investments in those countries, the companies that have had trade relations with those countries, the companies that produce goods for those countries. And, in the creditor countries, the state would not be hurt economically. To the contrary, they would raise their level of employment and use of industrial capacity; their banks would not have only losses; and their taxpayers would not have to pay any more taxes.

Listing some of the same unequal trade patterns, Fidel endorses the New International Economic Order and notes that the Third World countries, which for centuries were colonies and suppliers of exotic products, raw materials, and cheap fuels, are not to blame for their economic backwardness. The excessive fluctuations in the price of commodities, exchange rates, and interest rates, as well as the denial of needed forms of technology are to blame. He also notes that some nations "need to reform certain unjust structures and in particular political institutions, in order to replace corrupt, dictatorial, and authoritarian forms of government."

I have quoted extensively from Castro's own words for a number of reasons. Few readers will have direct access to them. Most of what we know of his views is filtered through distorted lenses. Even this brief summary will indicate the clarity of analysis and rhetoric that have made Castro such an effective spokesman for the nonaligned movement and the Third World.

The pope clearly has a quite different style and self-presentation. My interest here in Castro's approach has been in my perception of a stronger, more coherent and practical orientation which is not inconsistent with what I would hope is John Paul's purpose. It would have been more diplomatic to cite the significant number of bishops and theologians who speak a more familiar language than does this "godless communist."[4] But on the topic of development the Cuban leader has a sound analysis, which goes beyond the present encyclical, though not, I think, in ways that are contradictory to Catholic social teachings. If the fact that Castro says these things makes them off limits, then we are also saying something else. If we cannot genuinely learn from persons who do not share some of our fundamental beliefs, we have narrowed our options for understanding reality.

John Paul II has attempted to construct a universal document that speaks with one voice to the rich and the poor, and to guide both to do justice within the confines of the given structures of this world. In choosing such an inherently conservative stance, he has created a disappointing document. As the comparison I have made demonstrates, the pope has shown an inadequate ability, or perhaps willingness, to engage many of the central issues.

We desperately need a prophetic vision for our age. Our condition cries out for alternatives in the midst of the madness of sinful greed. The economic programs we are seeking require moral awareness and are best grounded on the belief that a new world is possible on earth as it is in heaven. Along with a reaffirmation of faith and general moral guidance, it would be so much better if we had a theology that studied the realities of the poor and reflected closely on them as the first step in understanding what God would have us do here and now.

NOTES

1. It may be that the IMF is beyond the scope of moral teachings. But this is a question of how one views the morality of IMF policies. It may be noted that John Paul II denounces terrorism, quite tangential in the context of his topic, in terms proposed by the rich nations, ignoring state terrorism that sponsors both military destabilization, so-called low-intensity war against countries wishing to break from the imperialist system, and the terror unleashed on the poor of debtor

nations by the policies of institutions like the IMF and the World Bank. The problem in the pope's eyes is the insufficiency of political will to help the poor. But the larger reality is the political power exercised by bankers to force every ounce of blood they can from the poor of debtor nations.

2. Gustavo Esteva, "Alternatives to Economics," a talk presented to the Eastern Economics Association annual meeting, Boston, March 11, 1988, reprinted in Don Cole, *Macroeconomics*, 89/90 (1989), p. 197.

3. Fidel Castro, "There's No Choice: The Cancelation of Debt or the Political Death of Democratic Processes in Latin America" (Havana: Ed. Política, March 29, 1985).

4. The character of the Cuban revolution is not irrelevant to the discussion at hand. In Latin America, clergy and laity divide over how they see Cuba. The charged nature of the issue is demonstrated by the very divided reactions to a letter addressed to Castro by Cardinal Arns to mark the thirtieth anniversary of the Cuban revolution in early 1989. The head of Brazil's largest Catholic archdiocese, Rio de Janeiro, Arns said that Cuba offered an example of social justice to the rest of Latin America, and added, "Christian faith discovers in the achievements of the revolution signs of the kingdom of God." "You are present daily in my prayers," Cardinal Arns told Castro, "and I ask the Father that he always concede you the grace of guiding the destinies of your country."

The archbishop's letter was not appreciated by conservatives in Brazil. In an editorial entitled "Adherence to Atheism," the Rio de Janeiro daily *O Globo* said it was "simply unbelievable that an archbishop should discover similarities between the kingdom of God and a totalitarian police state" that imposes atheism as official policy. Leonardo Boff argued that Cardinal Arns simply recognized in his letter that "Cuba carried out a revolution against hunger by ending prostitution, illiteracy, and misery." He added, "Dom Paulo is not a socialist, but a man of the poor and the oppressed" (Alan Riding, "Brazil Cardinal's Praise of Castro Stirs Protest," *New York Times*, February 5, 1989, p. 20).

I have not wanted to deal with the economic and political interpretation of Cuban realities. Readers may want to consult a popularly written and accessible, yet not uncritical, overview: Jean Stubbs, *Cuba: The Test of Time*, Latin American Bureau, 1989, distributed in the U.S.A. by Monthly Review Press, 122 West 27th St., New York, NY 10011.

8

Conflicting Paradigms in Social Analysis

Mary E. Hobgood

This essay seeks to join discussions that are going on in two separate bodies of analysis. The first is the Catholic social justice tradition, a series of papal encyclicals and episcopal pastoral letters that have sought to address growing conditions of poverty and socio-economic marginalization. This tradition begins in 1891 with Leo XIII's letter *Rerum Novarum*. Its most recent manifestation is the 1987 encyclical by Pope John Paul II entitled *Sollicitudo Rei Socialis* or *On Social Concern*.

A second body of analysis that my discussion draws upon is that of social analysis within the field of social theory. Social analysis seeks to interpret how the primary social structures of capitalist societies (including production, labor market structures, government policy and spending, and welfare and unemployment programs) actually work. Because there are primarily two explanations about the way these structures are related—the capitalist explanation and what I will call the liberation explanation—the field of social analysis is involved in a major ideological debate. At issue is how best to interpret how the various institutions of political economy are related to the creation of wealth and the existence of poverty. I will argue that, until most recently, this debate within the field of social theory has been reflected in an ongoing way within the tradition of Catholic social justice teaching as it has sought to analyze structures that keep persons in socio-economic marginalization.

As a way of focusing in on this debate, I will compare the social analysis of Pope John Paul II with the wider body of Catholic social analysis since 1891. I will focus especially on the recent papal encyclical *On Social Concern*, issued to commemorate the twentieth anniversary of Pope Paul VI's well-known encyclical *Populorum Progressio*, or *On the Development of Peoples* (1967).

Since "underdevelopment" and human economic suffering have increased, not diminished, in the ensuing twenty years, John Paul II desired in this commemorative document to "extend the impact" of Paul's encyclical by "bringing it to bear upon the present historical moment." Because Third World conditions of poverty and unemployment are being manifest now "even in the rich countries," John Paul II is impelled to apply Paul's teaching in what he considers to be a "fuller and more nuanced" way.[1] It is my thesis, however, that John Paul II does not enunciate Paul's teaching more fully. Rather, I will argue that this "traditionalist" pope has taken a noticeable departure from traditional or mainstream Catholic social teaching by ignoring structural criticisms concerning the causes of poverty, and by disregarding radical prescriptions of what might be done about poverty. Such structural criticisms and radical prescriptions, which may be aligned with a liberation social theory, are present not only in Paul's encyclical, but can be found consistently within the Catholic social justice tradition itself.

Before placing this letter within the context of the wider tradition, I wish to give some reasons why attention to social analysis is so important in the development of social ethics or a social justice tradition. One of the central tasks of social ethics is to apply norms of social justice to the use of social power. Over the years papal encyclicals and letters by Catholic bishops have developed such moral norms as economic democracy, universal dignified social participation, and a preferential option for the poor.

While some of the normative values in the Catholic social

justice tradition have enjoyed a fairly wide consensus, the interpretation in this tradition as to how these moral norms or values
are to be applied in actual societies has been fraught with tensions and contradictions. This situation is a result of the fact
that within the Catholic Church, as in society at large, there is
a lack of consensus about how the social, political, and economic
structures of late twentieth-century capitalist societies actually
work. If there is no consensus on the way the world works, there
is no consensus on the causes of poverty, the chief concern of
the Catholic social justice tradition. If there are inconsistent
interpretations of the problem, there is confusion about the concrete actions needed to achieve economic justice. Indeed the
social analysis in Catholic social justice documents reflects a
major contemporary ideological debate between liberation and
capitalist interpretations of capitalist dynamics.

To illustrate my point, I will first briefly outline major differences in the liberation/capitalist debate concerning how social
power is distributed in capitalist societies. I will argue that, from
the late nineteenth century through the papacy of Paul VI, the
social justice tradition of the Catholic Church has been engaged
in an ongoing analysis of modern capitalism that may be aligned
with both capitalist *and* liberation interpretive models. It is important to address the presence of incompatible interpretations
of social power within this tradition because such moral norms
as universal dignified social participation, democracy at the
workplace, and a preferential option for the poor necessitate
different moral action when they assume one social model, or
interpretive framework, than they do when the other model is
understood.

THE CAPITALIST-LIBERATION DEBATE

Capitalist or neoclassical social theory, that interpretation of
so-called free market economies inherited from the eighteenth-
century political economist Adam Smith, is a view of capitalism
that most of us have assimilated unconsciously. It assumes that
persons function autonomously in their economic lives and that
they are primarily interested in increasing their own economic
consumption and in maximizing profit. The capitalist market is

the logical extension of this theory about persons, and the so-called free or privately controlled market is believed to be as "natural" as the human body. Capitalist theory assumes that persons have the resources and skills to enter the market and that people operate in the market out of the desire to make profit, not out of the need to sustain themselves. Therefore, the presence of sufficient food, shelter, and clothing is simply assumed by the capitalist model.

Capitalist theory also assumes that self-interest operating through the market will guide resources to their most efficient use and distribute goods and services in a reasonably just manner. If the capitalist market does not create and distribute socially useful wealth perfectly, at least it does it better than any other system possibly could. Capitalists further argue that persons in traditional societies, due to particular cultural values or political instability in the region, are often unable to make choices to ensure their economic advancement.

The capitalist model assumes that poverty and unemployment are individual social problems that are most often due to a temporary disequilibrium or malfunctioning in the market, which will eventually iron itself out. If not, these "problems" are due to forces outside the economic system such as ignorance or prejudice, disturbances of free exchange by labor unions or government interference, or to the personal qualities of the poor themselves.

Finally, in the capitalist understanding of socio-economic reality, political and cultural organizations are thought to function separately from the economic arena. Consequently, such presumably "autonomous" organizations as the liberal state and religious bodies are thought to be capable of reforming or mitigating excesses of economic power, should they occur in the market. Liberals who espouse capitalist theory believe that the government can help solve such problems as racism, sexism, and unemployment through job creation, affirmative action, the increased availability of education, and the like.

When the Catholic social justice tradition reflects the capitalist model of social analysis, it advocates the superiority of the capitalist system and supports capitalist "development" of Third World markets and increased capitalist penetration in depressed areas. For example, in the late nineteenth and early twentieth centuries, Leo XIII and Pius XI, contrary to earlier church tradition, held that the right to private ownership was more fundamental than the duty to use property in a socially responsible way.[2] Every pope from John XXIII to John Paul II has indicated that the application of private economic initiative and the latest Western technology could eradicate poverty in most instances. Their writings assume the existing structures of capital and labor, the inevitability of a society structured by class, and the naturalness of a gender-based division of labor. Further, all papal documents have contained primarily, if not exclusively, the advocacy of liberal agents and liberal strategies for social reform that assume the capitalist model. For example, in most of the documents of the Catholic social justice tradition, the prescribed social change agents are primarily those who already hold power in the system—that is, governments, international agencies, and corporate elites. Similarly, the strategies for social change the popes and bishops most often propose are those based on strengthening the welfare aspects of the system as it currently exists, such as job training, affirmative action, and increased education.

However, in its analysis of poverty and in its prescriptions for social change, the Catholic tradition has also reflected assumptions that may be aligned with the liberation social model. Liberation social theory is a radical social theory, rooted in the work of the classic economists of the eighteenth and nineteenth centuries, particularly in the work of Karl Marx. In the late twentieth century, this social theory finds expression in critical forms of neo-Marxism and antiracist and socialist feminist analysis. Liberation social theory claims that production for satisfying human needs, not production for profit, is the "natural" economic activity. Contrary to the capitalist model, a liberation analysis of capitalist political economy claims that political, cultural, and market institutions do not function autonomously but form one interlocking structure in the service of private capital accumulation. Liberation theorists argue, for example, that those who prosper in the capitalist market depend for their economic well-being upon such political structures as the militarized state, such economic structures as the secondary labor market, and such cultural structures as the race and gender systems.

Through the militarization of economies and vast public expenditures for expensive weapons systems produced for private profit, the state has sustained sufficient aggregate demand — which decreasing wages cannot — to keep corporations profitable and to keep the world safe for expanding global capitalism. Liberation theory argues that in order for corporations to compete successfully, they must also reproduce such economic structures as the segmented labor market. The segmented labor market keeps women and minorities at the bottom, and an underclass of structurally unemployed in the poverty and welfare systems, which together keep wages and costs down. For example, government statistics yield that, despite the post-World War II economic boom, the civil rights movement and the feminist movement, 60 percent of blacks who were employed in 1970 and over 70 percent of women who were employed in 1985 occupy the gender and racially segregated labor of the secondary labor market — those poorly paid, low-benefit jobs in food service, peripheral manufacturing, clerical, and the lowest rungs of health and education work.[3] Radical theorists claim that the welfare system supports this gender and racially segregated labor market by creating an outcast welfare class, treated with contempt, which functions to make the worst jobs in the secondary labor market seem more attractive.

According to the liberation social model, these economic institutions — the segmented labor market and the welfare system — in turn depend upon the cultural institutions of racism and sexism for their structural legitimation. Racism and sexism serve to justify persons' unequal access to resources by explaining why some deserve what they get and others do not deserve what they lack. With racism and sexism alive and well, white women and people of color who populate the secondary labor market and the welfare system are less likely to resist their situations, because they do not identify with the mostly white men who populate the primary and better paid labor market. A liberation social theory claims that the wage differentials between men and women, and between whites and people of color, save capitalists enormous amounts of money and are necessary to the profits these businesses make and to their successful survival in the capitalist market system. Liberation theorists claim that coalitions of marginalized persons can organize themselves in the struggle to create a new society amenable to their welfare.

In contrast to the capitalist social model, then, a liberation or radical social model believes that cultural, political, and economic structures do not function autonomously to check and balance one another. It claims that the political economy is a unified entity in the service of the system of private capital accumulation. Liberation theory argues that capitalism is not "natural" or the logical extension of human nature but is created to serve the interests of those few—certainly less than 10 percent of the population in the U.S.A.—who own or control the social means of producing wealth. It understands that classism, racism, and sexism, and their reflections in such structures as poverty, unemployment, and the arms race are not autonomous "problems," as in capitalist theory, but are essential organizing mechanisms for the economic system itself. This social theory argues that the normal workings of capitalist social, political, and economic institutions reproduce—and now even intensify as the global capitalist arena has become more competitive—hierarchies of sex, race, and class that are indispensable to the profits of corporate business. In other words, private profit—the engine of the capitalist system—simply cannot be made without exploitation.

Whenever the Catholic social justice tradition reflects the liberation interpretation of society, it recognizes the interlocking nature of government and business in the exercise of social power in capitalist societies. In 1891 Pope Leo XIII lamented the vast concentrations of wealth in the hands of a few who were "powerfully represented in the councils of the state itself."[4] In 1931 Pius XI continued this social analysis and saw a direct relationship between economic power and political control, as well as significant opposition between the interests of capitalists and those who do not own or control capital. Pius XI said that the few who command wealth command immense power over the state and the "lifeblood" of the economy, including an immense number who live with "hand to mouth uncertainty."

Pius XI stated that there was no true free market, only "economic dictatorship."[5]

In *Mater et Magistra* (1961) and *Pacem in Terris* (1963) John XXIII also recognized the interlocking nature of government and economic interests when he noted that vast military expenditure by the state always accompanied capitalist expansion. He observed that public authorities often served the interests of the wealthy, that Western development led to domination and "another form of colonialism," and that economic advances grew in tandem with "increasingly pronounced imbalances" and inequalities between citizens.[6] Likewise, as we will see, Pope Paul VI, and even some elements of Pope John Paul II's earlier encyclical *Laborem Exercens* or *On the Priority of Labor* (1981), despite their extensive drawing upon the capitalist social model, also analyze the crisis of poverty and propose methods of social change in ways that can be aligned with the liberation social model.[7]

ON SOCIAL CONCERN: A DEPARTURE FROM MAINSTREAM TRADITION

In the remainder of this essay, I wish to consider how John Paul II's most recent encyclical, *On Social Concern*, represents a departure from this albeit divided, mainstream tradition. For the first time a pope has issued a social justice document completely lacking an analysis or prognosis that can be aligned with the liberation social model. *On Social Concern* does not give "a fuller and more nuanced" application of Paul's encyclical *On the Development of Peoples* to the present time, as John Paul II claims that he does. Rather, *On Social Concern* departs significantly from Paul's teaching by failing to appropriate or even acknowledge important liberation dimensions both of Paul's analysis of capitalism and Paul's understanding of the process of social change.

A first major difference in their social analyses can be seen in the ways these two popes account for the existence of poverty. In analyzing the economic crisis in Third World countries, Paul distinguished between political independence and economic dependence. Paul said that poverty in the Third World was due to the legacy of colonialism, especially the establishment of one-product economies. Despite political independence, nations were still kept in economic dependence through such neocolonial practices. Paul said that First World governments "under cloak of financial aid or technical assistance" sought to "maintain or acquire complete dominance."[8] He observed that poverty in the Third World was a result of the wide disparity between prices for Third World raw materials and prices for First World manufactured goods. Given this situation, Paul said that the promotion of "free trade" as a means to equity was ludicrous.[9] Paul identified "glaring inequities ... in the exercise of power" and said that trade is only free when "the parties involved are not affected by any excessive inequalities of economic power."[10] What was called for, argued Paul, was the emancipation of political structures from the economic interests of the wealthy. He advocated self-directed economic liberation at the local level or "a fitting autonomous growth."[11] According to Paul VI, then, one of the chief causes of poverty was the unequal distribution of global economic power and the control of that power by First World governments.

In the encyclical *On Social Concern*, John Paul II has a very different assessment concerning the roots of economic suffering, which he recognizes has escalated dramatically since the time Paul wrote. John Paul II claims that poverty is due to three factors: (1) the immoral economic decisions of individuals, which, multiplied enough times, creates "structures of sin" or "misguided mechanisms"; (2) the ideological or political conflict between the East and the West; and (3) the cultural value systems peculiar to the Third World.[12] In warning against an analysis that is "too narrow[ly] ... economic," and in enumerating what he believes to be the threefold nature of the problem, John Paul II shows his allegiance to the capitalist assumption that economic, political, and cultural social spheres function autonomously.[13]

When John Paul II locates the origins of poverty in individual decisions, he effectively denies that socio-economic systems are systems of social relations that specify certain relations between persons and groups, and preclude others. *On Social Concern* sees the relations in an economic system as entirely voluntary. It says:

Therefore, political leaders and citizens of rich countries *considered as individuals* ... have the moral obligation, according to the *degree of each one's responsibility,* to take into consideration in *personal decisions* and decisions of government this relationship of universality, this interdependence which exists between *their conduct* and the poverty and underdevelopment of so many millions of people [no. 19] [emphasis added].

On Social Concern does acknowledge the existence of "economic, financial, and social mechanisms" that "function almost automatically" on behalf of the richer countries. But it is clear that these mechanisms are not thought to be inherent in the economic systems themselves, but are "manipulated" by individuals and "favor the interests of the people manipulating them" (no. 16). These "misguided mechanisms" fall under the moral category of "structures of sin":

> [They] are *rooted in personal sin* and thus always linked to the *concrete acts of individuals* who introduce these structures, consolidate them and make them difficult to remove ... One can speak of "selfishness" and of shortsightedness, of "mistaken political calculations," and "imprudent economic decisions." ... [These structures are a result of] *individuals' actions and omissions* [no.36] [emphasis added].

Congruent with capitalist theory, John Paul II assumes that if individual human error, either through accident, prejudice, or ignorance, could be removed, then a capitalist economic system would be capable of eradicating poverty.

On Social Concern states that a second root of "underdevelopment" or poverty in Third World countries is the existence of "two opposing blocs, commonly known as East and West," which promote "antithetical forms of the organization of labor and the structures of ownership." These blocs pull other countries into their "spheres of influence" and in this process "help to widen the gap already existing on the economic level between the North and the South." The document gives two examples of how economic stagnation in the Southern hemisphere is presumably due to East/West conflict. The first one reduces internal strife in Third World countries to the East/West struggle over capitalism and Soviet communism. The document says that revolutionary uprising is due to the situation of countries "find[ing] themselves in and sometimes overwhelmed by ideological conflicts, which inevitably create internal divisions to the extent in some cases of provoking full civil wars." (no. 20, 21). A second example of how ideological conflict creates economic stagnation is John Paul II's view that First World countries would be doing more to help the situation of poor nations if they did not have to deal with defending themselves against communism. The document says:

Nations which historically, economically, and politically have the possibility of playing a leadership role are prevented by this fundamentally flawed distortion from adequately fulfilling their duty of solidarity for the benefit of peoples which aspire to full development [no. 23].

In blaming communism and a lack of political stability for Third World revolutionary uprising and for First World failures to deal with economic stagnation, this document falls comfortably within capitalist assumptions. It also illustrates a point made by the liberation view. Liberationists argue that in the Bretton Woods Agreements made after World War II, the U.S.A. and other First World elites created the cold war primarily for three reasons: to justify capitalist penetration of countries where significant numbers would protest their ensuing economic marginalization, to have a scapegoat on which to blame the failures of capitalist development, and to justify the extremely lucrative arms race in order to insure the successful future of the capitalist system.[14]

A third reason this document gives for the origins and persistence of poverty is the particular culture and value systems of Third World countries. John Paul II says that when these cultural values "do not always match the degree of economic development ... [they] help to create distances" between richer and poorer nations (no. 14). This reading accords with the capitalist view that persons in traditional societies are unable to make the individual choices that will insure their economic advancement.[15]

In analyzing poverty solely from a stance that claims that economic, political, and cultural institutions function autonomously, *On Social Concern* departs not only from the earlier tradition including Paul VI, but in a more limited sense departs even from John Paul II's 1981 encyclical *On the Priority of Labor*. While this earlier encyclical also rejects an analysis of the interlocking structures of political economy and claims that social injustice "does not spring from the structure of the production process or from the structure of the economic process," it nevertheless acknowledged the activity of international structures of oppression, which "exercise a determinative influence" on all socio-economic relationships.[16] It argued that the major cause of poverty and injustice in societies was due to the fact that capital was organized against labor.[17] The social vision of *On the Priority of Labor* was not out of harmony with Paul VI's advocacy of self-directed economic liberation when it promoted an economy in which capital served labor in a democratically organized and centrally planned economy.[18] This most recent encyclical, however, refuses to locate the origins of poverty in the conflictual nature of any political, social, or economic structures beyond what is created by the selfishness, shortsightedness, mistaken political ideas, or unfortunate cultural values of influential individuals.

In viewing the economic arena as a complex of voluntary associations, John Paul II departs from the social analysis of Paul VI, which said that the "concrete systems" of capitalism and collectivism, which he described as "technocratic capitalism" and "bureaucratic socialism," are incapable as systems of achieving economic justice.[19] Further, even though both *On Social Concern* and *On the Priority of Labor* make individual ethical choice the primary factor in determining the justice of an economic system, they also imply that the internationalization of advanced global capitalism has freed world capitalist leaders from being responsible to domestic political pressures that once worked to mitigate capitalist excesses. Both encyclicals state that on a global scale "there is something wrong with the organization of work and employment."[20]

Besides ignoring a liberationist structural diagnosis of the causes of poverty, *On Social Concern* also neglects the liberation prescriptions of what might be done about poverty in *Populorum Progressio*, and in Paul VI's later encyclical, *Octogesima Adveniens* (1971).

Elements aligned with a liberation perspective can be detected in several aspects of Paul VI's teaching about the methods and agents of social change. Paul said that because of the need for "bold transformations," "comprehensive structural changes," "daring and creative innovations," and "modern forms of democracy," the methods of social change would have to be determined by an analysis of the situation done by the local community.[21] Indeed, Paul noted that the degree of popular participation in shaping the economy was as important as the quantity and variety of goods produced.[22] He advocated democratic control of production with worker representation at every level of society.[23] Paul called for the creation of a visionary yet historically possible society when he advocated the use of a utopian imagination that would perceive in the present "the disregarded possibility" for justice and direct it "toward a fresh future."[24] This new society, then, would be created by the struggles of bold and imaginative persons united in "initiating their own strategies" and being "authors of their own advancement" and "artisans of their destiny."[25] Paul endorsed a "variety of possible options" in methods and left room for "some degree of commitment" with Marxists in achieving these.[26]

In contrast to Paul's "bottom up" model of social change through visionary struggle, *On Social Concern* advocates social change from the top down through consensus at the level of ideas. This encyclical implies that what the local situation can reveal in terms of needed reform is not as important as the emergence of ideas of solidarity and interdependence, and principles of cooperation and development that need to be implemented at the international level.[27] *On Social Concern* shows more confidence than Paul VI in the church's ability to make an "accurate formulation of the results of a careful reflection on the complex realities of human existence" (no. 41). It champions a solidarity seemingly without struggle that has to do with "gratuity, forgiveness, and reconciliation" (no. 40). It assumes that the major initiators of change will be individuals and leaders of nations and international bodies who already have social power and practice individual personal virtue.[28] As is true of that strain of Catholic social teaching more in harmony with capitalist social analysis, John Paul II assumes that moral conversion and consensus at the level of ideas will mobilize the political will necessary for social change.

But how can those who have produced the inequalities also provide the means for ending them? To expect partners in an unequal relationship to respond to appeals for cooperation and moral responsibility is to ignore the reality acknowledged in the teaching of Paul VI, that since vast differentials in power will decisively affect the outcome of any negotiations, there is no change without social struggle. The position of *On Social Concern* represents only liberal capitalist assumptions regarding the absence of fundamental conflict, the relative equitable distribution of social power, and optimism regarding reform within the present system.

Finally, *On Social Concern* selectively appropriates normative values from a tradition of social teaching aimed at the reform of economic institutions and reduces them to exercises of individual charity. In his earlier encyclical, *On the Priority of Labor*, John Paul II advocated such ethical norms as the dignified participation of all persons in socio-economic life, economic democracy, or centralized economic planning accountable to worker owner/managers at the local level, and a "struggle of the workers" and "solidarity of the workers and with the workers."[29] These normative values all had to do with changing government, economic, and labor structures.

In contrast, *On Social Concern* does not advocate economic democracy and universal dignified social participation. Perhaps they are already presumed to exist or to have the potential to exist in countries with parliamentary democracy.[30] Further, this encyclical not only abandons norms advocated in John Paul's earlier encyclical, but the values it does advocate have to do with individual charitable practices, not reforming structures. For example, as noted above, in contrast to John Paul's earlier encyclical, which linked solidarity with the struggle of workers, this document has an individualistic notion of solidarity. It says that it has to do with "total gratuity, forgiveness, and reconciliation" — regardless of configurations of social power — and that it has "many points of contact [with] charity" (no. 40). Similarly, the preferential option for the poor has little if any resonance with Paul VI's awareness that people struggling for a new society are to be opted for because they are examples of human dignity at work. Rather, this value also has become "a primacy in the exercise of Christian charity . . . [for] each Christian" (no. 42). These norms are reinterpreted apolitically so as not to upset present structures, for the option for the poor must never endanger the common good.[31] Here we see how the meaning of social justice values is contingent upon social theory or the particular way of organizing society that is assumed.

In conclusion, I have argued that because *On Social Concern* is devoid of analysis that can be aligned with the liberation model, selective normative values have been abstracted from the liberation model and are radically transfigured into individual charitable acts that support rather than challenge the status quo. Moreover, this encyclical represents a significant departure not only from the teaching of Paul VI, which it claims to articulate more fully, but from the wider Catholic social justice tradition. John Paul II's rupture with and individualistic understanding of traditional normative values in fact violates a mandate central to the Catholic tradition since Pius XI. In 1931 this pope opposed "abandon[ing] to charity alone" the task of addressing economic structures that cause "the open violation of justice."[32]

What reasons can we posit for the promulgation of such an innovative document? One possibility is that *On Social Concern* represents a reaction by the Vatican to the growing strength of liberation movements and liberation social analysis within the late twentieth-century global Catholic Church. The institutional church perceives that these movements and this kind of social analysis threaten its institutional power over Catholics and its economic power in the global capitalist system. The growth of liberation movements in the Third World not only opposes capitalist power but promotes the formation of communities with more modes of operation. Latin America, for example, is birthing new egalitarian forms of the Catholic Church at odds with Vatican notions of hierarchy and authority.

This encyclical may also be reacting to the use of liberation social analysis by First World Catholic hierarchy who are faced with rising poverty and structural unemployment even in their own "developed" countries. It is not only the Latin American bishops but also the Canadian bishops in their 1983 pastoral letter who have said that capitalist development by its very nature creates the enrichment of an elite and increasing numbers without access to the market or dignified participation in the life of the society.[33]

Thus, the escalation in liberation movements and liberation social analysis challenges not only the institutional church's hierarchal social relations and power over Catholics; it also challenges the global capitalist system that has been the source of the Vatican's own economic power. Since the Lateran Treaty of 1929, the Vatican's financial administrators have given priority to making profit through the capitalist system, regardless of moral considerations.[34] The official church may at present be rejecting liberation forms of social analysis because, in a world of increasing revolution, it is not ready to give up social and economic privilege and face the socio-economic dilemmas of its own existence.

What might John Paul II have said were he to have truly articulated the liberation aspects of Paul VI's vision in a "fuller and more nuanced way"? As we near the end of the twentieth century almost 70 percent of the Catholic Church's 907 million members live in the Third World.[35] Most of them are very young and very poor. Many of them are involved in escalating national liberation struggles. What does Paul VI's liberation vision offer them that John Paul II does not?

First, Paul's liberation view sought a structural rather than a voluntaristic view of capitalist dynamics. If only at selective points, it nevertheless began to grapple with the historical and structural relationship between the evolution of the capitalist system and the realities of poverty, unemployment, and lack of dignified social participation for increasing numbers of persons. Second, in supporting a social analysis done at the local level, Paul's vision would encourage the marginalized to claim their power to interpret the socio-economic situation from their point of view. Third, Paul's view of solidarity is one that supports those who struggle together to challenge those social, political, and economic structures that keep them marginalized. Finally, Paul's understanding of the need for utopian imagination would encourage the experimentation of women and men who strive to create life patterns that support mutuality in human relationships. If John Paul II had truly held up the fullness of Paul's vision, he would have had to offer something like this to the majority of the world's Roman Catholics.

Even though the present pope has abandoned a liberation vision, the Catholic churches have not. More and more Catholics live in the Third World and are informed by a radical analysis, which has, until this most recent instance, always been present in the official church's teaching. It will move ever more swiftly to center stage as even First World bishops are now employing elements of its perspective. For not only are the Third World poor becoming increasingly numerous in the church, but late twentieth-century global capitalism is reproducing Third World patterns of rising poverty and structural unemployment even in the First World. Given this situation, liberal strategies for social change that assume the capitalist model, such as those articulated in *On Social Concern*, will seem increasingly beside the point. Only a liberation analysis and liberation movements for social change will touch the depth of the problem of human economic suffering that the Catholic social justice tradition has, at times, diagnosed so well.

NOTES

1. *Sollicitudo Rei Socialis* or *On Social Concern* (hereafter OSC). Translation is taken from *Origins*, 17:38 (March 3, 1988), paragraphs 4, 13, 17, 35.

2. *Quadragesimo Anno* (hereafter QA), 47; *Rerum Novarum* (hereafter RN), 10, 12, 35. Translation is taken from *Seven Great Encyclicals* (Glen Rock, N.J.: Paulist Press, 1963).

3. David M. Gordon, Richard Edwards, and Michael Reich, *Segmented Work, Divided Workers* (New York: Cambridge University Press, 1982), p. 210, and Ruth Spitz, "Women and Labor: Unfinished Revolution," *Democratic Left*, vol. 14, no. 5 (September-October 1986), 16.

4. RN, 35, 1, 2.

5. QA, 60–61, 105–9.

6. *Mater et Magistra*, 48, 102, and *Pacem in Terris*, 63, 109. Translation is taken from Joseph Gremillion, *The Gospel of Peace and Justice* (Maryknoll, N.Y.: Orbis Books, 1976).

7. For a more extensive discussion of this social theory debate as it is reflected in the Catholic social justice documents, see Mary E. Hobgood, "Paradigms in Conflict: Economic Theory in Catholic Social Teaching: 1891–1986," doctoral dissertation, Temple University, 1988.

8. *Populorum Progressio* (hereafter PP), 7, 52.

9. PP, 58, 57.

10. PP, 9, 58.

11. PP, 6.

12. OSC, 35–37, 20–22, 14.

13. OSC, 15.

14. Lee Cormie, "La Iglesia y la crisis del capitalismo: Perspectiva norteamericana," *Opciones* (Chile), no. 11 (mayo-agosto 1987), 9–30. In contrast to John Paul II's line of argument, the U.S. bishops' pastoral letter on the economy says that the tendency to evaluate "North-South problems" in terms of an "East-West assessment" must cease because it is done at the expense of meeting basic human needs in the Third World. See "Economic Justice for All: Catholic Social Teaching and the U.S. Economy," *Origins*, 16:24 (November 27, 1986), 262.

15. See Walt W. Rostow, *The Stages of Economic Growth: A Non-Communist Manifesto* (New York: Cambridge University Press, 1960).

16. *Laborem Exercens* or *On the Priority of Labor* (hereafter OPL), 16, 17. Translation is taken from Gregory Baum, *The Priority of Labor* (New York: Paulist Press, 1982).

17. OPL, 12, 14.

18. OPL, 14, 18.

19. *Octogesima Adveniens* (hereafter OA), 37, 35. Translation is taken from Joseph Gremillion, *The Gospel of Peace and Justice*.

20. OPL, 16–18, and OSC, 18, 43.

21. PP, 32, and OA, 42–43, 47.

22. OA, 41.

23. PP, 34, 65, 74, and OA, 42, 47.

24. OA, 37.

25. PP, 34, 65.

26. OA, 31, 50.

27. OSC, 19, 26, 38.

28. OSC, 26, 42–43.

29. OPL, 14, 18, 8, 20.

30. OSC, 44.

31. OSC, 39.

32. QA, 4.

33. Canadian Conference of Catholic Bishops, "Ethical Reflections on the Economic Crisis," in Gregory Baum and Duncan Cameron, *Ethics and Economics* (Toronto: James Lorimer, 1984).

34. See Penny Lernoux, *In Banks We Trust* (Garden City, N.Y.: Doubleday, 1984).

35. Penny Lernoux, "Shadow Darkening Church of the Poor," *National Catholic Reporter* (June 17, 1988), 8.

9

Feminist Analysis:
A Missing Perspective

Maria Riley, O.P.

> The decision to feed the world
> is the real decision. No revolution
> has chosen it. For that choice requires
> that women shall be free.
>
> Adrienne Rich[1]

Sollicitudo Rei Socialis speaks so clearly and forcefully of the failure of development and the consequent sufferings of so many persons, it is difficult to be critical of it without appearing to nitpick. John Paul II's powerful moral message declares that the right to a dignified human life supercedes all the justifications our political and financial activities put forward to cloak our unbridled desire for profit and drive for power (no. 37). It is a bracing corrective to the evolution of human society as we have lived it during the past three decades. However, the very importance of this encyclical demands that its blind spots be illuminated so that it is not dismissed out of hand for some of its obvious failures.

In the opening section of the encyclical, John Paul II states that his objective is twofold: (1) to affirm the continuity of the social doctrine with special reference to *Populorum Progressio*; and (2) to renew that social teaching as "suggested by the changes in historical conditions" (no. 3). It is in his selective reading of the changes in historical conditions that I take issue with the encyclical. John Paul II does not recognize the subtle but profound shifting in human consciousness and in social structures that is occurring globally as a result of the women's movement. Most major critiques of the process of development over the last twenty years now recognize the essential role of women in society. They also recognize, at least in their rhetoric, that a significant cause of the failure of development has been the ignoring of women's role. For example, the UNICEF report, *Within Human Reach: A Future for Africa's Children*, states:

> Women remain the providers of 60 to 80 percent of the household food needs in many parts of sub-Saharan Africa. Women are the key actors in ensuring the survival and well-being of children, and their educational level is the single most important factor related positively to high infant survival rates. Expanding women's social and economic opportunities and increasing their control over household finances and their participation in community affairs, therefore, are the most significant measures that can be taken to enhance children's health and the welfare of families.[2]

The conclusions of such studies continue to illustrate that the promotion of women is not only a matter of justice to women, it is also essential to the survival and well-being of societies.

In *Pacem in Terris*, 1963, John XXIII identified the then incipient women's movement as one of the "signs of our times." He wrote:

> It is obvious to everyone that women are now taking a part in public life. This is happening more rapidly perhaps in nations with a Christian tradition, and more slowly, but broadly, among peoples who have inherited other traditions or cultures. Since women are becoming ever more conscious of their human dignity, they will not tolerate

being treated as inanimate objects or mere instruments, but claim, both in domestic and in public life, the rights and duties that befit a human person [no. 41].

Since 1963 the global women's movement has continued to grow and mature in its appreciation of the necessity to make its voice and agenda known, particularly in relation to development.

The United Nations declared 1975 the International Women's Year (IWY) in response to the early indicators from women in Africa, Asia, and South America that something was awry in the development process that many nations were pursuing under the direction of Western-dominated agencies, such as the World Bank and the International Monetary Fund. Women, who throughout the world are responsible for the daily sustenance of the family, were the first to feel the lack of resources, particularly in food and in availability of land for subsistence farming, that followed upon the changes initiated by development processes. One of the primary purposes of the International Women's Year, subsequently extended to the International Women's Decade, was to examine the development process and its effects upon women and those dependent upon women, the young and the old.

The history of thinking about women's role in development illustrates the growing maturity of analysis over the last twenty years. In the early 1970s, development planners talked about "integrating women into the development process." Women from the so-called developing countries were quick to point out they did not need to be integrated into development, they already were the primary subsistence food producers and petty traders of most economies. By the late 1970s, the language had changed to "supporting women in development." But as the quality of life continued to deteriorate in so many countries during the 1980s, it became more and more evident how integral women are to the sustaining of life in all societies. This reality is especially apparent in less industrialized countries. The failure to include women in all phases of the development process insures the failure of that process, as history and experience have proven.

Feminist critiques of current development models and of current planning, programming, and evaluation of development projects are among the most creative and promising of all development work today.[3] The literature is expanding rapidly. Not all the literature is written by feminists; much of it is written by other groups concerned with addressing the needs of the poor.[4]

Sollicitudo Rei Socialis shows no awareness of this body of material. This is a serious and debilitating lacuna in the encyclical. There are a number of ways in which this lacuna is evident. In developing my feminist critique of the encyclical, I will concentrate on three problem areas: its methodology, analysis, and strategies. In so doing, I am not arguing so much with what the encyclical says, as with what it does not say.

METHODOLOGY

Feminists are not the only group of persons to raise questions about the methodology used to write papal encyclicals. But given the absence of any awareness of women's experience and critique of development in this document, the question of methodology must be addressed from a feminist perspective.

John Paul II speaks of the church's threefold approach to developing social teaching: (1) its "principles of reflection," (2) its "criteria of judgment," and (3) its basic "directive for action." The methodology is fundamentally deductive. Women ask, who defines these principles, criteria, and directives? From where do they come? Historically, women's voices and experience have not been formative of Catholic social thought. This, of course, is not a new insight. Women's voices and experience have been absent from all authoritative teaching and deliberation in the church.

The absence of women is symbolic of a fundamental flaw in the methodology for developing this encyclical. The process of feminist analysis continues to emphasize two key principles of analysis: (1) how a person arrives at a particular perspective powerfully influences that perspective; and (2) who is included and who is excluded in the process shapes the content of the analysis. In a way, the process used for developing this encyclical contradicts its content. To contribute to building a society that is just, equitable, and life-affirming for all, the methods in constructing it must be correspondingly open and respectful of differences. They must attempt to break down existing stereotypes and oppressive hierarchies of power and control. The process is integral to the justness of the product. Such an insight demands models that are participatory and inclusive—inclusive not only of women but also of representatives of all groups outside the dominant culture, which in this case is predominately white, male, clerical, and European.

This insight is not restricted to feminist thinking; liberation theologians would raise similar critiques. However, it is important to include it in this analysis because women are often not consciously included in the call for inclusiveness among male liberation theologians. Unfortunately, this works out in practice to be the equivalent of unconscious exclusion of women. At this moment in history, women need to assume a "hermeneutic of suspicion" in the face of the pandemic patriarchy that shapes our cultures, especially the culture of the church. It plagues even liberation theologies.

ANALYSIS

There is much in *Sollicitudo Rei Socialis* with which feminist analysis finds common cause, in particular in its effort to extend the meaning of the word "development" beyond economic categories. John Paul II continues and enlarges upon Paul VI's reflection on the meaning of development in *Populorum Progressio*. Paul VI defined development in human terms, including not only economic but also social, political, personal, and spiritual dimensions of life.

The International Women's Decade 1975–1985 declared equality, development, and peace as its three goals. The early documentation clearly analyzed the linkages among these goals, particularly from the experience of women:

Equality is here interpreted as meaning not only legal equality, the elimination of *de jure* discrimination, but also equality of rights, responsibilities, and opportunities for the participation of women in development, both as beneficiaries and as agents. The issue of inequality as it affects the vast majority of women of the world is closely related to the problem of underdevelopment, which exists mainly as a result of unjust international economic relations. . . .

Development is here interpreted to mean total development, including development in the political, economic, social, cultural, and other dimensions of human life, as also the development of economic and other material resources and also the physical, moral, intellectual, and cultural growth of the human person. . . . It [development] also requires a change in the attitudes and roles of both men and women. Women's development should not only be viewed as an issue in social development but should be seen as an essential component in every dimension of development. . . .

Without peace and stability there can be no development. Peace is thus a prerequisite to development. Moreover, peace will not be lasting without development and the elimination of inequalities and discrimination at all levels.[5]

This vision of development resonates with John Paul II's reflection on "Authentic Human Development" (nos. 27–34).

Feminist analysis also resonates with the pope's condemnation of militarization and its consequent squandering of resources that could be directed toward fulfilling human needs. DAWN, the Third World women's network on women and development issues, identifies militarization and violence as one of the major causes of the current crisis.[6] The pope recognizes the living victims of war—refugees. However, feminists would add the concrete observation that 80 percent of all refugees are women and their dependent children.[7]

Women also find common cause with John Paul II's identification of the preferential option for the poor. Once again, however, they would move beyond generalities and abstractions to put a human face on the poor. That human face is disproportionately female. Women and their dependent children make up more than 66 percent of the world's poor and the number is growing. Women's poverty consists not only in the lack of resources, but also in the lack of opportunity and in the growing incidence of women worldwide who are the sole responsible parent to children. This trend has been identified as the "feminization of poverty."[8] It is more correctly understood as the pauperization of women and children.

Women join others in applauding the growing concern for the environment in recent social teaching. In addition to the encyclical's stated reasons for that concern—the protection of the ordered system of the cosmos, the limitation of our natural resources, and the deterioration of the quality of life—more and more ecologists and feminists speak of a growing awareness of the "community of creation." In identifying with the "community of creation" they are pointing out the mutual dependence of all life—human, animal, plant. This shift toward understanding that we are all mutually linked enables the human community to realize that its ecologically destructive habits are slowly destroying the very foundation of all life, including human life.

A feminist analysis of the failure of development over the last several decades would agree with many of the generalizations in *Sollicitudo Rei Socialis*, but differences begin to emerge in the identification of some of the causes of that failure. Feminist analysis would point not so much to what the encyclical says, but to what it does not say, because it lacks a gender analysis. I will develop several examples: some root causes of the failure of development, reflections on the demographic "problem" as developed in the encyclical, and an analysis of the culture of militarism. In so doing I hope to illustrate how Catholic social teaching would be enriched and enlarged by including feminist analysis and reflection.

Sollicitudo Rei Socialis identifies the failure of development primarily in global terms: East-West conflict, militarization, international debt, homelessness, and unemployment. It affirms the profound insight of Paul VI in *Populorum Progressio* that the social question has become worldwide in dimension. It briefly alludes to the national and local social questions but chooses to analyze the current situation from a global perspective (no. 9).

Feminist analysis, on the other hand, asserts that local or micro questions are integrally linked with global or macro questions. It insists that we will never move to a more successful theory and practice of development until we recognize and attend to those linkages.

Moreover, feminist analysis consciously seeks to illustrate that all issues have a political, economic, social, and cultural dimension in contrast to some analytical thinking that tends to define issues as political, or economic, or social, or cultural, or to ignore the intrinsic links among these dimensions. Using women's experience as a lens, feminist analysis rejects dualistic approaches that "dichotomize relationships between private and public sphere, production and reproduction, the household and the economy, the personal and the political, the realms of feeling and intuition and those of reason."[9] Recognizing that all is connected, it seeks a more holistic approach to the analytical process.

In analyzing the failure of development, feminists focus on three areas usually overlooked in development theory: the household, women's work, and women's multiple roles. They focus on poor households — and on women within those households — insisting that they are a good starting point for an understanding of the situation of women in development because it "enables us not only to evaluate the extent to which development strategies benefit or harm the poorest and most oppressed section of the people, but also to judge their impact on a range of sectors and activities critical to socio-economic development and human welfare."[10]

For example, assessing the International Monetary Fund's structural adjustment requirements for new or refinanced loans to debtor nations by its impact on the household economy, gives an immediate indicator of the human failure of that policy. It is not adequate to evaluate development on abstractions such as the gross national product. It must be evaluated on its impact on ordinary people, especially the poor.

This particular policy demands cuts in public expenditures on social programs such as health, housing, and education, as well as such needs as water, utilities, roads. These cuts are accompanied by a devaluation of the currency. Such policies particularly affect women by reducing their sources of income and services while simultaneously increasing the demands upon their time and creativity to fill the gaps left by the diminishment of social services. That there is survival at all in this situation is in great measure due to the resourcefulness of women in developing income-generating and income-saving projects, and in developing cooperative ventures with friendship and extended family networks.[11] But that women-resource is under terrific stress in many societies today and cannot sustain the burden of survival much longer.

Another example of failure of development strategy because it ignored the work of women has been in the economic policies aimed at developing an agricultural economy for export. If those plans are critiqued from the point of view of women, we discover one of the causes of widespread hunger. Africa presents a clear case in point. African women are the subsistence farmers of the societies. Communal farm land commandeered into export cropping often leaves women with no access to land. Consequently they are unable to fulfill their traditional obligation of feeding the family.

These examples illustrate that by failing to take into account women's roles in socio-economic development, the policies adopted often exacerbate the very problems they seek to resolve.[12] In a very real sense we can say that women and children are the early indicators of the failure of a development policy.

This failure to recognize women's essential and multiple economic roles in a society reflects a "deeply gendered ideology, which simultaneously minimizes the value of the tasks necessary for social reproduction, while promoting a pattern of economic growth based on the exploitation of the socio-economic vulnerabilities of a female population."[13] It is also one of the causes of the failure of development and the continuing deterioration of the quality of life for growing numbers of persons worldwide. *Sollicitudo Rei Socialis* fails to recognize this dynamic in the development process. I would argue that it fails to do so because it too is shaped by a "deeply gendered ideology."

This ideology reveals itself in the rather cursory treatment the encyclical gives to the "demographic problem" (no. 25). This question is at the heart of all feminist analysis, because it is primarily women who carry both the glory and the burden of children worldwide. No other reality has such impact on women's lives. The encyclical reflects absolutely no understanding of women's experience in reproduction.

While briefly alluding to the difficulties for development due to population growth in the countries of the Southern hemisphere, it offers no analysis of that growth. Yet population studies over the years have identified clear linkages between poverty and the number of children in a family in developing countries. There is a ratio between the number of children a couple have and their search for economic security in old age in societies that have no social security programs. There is also a ratio between the number of children who survive early childhood and the number of children a family has. If infant and youth mortality is high, couples will continue to have children to ensure that some survive into adulthood.

But the most important statistic that demographers have identified is the connection between increasing women's educational and life opportunities and the lowering of the birth rate per woman. In *Women . . . A World Survey*, Ruth Leger Sivard writes:

> Since education influences women's economic participation and earning power, and also the number of children they have and the health their children will have, progress here can be the harbinger of expanding opportunities in the future. Education develops the human potential. In the modern world it is seen as vital for a fully productive role in life for women as well as men.[14]

The population question must be analyzed within the social, economic, political, and cultural structures that shape women's lives. This statement is valid in the so-called developed countries of the Northern hemisphere as well. As long as the church continues to ignore the context of women's lives when it raises the issues of childbirth, its voice in this profound human concern will not be heard.

The question of militarization is critical in feminist analysis. *Sollicitudo Rei Socialis* condemns the growth of militarism in the world on political, economic, and social grounds. It decries the East-West conflict with its surrogate wars in developing countries (nos. 20–23). It names arms production and arms trade as a "serious disorder" (no. 24). It identifies the stockpiling of atomic weapons as a symbol of the death-dealing direction of the contemporary world. It speaks to the victims of conflicts, refugees, and it condemns terrorism.

Sollicitudo Rei Socialis is in continuity with the church's long history of teaching that seeks to promote peace and justice in our world. It is a history, however, that for the most part concentrates on the problems of war between nation states, the possibility of a just war, the morality of deterrence, the immorality of the destruction of innocent noncombatants.

Feminism enters the question of militarism through its analysis of the culture of patriarchy.[15] Its analysis of war is shaped by the critical feminist insight that the "personal is political." The simplest definition for this insight is to assert that men's power and women's subordination is a social, economic, political, and cultural reality—that what happens in personal relationships between women and men reflects social structures. Those structures are patriarchal.

According to feminist analysis, the root cause of war is the will to dominate. John Paul II speaks of the dual sin shaping our world, "the all-consuming desire for profit" and the "thirst for power, with the intention of imposing one's will upon others" (no. 37). Radical feminist analysis identifies the root of the will to dominate in men's will to dominate and control women. It is the "original sin." From this root come all other forms of domination. The will to dominate appears subtly in patriarchal social structures and in the cultural ideology that supports those structures.[16] It appears overtly in all acts of violence: rape, torture, sexual abuse, incest, pornography, domestic violence, terrorism, the destruction of the earth. It finds its ultimate expression in war, as one nation, usually governed by men, seeks to dominate other nations.

Feminism in particular criticizes militarism, pointing out how the military mind-set is shaped with an emphasis on domination of the "other," the weak ones, of which women are primary symbols. It points to the history of women and land being considered the booty of the victorious army. Today it points to the prostitution of women that so commonly accompanies a military presence in a country. Feminists' anger toward militarism and war is deep and abiding.

Feminist analysis brings a cultural analysis to the problems of militarism and war that would enrich and enlarge the reflections of *Sollicitudo Rei Socialis*. It also points to some of the directions that would promote it—namely, the transformation of dominant structures to structures of mutuality. However, until women and their insights are included in the framing of Catholic social teaching, it is difficult to project that it will ever include a critique of the culture of patriarchy.

The insights of feminist analysis on the failure of development are slowly moving from the margins into the mainstream of development thinking. This movement illustrates the growing realization of women's essential role in society. Future evolution, we hope, will know how to use the new insights gained from gender analysis to become the basis for framing policy. The clear message of the results of the International Decade for Women 1975–1985 is that the movement of women beyond poverty, dependence, and violence is contingent upon the evolution of societies, both national and international, beyond the current imbalances of economic and political power that shape our world. But concomitantly, a society's ability to move toward justice for all is contingent upon the liberation of women. Because *Sollicitudo Rei Socialis* reflects none of this thinking, it must be judged a dated document.

STRATEGIES

John Paul II calls for a response of solidarity to overcome the structures of sin that currently shape the interdependence of our world. He recognizes that interdependence in an unequal world begets structured inequality. He recommends the "virtue" of solidarity—that is, a "firm and persevering determination to commit oneself to the common good, that is to say, to the good of all and to each individual because we are all really responsible for all" (no. 38).

In seeking to define solidarity he uses several key words and phrases: "moral responsibility," "to see the 'other' as neighbor," "the path to peace and to development," "a Christian virtue," "goes beyond itself, to take on the specifically Christian dimension of total gratuity, forgiveness, and reconciliation," "new model for the human race, the communion of the Trinity," and "on the individual, national, and international level."

He further delineates the appropriate responses of different persons in seeking solidarity:

> The exercise of solidarity within each society is valid when its members recognize one another as persons. Those who are more influential because they have a greater share of goods and common services should feel responsible for the weaker and be ready to share with them all they possess. Those who are weaker, for their part, in the same spirit of solidarity should not adopt a purely passive attitude or one that is destructive of the social fabric, but while claiming their legitimate rights, should do what they can for the good of all. The intermediate groups, in their turn, should not selfishly insist on their particular interests, but respect the interests of others [no. 39].

The exercise of solidarity is the pope's strategic moral response to the problems of injustice he has identified throughout the encyclical.

A feminist reflection on the meaning of solidarity moves beyond the concept of interdependence and even the common good to recognize an essential unity within the community of creation. This understanding of solidarity is rooted in several key feminist moral insights: the centrality of relationship in life, mutuality, and the underlying integral unity of experience.

A key foundation of a feminist moral ethic is to recognize the centrality of relationship in human experience. This insight arises from women's experience as primary nurturers of the family. Reflection on this experience opens new understandings of the presence of God in history. For Christian feminists, this reflection focuses on Jesus' radical acts of relationship, especially with the outcasts of society—the lepers, the woman at the well, the Syro-Phoenician woman, tax collectors, and prostitutes. He joined them in solidarity, and for that reason he too became an outcast in his society. Jesus' journey toward Calvary was not a journey toward self-sacrifice so much as it was a journey of radical acts of love that deepened relationships, embodied and extended community, and passed on the gift of life.

In concluding her reflection of a Christian feminist ethic, Beverly Harrison writes: "We are called to express, embody, share, celebrate the gift of life and to pass it on. We are called to reach out, to deepen relationships or to right wrong relations—i.e., those which deny, distort, or prevent human dignity from arising—as we re-call each other into the power of personhood."[17] In a feminist understanding, solidarity is first of all an experience of relationship, rather than an abstract virtue.

But if relationships are to express true solidarity, they must be built on mutuality. *Sollicitudo Rei Socialis* condemns the relationships of domination that presently rule our world, particularly in the "desire for profit . . . and the thirst for power" (no. 37). As I stated before, feminism identifies this will to dominate as part of the culture of patriarchy. Mutuality in relationship is the feminist alternative to domination. Mutuality moves beyond equality to recognize the reciprocity of giving and receiving, caring and being cared for. In its negative expression, it recognizes the reciprocity of evil, of harming and being harmed, of hating and being hateful. Solidarity, without mutuality, easily slips into paternalism or maternalism.

Finally, a feminist ethic would argue for a renewed understanding of the integral unity that underlies all experience. This unity transcends all the rational categories of dualism, which systems of philosophy have developed to explain experience, such as body/soul, intuition/knowledge, thinking/feeling, public/private, church/world, sacred/secular.

Applying these key insights of a feminist ethic to our understanding of solidarity extends and deepens its meaning as developed in *Sollicitudo Rei Socialis*. A feminist perspective on solidarity would insist that our very salvation as persons is linked. For example, a feminist ethic understands that racism is not only unjust to persons of differing racial and ethnic backgrounds; it destroys the soul of the racist. Likewise, sexism is unjust not only to women; it destroys the soul of the sexist. In the context of this essay, economic and political domination of so-called developed nations is not only unjust to weaker, poorer nations; it is destroying the soul of the powerful nations. Solidarity in the liberation struggles of peoples is a mutually salvific act. For us of the developed world, it is at the heart of our redemption.

Sollicitudo Rei Socialis is an important but dated document. Its failure resides in its blindness to the essential contribution that feminists, both women and men, are making to the development debate. I suggest that the framers and consultants of this document are trapped by the myopic position that "women's issues" are marginal to the so-called great issues of our day. This particular myopia results from a patriarchal mind-set. Mainline development theory and practice has also been shaped by patriarchal thinking. Ironically, it has been the very failure of that development over the last several decades that has opened the way among some groups to reassess the development process from women's perspectives. It is becoming clearer that "women's issues" are not marginal; they are central to the search for the kind of development in which people matter. *Sollicitudo Rei Socialis* would have been enriched by the voices and insights of women.

NOTES

1. Adrienne Rich, "Hunger," *The Dream of a Common Language* (New York: Norton, 1978), p. 13.

2. *Within Human Reach: A Future for Africa's Children*, a UNICEF Report (New York: United Nations Publication, 1985), p. 52.

3. The word "feminist" carries a variety of meanings for readers. Because in its root form it refers to the female, it can be considered exclusionary of men. However, current, but not universal, usage includes both women and men. In the context of this essay, I am using feminist to mean a person, woman or man, who believes in the essential equality between women and men, and seeks to create social attitudes, policies, and structures that reveal and sustain that equality.

4. See, for example, Gita Sen and Caren Grown, *Development, Crisis, and Alternative Visions: Third World Women's Perspectives* (New York: Monthly Review Press, 1987); and *The State of the World's Children, 1988* (Oxford: Oxford University Press, 1988).

5. *Report of the World Conference of the United Nations Decade for Women: Equality, Development, and Peace* (New York: United Nations Publication, 1980), pp. 3–4.

6. Sen and Grown, *Development*, pp. 67ff.

7. Joni Seager and Ann Olson, *Women in the World Atlas* (New York: Simon and Schuster, 1986), p. 27.

8. This term was first used by Diana Pearce in "The Feminization of Poverty: Women, Work and Welfare," *Urban and Social Change Review* (Feb. 1978) and later popularized by the *Final Report of the National Advisory Council on Economic Opportunity* (Washington, D.C.: Government Printing Office, 1981). Although it was first used in reference to the growing poverty of women in the United States, it has also been applied to the growing poverty of women worldwide.

9. Peggy Antrobus, "Gender Analysis," unpublished manuscript.

10. Sen and Grown, *Development*, p. 24.

11. Peggy Antrobus, "The Empowerment of Women," unpublished manuscript.

12. Ibid.

13. Ibid.

14. Ruth Leger Sivard, *Women . . . A World Survey* (Washington, D.C.: World Priorities, 1985), p. 18.

15. I am using the term "patriarchy" in its current understanding as the system of male control over all the structures of a society— political, economic, social, and cultural.

16. Feminism also points out that religion has served to legitimate patriarchal culture.

17. Beverly Harrison, "The Power of Anger in the Act of Love: An Ethic for Women and Other Strangers," *Union Seminary Quarterly Review*, 36, Supplementary Issue (1981), p. 53.

10

Sollicitudo Rei Socialis:
A View from the Philippines

Bishop Francisco F. Claver, S.J.

Perhaps it is self-flattery of the crassest kind to say so, but *Sollicitudo Rei Socialis* could have been written with precisely the Philippines in mind. For the North-South, East-West tensions, among other things, that the encyclical uses as its framework of analysis of global injustices, have plenty to do with the most serious political and economic problems of the Philippines today; and its principal concerns and thrusts coincide to quite a large extent with those the Philippine church as a whole has been painfully struggling with and evolving these past twenty years.

Whether it is deluded self-congratulation for what we believe we have done rightly or honest evaluation of the sorry state of underdevelopment we still are in as a nation, the unadorned fact is that the encyclical is right on target as far as we in the Philippines are concerned. And where it touches our present condition as a church, I have no hesitation saying the encyclical is strong confirmation of all we have been striving to do in that part of our pastoral work that goes under the rubric of "social action."

THE ENCYCLICAL AND THE PHILIPPINE CHURCH

The ready applicability of Pope John Paul II's thoughts to the Philippine situation is no accident: we as a nation belong to that vast brotherhood of poverty whose plight the encyclical seeks to address; and *Populorum Progressio*, whose twentieth anniversary it celebrates and whose ideas it seeks to further, has been a guiding force of no little moment in the Philippine church's approach to development and justice questions.

Point by point, insight by insight, we can take the encyclical and cast it against the background of events in the nation—and the progression in the Philippine church's thinking and acting on those events—and we cannot fail to note a most striking parallelism and convergence of thought. There is little space here for showing that congruent development in its entirety. But we can dwell on a few dominant ideas from the encyclical, which, to my mind, speak directly to current concerns in the church's social action work in the Philippines today. The following five topics, I believe, are of signal importance: ecology, culture, nonviolence, moral values, and discernment.

1. Ecology

The pastoral letter of the Philippine bishops in January 1988 on environmental and ecological despoliation has been hailed as a ground-breaking first as far as statements by national episcopal conferences on the subject go. The encyclical antedates this letter by a month and it is unfortunate that the bishops had no inkling of its clear bias for ecological conservation or the letter, "authoritative" enough as it is on its own merits and by their unanimous issuance of it, would certainly have gained in strength. Still the pope's urging on Christians to take seriously and do something about the destruction of our world's environment is going to be potent support for what we as a church here in the Philippines are going to do ourselves about reversing that destruction, preserving what is left of our life-supporting processes, and restoring what has been destroyed.

2. Culture

If the health of our physical environment is a gospel concern, so too is that of our social environment, that part of it especially that conditions the way we think, the way we behave, the way we look at life, in a word, our *culture*. The constant reference to culture and the need of consulting it in the process of human development is another highly significant aspect of the encyclical. Its preoccupation with culture is mirrored here in the Philippines in the growing appreciation of the necessity of taking a closer look at cultural verities and how they hinder or support efforts at reform and nation-building. The rather general interest in values-transformation and -education not only in schools but in various government departments and other sectors of Philippine society as well did not just occur out of the blue. For a long time—especially in church circles, with the widespread use of "structural analysis"—there was a one-sided stress on structural change, little attention, if at all, being paid to cultural values and attitudes that underpin social structures and govern their very working.

3. Moral Values

Insuring the right physical and social environment is a must for true human development. But so too is a third kind of environment—the moral-spiritual. If there is anything that can be said to be the encyclical's one major preoccupation, it is that moral values—faith values—should be paramount and all-pervasive in the Christian's perspective on and approach to human development and liberation (see esp. nos. 37-40, SRS). What it proposes, in effect, is a spirituality of social involvement, something which, of late in the Philippines, bishops and priests, religious and laity—especially those heavily immersed in justice work—have been grappling with. Again, the convergence of thinking in the encyclical's stress on moral values and ours in the Philippines on a social justice spirituality is most startling and is strong affirmation of the efforts of such in the Philippine church as have been trying to put flesh on the church's social teachings in direct work on justice problems without allowing themselves to be swallowed up by ideological (especially Marxist) presuppositions on societal change.

4. Nonviolence

There was a time when concern in the Philippine church for nonviolent action for justice seemed to be a peculiarity of the Catholic bishops alone (see their pastoral letters in October 1979, July 1984, and February 1986). But not now. With the nonviolent revolution of 1986 followed by the clear vote for peaceful, democratic change in the resounding approval of the new Constitution in 1987, the approach to justice by nonviolence is to all intents and purposes *the* dominant ethic.

This repudiation of violence (no matter how justified) as a way of social reform finds strong resonance in the encyclical. Time and again it speaks of peaceful, nonviolent action. Not once does it advert to the possibility and moral acceptance of violence in extreme cases — as did *Populorum Progressio*, following ordinary Catholic moral theology. Not that it negates altogether our traditional morality on violence in a last resort situation. But its total silence on the subject is in glaring contrast to its strong insistence on nonviolence. What to make out of the fact? We can only deduce it means firm support for the direction we have been taking all these years.

5. Discernment

The word is hardly used in the encyclical but if there is any action that it urges on the church — and that is itself a practical and excellent example of — it is spiritual discernment. I take the term to mean the joining of a hard-nosed analysis of social realities (using to the full whatever scientific tools are available) and a perspective that comes wholly from faith, to the end that God's action in persons and events be more clearly understood, more consciously cooperated with, and more faithfully advanced. Discernment as here understood was practically forced on the church of the Philippines in response to the heavily ideological reading of national social problems issuing from the kind of structural analysis promoted in the late 1970s by supporters of the National Democratic Front. When the encyclical says it is not proposing a third way (an alternative, that is, to the two dominant ideologies of our times, liberal capitalism and Marxist collectivism—see no. 41), what it is offering instead is a way of interpreting social realities from the standpoint of the faith of the gospel regardless of specific political ideologies and programs. That, I believe, is precisely what spiritual discernment is all about and the encyclical itself is a fine model of such a discernment.

THE ENCYCLICAL AND SOCIAL CHANGE

The choice of the five topics above for discussion is not exactly haphazard. All too often, in discussions on social change—and integral, human development and liberation *is* social change—the problem does not revolve around the *what* and the *why* of change so much (although these are, needless to say, essential considerations) as on the *how* of it. It is for this reason that the faith and ideology problematic has been a live one in the Philippines for some time now. (Would it be an unwarranted extrapolation from this Philippine experience to infer that the concern is basically what is at the root of much of church anxiety about versions of liberation theology that give rather easy acceptance to the use of violence to correct entrenched social injustices?) In the light of the above fact, the five topics chosen for comment here constitute as a whole a strategy of—or at least an approach to—social change.

Here I would like to expand the idea a bit further using as pegs for discussion a few points that were touched on earlier but not fully explicitated as pivotal from the perspective of social change. These points will center on the following: structures and values, holistic social transformation, analysis and discernment, and faith and change strategies.

1. Structures and Values

Liberation theologians make much of "sinful structures" (the encyclical uses "structures of sin," and as far as can be ascertained, the slight change in terminology is intended, it seems, to bring out the analogical nature of sin when applied to structures) and their emphasis on them sometimes leads to the impression—if not outright belief—that changing social structures is *the* secret to any meaningful social change: "Reform social structures and you reform society." Opposed to this line of thinking is the view that the inner make-up of people, their cultural values and attitudes, are *the* key to real social change: "Transform values and you transform society."

The debate is a dated one, at least for us in the Philippines. After the successful revolution of 1986 (a structural change of some kind, at least in the political system) and the persistence of old problems even after the revolution (violence, graft, and corruption, elitist politics and economics), what sociologists have said all along about the mutuality of social structures and cultural values is now seen and understood more widely, making the debate academic. To be more concrete: the new Constitution more or less sets forth the framework, i.e., the structures, of societal reform. But most Filipinos see that the fleshing out of those structures in good laws, not to say these laws' faithful implementation, will not occur unless there is a corresponding change in mentalities, in cultural values, a moving away from individualistic, family-centered values to more social, community-centered ones. It is a task the enormity of which few of us have any illusions about.

2. Holistic Social Transformation

As has been pointed out already, it is one of the great merits of the encyclical that in its analysis of global economic and political structures it keeps pointing to the critical part culture plays in the process of development and liberation. This takes cognizance not only of the crucial sociological fact adverted to above, that in holistic social change both social structures and cultural values from the sheer fact of their interdependence must be attended to; but also of another just as crucial sociological fact—and one that is of paramount importance in any effort at social engineering—that what people, the subjects of change, think and what they do about change itself, is an aspect of development processes that cannot be disregarded except at great cost or risk of failure.

Is this reading too much into the pope's words on culture in his encyclical? But the simple fact is when in the process of social change a people's culture is respected, the following are taken into consideration almost as a matter of course — or should be: (a) Every people with a culture of its own has an idea (unarticulated in most cases, it is true) of the kind of society it wants for itself. Ignoring this cultural vision will not guarantee success — just the contrary, difficulties, opposition, disinterest — in the change process. (b) Consulting a people's cultural vision of a good society should also mean their active participation both in the decision- and implementing-phases of the work of development. Again, a sine qua non in social change. And (c), involving people in defining goals and in participative action toward their attainment is to treat them as people of dignity — something which technocrats are not well known for remembering but which, remembered or forgotten, can make or break a whole development scheme. In the pope's making of *solidarity* a key concept of his encyclical, all the above, I believe, is implied.

3. Analysis and Discernment

A social analysis that includes a careful appraisal of both structural and value components of society has this one practical effect: that by it people know at any given time where they are, what current difficulties they suffer under, and most importantly *why*. One inherent problem in the process of change is the time differential between structures- and values-change: social structures, in that they are by nature relational, can change rather more easily and within a shorter time span. Not so cultural values: they are internal to people, imbibed in a long socialization process, and hence by their very nature take longer to change. The problem is especially acute when drastic social change takes place overnight — as in a revolution: How to instill in people cultural values that will be supportive of the new order, given the time-differential mentioned above? Outside of brainwashing techniques and massive indoctrination through controlled information and reeducation camps, it seems to me the gap between structures- and values-change will be bridged only by a process of ongoing and holistic social analysis by the people. That bridging will be further advanced if the analysis is not merely social but is guided as well and motivated by faith—the spiritual discernment we spoke of above. For what discernment does is to make the process of *metanoia* more deliberate—i.e., more consciously a human enterprise but just as consciously dependent on the action of the Spirit. This sounds like unduly spiritualizing what is in essence a mundane task and attributing to the exercise a power for change not accorded its purely secular character. Perhaps. But then what would it mean for the Christian to transform the world in faith?

4. Faith and Change Strategies

In a very real sense the question just asked is what the encyclical is providing an answer to. And I think we can summarize that answer thus: it is our task as individual Christians and as communities to bring our faith and its values to bear on our world and its problems—such problems especially as make people less human, less free, less moral—to thereby transform it more and more into the image of Christ's kingdom. The summation, I admit, fails terribly to put together all the great insights of the encyclical. But, I submit, from the narrower perspective of how to bring about social change as Christians, it is as good a working summary as any. Only two further points need be made, and I propose them here as points of departure for the further elucidation of the encyclical's ideas and for their advancement in real praxis.

(a) Values—those of faith especially—are not mere mental categories that we use as criteria for judging or deciding. They are that, of course, but they are also much more: they are dynamisms impelling to action for the attaining of whatever is defined as good. A little fact—but it prompts us to ask this question: the encyclical makes much of faith values, but how ready are we to move from them as mental constructs and to make them real forces for change?

(b) By the same token we look at the faith itself primarily from and for its intellectual content—rarely do we take it as power, and indeed as the power that we need (and is ours as Christians) in our task of transforming the world. We accept the task from faith, but we make little of the *power* of faith itself in accomplishing it. Another way of putting the problem: we do not make enough space for God's action in our schemes—human schemes—for development and liberation of people, thus severely delimiting our capacity to be surprised!

The encyclical does not in so many words make the two points just made. But in its insistence on how we must bring the values of the kingdom into our world, it does just that, it seems to me, and in no uncertain terms.

11

Sollicitudo Rei Socialis:
A Latin American Perspective

Ricardo Antoncich, S.J.

The message of the encyclical *Sollicitudo Rei Socialis* is universal. Pope John Paul II is issuing an urgent call both to developed countries, threatened by the dehumanization of over-development, and to underdeveloped ones, whose socio-political misery and chaos have brought them, too, to the brink of dehumanization. In certain ecclesial contexts, however, this papal document will touch a special nerve. Latin America is a case in point.

The particular enthusiasm that *Sollicitudo Rei Socialis* has stirred in Latin America is due to the fact that it rehearses so many of our own ideas. A great deal of the theological reflection that has developed in Latin America over the course of the two decades since Medellín now appears in the encyclical.

I should like to focus here on this Latin American thinking as we find it embodied in the encyclical. First, let me remark on the document's method. Then I shall turn to content.

METHOD: SEEING, JUDGING, ACTING

It could seem a matter of scant importance, but the question of order and method in theological reflection is crucial. In Latin

America—at Medellín, at Puebla, and in a great many church documents issuing from the widest variety of sources here (bishops, priests' movements, lay apostolic organizations, and so on)—theological reflection is organized in terms of what we call *seeing, judging,* and *acting.* The implication is that theological reflection should be rooted in concrete life, thereupon to guide us back once more to that concrete life. Our way of doing theology reflects our concept of the theological ministry as a service to the pastoral praxis of the church—an aid to the church in its mission of evangelization.

It seems that the encyclical *Sollicitudo Rei Socialis* takes this same three-step approach. After an introduction, and a reference to *Populorum Progressio* (chap. 1–2), the pope presents us with three major series of ideas. First he *sees:* he contemplates the panorama of the contemporary world (chap. 3). Then he *judges,* in terms of the Christian concept of development (chap. 4) and a theological reading of history (chap. 5). Finally, he *acts*—he makes a commitment of solidarity to the impoverished (chap. 6, 7).

The pope introduces all these considerations with a reminder of the importance of *Populorum Progressio* as an expression of a social teaching along the lines of Vatican II. But new elements have entered the picture now, dashing the hopes that soared in the developmentalistic climate in which Pope Paul VI had written his encyclical: "If development is the new name for peace, then wars and military buildup are the most fearsome enemy of an integral development of peoples" (SRS, no. 10).

Seeing

The first step, then, will be to *see* the reality of worldwide economic underdevelopment. Here the pope issues an emphatic warning. The economic problem is a complex one. It is tied to other problems. Side by side with the economic elements to be considered, we find additional factors, which frequently aggravate our economic problem. Among these the pope cites culture (SRS, no. 15), and forms of poverty other than economic—anthropological poverty, for example (ibid.).

The economic issue is further complicated by the incidence

of political and ideological elements on economic problems. Third World problems are not without their ties to the ideological tensions between East and West—those sectors of the Northern world vying with each other for influence and geopolitical control in the Third World (SRS, no. 20).

But the social teaching of the church guides us to another level of consideration: the moral level. Religious ethics invites us to adopt a new outlook—one that depends on an encounter with concrete human beings rather than with abstract statistics. The pope speaks of "faces"—the faces of the men, women, and children who, "in a divided, inhospitable world, fail to find so much as hearth and home" (SRS, no. 24), or the human faces of the victims of terrorism, often innocent persons who have had no part in the conflicts that now prove their cruel undoing (ibid.).

To convert this act of seeing, the sight of these human faces, into an act of religious contemplation, we turn our gaze to the suffering Christ:

> Omitting any analysis of numbers and statistics, we need only regard the reality of such an enormous multitude of men and women, children, adults, and the elderly—crowd upon crowd of concrete, unique persons, then—who must suffer the unbearable weight of all this misery. Millions upon millions of people are simply without hope today. After all, in so many places on earth, the situation of the afflicted has grown more terrible still. As we assist at these dramas, as we witness the utter indigence and need in which so many of our brothers and sisters are forced to live, suddenly we behold the Lord Jesus himself, standing before us and issuing his challenge (see Mt 25:31–46) [SRS, no. 13].

For the church, the poor are not primarily an "economic problem in the developmental process," or a "political force for the organization of the masses." For us, the poor are first and foremost Jesus Christ in our midst.

Judging

It is from this faith perspective of ours that we now embark on the moment in our reflection that we call *judging*, which is carried out in the encyclical, as I read it, in two clearly differentiated moments. First, the pope reviews the concept of development. Then he undertakes a theological reading of reality.

Review of the Concept of Development. The concept of development has a prescriptive function. Therefore its correct definition is important for the very process of development. Here the encyclical criticizes inadequate notions of development, offering instead a concept calculated to correct their deficiencies.

The first notion the pope criticizes has its philosophical roots in a certain illuminism, regarding development as a mechanistic, quasi-automatic process. Today this conception is seen to be simply indefensible, as wars rage around us and the specter of nuclear destruction looms over our lives.

The second notion is, at all events, a more plausible one: development as the mere accumulation of goods and services. Here the pope embarks on a line of thought calculated to liberate us from the materialism of the affluent society. Not only must we deplore the inequality involved (between the affluence of a few and the destitution of so many), but the very affluence of the few who enjoy it, which is in itself an instance of human degeneration. Overdevelopment is crass materialism (SRS, no. 28), a materialism without explicitly philosophical underpinnings, to be sure, but a materialism nonetheless in practical life, occurring when, "in function of a particular scale of values, a determinate hierarchy of goods based on the immediate attraction of the material, [this materialism] is regarded as capable of satisfying human needs" (SRS, no. 13c).

Materialism can be examined in terms of the polarity between *being* and *having.* The pope cites *Gaudium et Spes,* no. 35, and *Populorum Progressio,* no. 19, to this effect. But Pope John Paul II has himself appealed to this polarity or tension. In *Redemptor Hominis,* no. 16a, he characterizes the human vocation to subdue the earth as a call to accord ethics its rightful primacy over technology. The person has priority over things. Spirit is superior to matter:

We see an inversion of these priorities when things turn against man who has created them. Is this not the very essence of alienation? [John Paul II, *Redemptor Hominis,* no. 15b].

A materialistic civilization accepts the primacy of things over persons (idem, *Dives in Misericordia,* no. 11).

Out of this same logic of human priorities springs the priority of labor over capital (idem, *Laborem Exercens,* no. 12a), which is the "primacy of man in the production process, the primacy of man over things" (ibid., no. 12f). The priority of work vis-à-vis capital is a postulate of the social order itself (ibid., 15a). The degree of recognition any given civilization accords the priority of labor over capital is a particularly revealing indicator of the humane quality of that civilization. As human activity, work is an expression of being, and contributes to the development and growth of being by actualizing the potencies of being. All work, as immanent activity, perfects being—the being of the agent performing it. But as transitive activity, work is a transformation of the reality upon which it is brought to bear, and is ordered to the perfection of "having," as it strives to increase the number and quality of objects or perfections at hand with a view to satisfying the necessities of being.

Work involves tools, raw material. Work is a chain of *having* in order to satisfy the necessities of *being.*

Being asserts itself over having when it sets limits to the absolutizing tendencies of the latter and directs them to higher values. Mature persons, responsible human *beings,* can channel their particular *having* along ethical routes. This calls for respect for a hierarchy of personal and social values. Ethics requires that *having* be subject to the values of charity and justice—that is, that it always be lived in accordance with the demands of solidarity in *being.*

Gaudium et Spes, no. 69, regards ownership (having) as a kind of protective coating, or buffer, for being. In practice, however, ownership ultimately destroys its own positive function, the positive function of having. Persons wrapped up in having are closed in upon themselves, unable to communicate *what they are* with other persons. Thereupon they tend to see in others, as well, not what they are, but what they have. And all of this occurs not only at the individual level, but at the level of society itself. A "having society" becomes a dehumanizing, selfish, consumer society.

Having can only find meaning, individually or socially, in the human being. Therefore John Paul II speaks of an "internal parameter" consisting in the nature of this being.

The biblical foundations offered by John Paul II here in his description of being, together with his insistence on the priority of being over having, are similar to those of his encyclical *Laborem Exercens*. They strike us by their emphasis on dominion over nature, as well as on the quality of the human being as image of the creator to the point of positing in human solidarity the basis of a likeness to the holy Trinity. And this point leads us at once to the second aspect of "judging": a theological reading of reality.

Theological Reading of Reality. In contrast with chapter 4, which is doctrinal, and concerned with a consideration of the concept of development in the light of faith, chapter 5 sets us squarely before concrete history. The perspective of chapter 5 implies the conviction that forces appear in concrete human history that do battle for the reign of God. Hence the encyclical refers to the social teaching of the church as an "interpretation" of the historical realities within the field of the church's evangelizing mission. That mission includes a genuine "ministry of evangelization in the social field, which is an aspect of the prophetical function of the church" (SRS, no. 41).

As we contemplate concrete history, we discover signs of the presence or absence of the reign there. Chapter 5 once more places us before the facts, that we may read them in the light of God's word. And here we find the encyclical's richest contribution to theological thinking: the pope sees human history as the battlefield of sin and grace, the theater of the war between the antireign and the reign of God.

Of course, the reign of God has both an eschatological fullness and a historical concretion:

The church well knows that no temporal realization is identifiable with the kingdom of God, and that none do more than reflect, and, as it were, anticipate, the glory of this kingdom, which we await at the term of history when the Lord returns [SRS, no. 48].

On the one hand, this could seem to dilute the historical density of the present moment in terms of the presence of the reign of God. The pope speaks of a reflection, or anticipation, of the reign of God. If human history does no more than "reflect" the definitive reign of God, as a mirror reflects a ray of light, then is history of any more importance than the mirror as compared with the ray of light? Or again, the blueprint for a building to be constructed might surely be said to "anticipate" the final form of the building. But one cannot live in the blueprint. Only the building itself is of any real value.

This would be a poor translation of the pope's thought, as he goes on to speak of the importance of the present life for conditioning the future one, and, especially, of the organic continuity between history, however imperfect and provisional, and eschatology:

However imperfect and provisional, nothing that can and should be realized by way of an effort of universal solidarity, with the divine grace, at a given moment of history, that the life of human beings may be rendered more humane, will have been lost or in vain [ibid.].

And the pope goes on to cite *Gaudium et Spes,* no. 39 — the last words pronounced by Archbishop Romero before he was murdered — in which we are told of certain goods (human dignity, a union of brothers and sisters, and freedom, along with many other things) that will be found to be without any blemish when Christ hands over his reign to his Father.

I should like to emphasize two elements of the Holy Father's theological reading of history: the mystery of the eucharist, and the struggle between the forces of the antireign and the reign of God.

(a) The Eucharistic Mystery. The eucharistic mystery is the eschatological reign of God, present in history. The historical presence of the eschatological reign is inaugurated in the incar-

nation, and the eucharist is its permanent, ongoing memorial. Now, if the goods we fashion in this world, by means of our work, contain an element destined to endure in the eschatological reign, and if the definitive reign, in turn, is to be found already present today in the eucharistic mystery, then theology must uncover the precise nature of the intimate relationship between the mystery of the eucharist, on the one hand, and human dignity, a union of sisters and brothers, and freedom, on the other.

In its quality as the eschatological reign of God already present, the eucharist is a mystery of faith. But faith, in turn, understands that the struggle for human dignity, communion, and freedom has an eschatological meaning. The vision of faith opens our understanding to the insight that something of the definitive "heaven" is present on our earth, and something of our effort on this "earth" will forever abide as a value of heaven.

But there is an even more intimate relationship between the eucharist and the dignity, unity, and freedom of the daughters and sons of God. The eucharist is the perpetually renewed memorial of Jesus' self-surrender for human salvation—that is, for the basic dignity of all God's children, for their oneness as sisters and brothers, and for their freedom to love. These boons are therefore inseparable from their source and origin, which is Jesus' redemptive surrender. Latin Americans intuit this, in all simplicity, when they celebrate in the eucharist the eschatological fruits that gradually come to maturity in current history. The eucharist is more than a religious symbol of a temporal, historical fact. In the intuition of faith, our people know that this mystery is a mystery of justice, freedom, and human solidarity.

The whole of chapter 5 moves along these same lines of theological reflection. We are still dealing with a theological reading of reality, which is articulated around two concepts: sin and solidarity, the absence or presence of grace, the forces of the antireign and those of the reign.

(b) Antagonism between Antireign and Reign. The encyclical's approach to the thematic of sin is enriched by its emphasis on the relationship between sin and social structures. With an explicit reference to the apostolic exhortation Reconciliatio et Paen-

itentia, the pope rehearses the authentic sense in which we may speak of "social sin."

It is a classic principle of theology that where there is neither freedom nor responsibility, there can be no sin. The moral quality of freedom and responsibility does not attach to structures as such. As it is we human beings who are responsible for these structures, it is we who fall under the imputation of sin when these structures are evil. Social problems, the pope insists, are not the outgrowth of some blind, irresistible interplay of sociological forces. Human beings are genuinely responsible for these problems. Thus the social problem is posited on an ethical level—a level that, as the encyclical emphatically states, indeed belongs to it.

Puebla had adopted this same outlook when it pointed out that social problems do not simply occur, that they do not descend on the human scene for no particular reason. They are bound up with a causality, of a technological order, to be sure, but of a moral one as well. The bishops at Puebla warn of extremely grave situations of human poverty (Puebla, Final Document, no. 29), situations constituting a genuine scandal incompatible with Christian faith (no. 28). They warn of the crisis (no. 50) of an unbridled lust for gain, and identify this kind of greed as an obstacle to communion (no. 69). They warn against the appropriation of wealth by privileged minorities (nos. 1208, 1263) and the consequent widening of the poverty gap (no. 1260). Faced with a like situation, faith is constrained to speak its word (no. 15). The eyes and hearts of shepherds must react (nos. 14, 127, 163)—not with a determination of the technological nature of the problem (no. 70), but with a discernment of the facts at hand as signs of the times (nos. 379, 420, 473).

It is in this perspective that one does a theological reading of the presence of sin in social mechanisms (no. 70). This sin is the occasion of enormous frustration (no. 73), as it destroys communion and the common life (no. 185). Sin is found not only in interpersonal relationships, but in the phenomenon of oppression as well (no. 328), and is an obstacle to communion (no. 281). Christ delivers us from sin, the root of oppression (no. 517), as well as from all situations of injustice (no. 1288).

Social sin does not exist independently of concrete human

responsibility. The structures of sin are the authentic point of reference for moral action. To create these structures despite their injustice, or to tolerate and accept them without any intention of changing them, implicates us all in the sin of which these structures are the vehicle (in the sense of being both its fruit and its temptation).

The reference to sin in *Sollicitudo Rei Socialis* is even more concrete when the pope begins to specify the idols of power and of "having" that lurk in social processes and mechanisms:

Were we to consider certain forms of modern "imperialism" in the light of these moral criteria, we should discover that, beneath certain decisions seemingly inspired solely by economics or politics, genuine forms of idolatry lie concealed: money, ideology, social class, and technology [SRS, no. 37].

Then the pope invites us to consider, at the opposite pole, the forces of the reign, the power of grace. Just as sin is concretized in unjust wealth and enslaving power, so grace becomes present in a liberating solidarity. I add the word "liberating" to emphasize the authentic meaning of solidarity. After all, imperialist mechanisms, too, have recourse to their solidarities and alliances. Authentic solidarity is solidarity that sets the oppressed, the victims of the mechanisms of oppression, free.

Ever more clearly, then, social structures are a function of human agency, and vice versa. But this interdependency is a happy quality of solidarity, as well, when the result is a commitment to the quest for the common good—the good of each and all, that each may be responsible for all:

This determination is based on the firm conviction that the great obstacle to full development is the lust for gain and thirst for power of which we have been speaking. These "attitudes and structures of sin" are overcome—with the help of divine grace—only by way of a diametrically opposed attitude: total dedication to the good of our neighbor, with a readiness to "lose ourselves," in the evangelical sense, for others instead of exploiting them, and to "serve" them instead of oppressing them for our own advantage (see Mt 10:40–42, 20:25; Mk 10:42–45; Lk 22:25–27) [SRS, no. 38].

Solidarity is a moral imperative for those who "must feel responsible for the weakest, and be ready to share what they possess" (ibid., no. 39). It is likewise a necessity for those who have nothing, who must struggle for justice "on the social scene, not by having recourse to violence, but by confronting the ineffectiveness or corruption of public authorities with their needs and rights" (ibid.).

But above all, solidarity is a moral imperative for the church. And the following sentences in the encyclical are of great pastoral significance for Latin America:

> By virtue of its evangelical commitment, the church feels called to the side of these multitudes of the poor. The church must discern the justice of their demands, and help respond to them, without ignoring the contribution of other groups toiling for the common good [ibid.].

A theological reading of reality interprets solidarity as charity. Therefore it is to be offered to enemies. Here we are in a specifically Christian perspective. The Old Testament demonstrates great social sensitivity, favoring the underprivileged with its institutions and laws (the year of grace, the distribution of the fruits of the earth in sabbatical years, and so on). But it maintains no attitude of reconciliation with enemies. Here Jesus posits one of the basic differences between the Old Testament and the New (see Mt 5:38–45), as well as between pagans and the disciples of the reign (Mt 5:46–48). When solidarity reaches the point of recognizing in an enemy a beloved child of our own divine Parent, it has finally attained to the essence of charity: now solidarity "transcends itself" (SRS, no. 40), and becomes intelligible in function of the grace of the Spirit, who shows us the love of the Father and bestows on us our certitude of the faithfulness of the Son (see Rom 8). Solidarity, as a communion of human persons with one another, is a particularly transparent example of the grace of God imparted in the present moment:

after all, it is a reflection of the mystery of the very life of the triune God.

A theological reading of reality rests not so much on a "science" (theology) as on a "con-science," in the original sense of the word: a consciousness, an awareness. The following passage from the encyclical merits particular attention:

Thus a consciousness of the common parenthood of God, of the state of sisters and brothers obtaining among all human beings in Christ (all of them being "sons in the Son"), and of the lifegiving presence and activity of the Holy Spirit, will bestow on our view of the world a new criterion for interpreting that world. Above and beyond all human and natural bonds, strong and deep as they are, one perceives in the light of faith a new unity of humankind, in which all solidarity ought ultimately to take its inspiration. This supreme model of unity, this reflection of the interior life of one God in three Persons, is what Christians express in the word "communion." This specifically Christian communion, zealously attained, propagated, and enriched with the help of the Lord, is the very soul of the vocation of the church to be a "sacrament" in the sense that we have indicated [SRS, no. 40].

Sin and grace struggle to possess the human heart. Our theological reading of reality perceives the mystery of these forces at work in that reality. Modern development is one of the theaters of that struggle.

Acting

The moment has come to *act*. The pope proposes a number of courses of action. One of these is the revitalization of the social teaching of the church, which is not reducible to a body of doctrine, but must be the instrument of a reading of history as prophetic praxis.

Basing our considerations on this reading, we understand that solidarity with the oppressed is the privileged, prioritarian route of escape from both the misery of underdevelopment and the indifference and selfishness of overdevelopment. The great prophetic act, the deed of prophecy par excellence, is the option for the poor as a concrete expression of the primacy of charity. All economic problems—like the international reform of trade, a reform of the world monetary and fiscal system, the exchange of technology and its adequate use, a revision of the structure of international organizations, and so on—must be reconsidered from the standpoint of a position taken in favor of the poor. Creative initiatives must prevail. Solidarity must be fostered with and among underdeveloped peoples, to the advantage of the poor.

One of the pope's concrete suggestions could unleash a veritable Christian revolution. He recommends we turn back to patristic tradition, and the practice of the early church, which served the poor by the sacrifice not only of superfluities, but of necessities. The pope is citing a practice of long ago, but its operative ethical principle is still valid today. After all, what is at stake is a life based on a Christian scale of values. Here are the pope's actual words:

> And so, in the earliest teaching and practice of the church, the conviction prevailed that the church itself, its ministers, and each of its members are called to alleviate the misery of the suffering, near and far, not only with their "superfluities," but with their "necessities," as well. The superfluous adornment of temples or the precious objects used in divine worship are not to have priority over the requirements of those in need. On the contrary, it may well be a matter of obligation to alienate these goods in order to be able to procure food, drink, clothing, and housing for those in need of the same. As we have stated above, we are presented with a "scale of values" here—in the framework of the right of ownership—between having and being, especially when the having of some may be at the expense of the being of so many others [SRS, no. 31].

The pope hopes that this encyclical will stimulate new practices in the church, practices that would actually only be a continuation of the purest church tradition. The word of doctrine, which elucidates the concept of development, must be conjoined to the church practice of being a sign of the unity of the human race (a unity set at nought by division into blocs, and into a First, Second, and Third World) through solidarity with the poor to the point of detachment from its own goods. If the traumatic situation described in chapter 3 does not meet the requirements of a case of need—extreme need—then one wonders what situation ever could.

This deed of solidarity on the part of a church stripping itself of its wealth in the face of the crying needs of the daughters and sons of God is all the more incumbent on a church of the Third World. Not that it is the exclusive obligation of this part of the church. The problem is universal, and the universal church must feel challenged by it. Indeed, what *Populorum Progressio* and *Sollicitudo Rei Socialis* seek to point up are precisely the worldwide dimensions of the problem and the importance of worldwide deeds calculated to find a solution. And yet, let us observe, among the destitute peoples of Africa, Asia, and Latin America, the wealth of the church in the midst of situations of such abject misery may more easily constitute a scandal—the scandal cited by Puebla in the gap between wealthy Christians and their impoverished Christian brothers and sisters (Puebla Final Document, no. 28).

CONTRIBUTIONS IN TERMS OF CONTENT

In the sociological debate on Latin American reality, "developmentalism" has been scored as "reformist" and ineffective. The developmental model itself has been criticized as a breeding ground for profound inequalities and imperialistic oppression. Again, it is alleged that access to development on the part of the Third World is structurally impossible, owing to the utter dependency of underdeveloped nations on developed ones. The gravity and magnitude of the international debt is crystal clear evidence that these criticisms are well-founded.

In this context, an encyclical on development could seem to represent a step backward, a backsliding to stages once upon a time attained and now transcended. This fear is baseless. *Sollicitudo Rei Socialis* explicitly rejects a purely economicist, imperialistic concept of development, and recognizes the structural inevitability, in this concept, of mechanisms of dependency.

Consequently, we must say: the concept of development is still valid, and can serve as a platform for a dialogue between opposing parties who both use this term. Not that we must abandon the language and practice of a theology of liberation. Rather we must show that authentic development implies the greatest possible fullness of human freedom in the sense of an integral freedom, and therefore that the coordinates of a development of freedom, and a freedom in development, determine, for liberation as a process, the crucial point of reference.

An enriched concept of development can scarcely be regarded any longer as moving along the lines of the "developmentalism" criticized by the theology of liberation, once it begins to share that theology's concern for the world of the oppressed.

And once a theological reading of liberation has discovered the relationship between sin and the structures bound up with sin, it has discovered the meaning of liberation as the term is used by Pope John Paul II in *Sollicitudo Rei Socialis:*

> The principal obstacle that genuine liberation must overcome is sin, and the structures leading to the same, with their striking tendency to multiply and spread. The freedom with which Christ has set us free (Gal 5:1) moves us to be converted in such a way that we become servants of all. Thus the process of development and liberation is concretized in the exercise of solidarity—that is, in the practice of love of and service to our neighbor, especially the very poorest [SRS, no. 46].

The encyclical makes another important contribution, this time from the viewpoint of another theology, that of reconciliation. A theological reading of history enables us to identify the oppression introjected into structural mechanisms as sin. Accordingly, the persons who create, defend, and perpetuate these mechanisms are committing sin (in the objective sense of what offends God, saving, of course, the intentionality of the subjective conscience). But then this same theological reading demands that these persons be regarded in the light of the redemptive attitude of Jesus, who has come not for the healthy but for the sick, and who loves his enemies (sinners) and returns them good for evil. This he taught in both word and deed (see Mt 5:38–48, Lk 23:34).

The liberation process that animates the efforts of the oppressed, detecting the barriers that frustrate those efforts, regards persons and social groups not as mere antagonistic forces in an inevitable conflict, but as responsible, free persons, capable of being converted.

A preferential option for the poor, then, calls for simultaneous efforts at all levels of society. It demands we support, defend, and encourage the mutual solidarity of the poor. It likewise demands we educate the poor, exhort them, and manifest to them with unequivocal clarity that the oppressive conduct of other social groups is antievangelical, and that God's grace and pardon are offered to those other groups with a view to assisting them to abandon their lives of oppression and to live lives of solidarity with the very poorest instead. This is the nature of the conversion of those who have enslaved others: they overcome their oppressive impulses and become servants of the poor. Once more we may cite *Sollicitudo Rei Socialis*: "The freedom with which Christ has set us free encourages us to become servants of all" (SRS, no. 46).

I have sought, in these pages, to offer a reflection on the encyclical *Sollicitudo Rei Socialis* from a Latin American viewpoint. My purpose in calling attention to certain aspects in its method and content is to encourage our brothers and sisters in Christ to read this document more attentively and implement its directives more assiduously. The urgency of current problems makes this incumbent on us.

— Translated from the Spanish by Robert R. Barr

Contributors

Ricardo Antoncich, S.J. was born in Peru and did his theological studies in Spain and Germany. A professor of theology at the Catholic University in Lima, he has served as an advisor to the Latin American Conference of Bishops (CELAM). He is the author of *Christians in the Face of Injustice: A Latin American Reading of Catholic Social Teaching* (Orbis Books, 1987).

Gregory Baum teaches theology at McGill University in Montreal. He is editor of the journal *The Ecumenist* and serves as one of the editorial directors of the international journal *Concilium*. He has published widely in theology, ecumenism, sociology, and Catholic social teaching. Among his books are *Religion and Alienation*, *The Priority of Labor: A Commentary on "Laborem Exercens,"* and *Theology and Society* (all with Paulist Press).

Francisco F. Claver, S.J. served as bishop of Malaybalay, Bukidnon, in the Philippines from 1969–1984. He has served as a member of the Pontifical Commission on Non-Believers, and is currently director of the National Secretariat of Social Action in the Philippines. He is the author of *The Stones Will Cry Out: Grassroots Pastorals* (Orbis Books, 1978).

John A. Coleman, S.J. teaches theology at the Jesuit School of Theology and the Graduate Theological Union at Berkeley. He is the author of *An American Strategic Theology* (Paulist Press, 1982) and editor of a forthcoming collection of essays marking the centenary of Catholic social teaching (Orbis Books, 1991).

Donal Dorr is an Irish missionary priest with extensive pastoral and academic experience in Africa and Latin America. His books include *Option for the Poor: A Hundred Years of Vatican Social Teaching* (1983), *Spirituality and Justice* (1985), and *Integral Spirituality* (1990), all published by Orbis Books and Gill and Macmillan.

Robert Ellsberg is Editor-in-Chief of Orbis Books. A former managing editor of *The Catholic Worker*, he edited *By Little and By Little: The Selected Writings of Dorothy Day* (Alfred A. Knopf, 1983). He is a doctoral candidate at the Harvard Divinity School.

Denis Goulet is O'Neill Professor in Education for Justice at the University of Notre Dame. An expert on development, his recent books include *The Uncertain Promise: Value Conflicts in Technology* and *Incentives for Development: The Key to Equity* (both published in 1988 by New Horizons Press).

Peter J. Henriot, S.J. recently retired as executive director of the Center of Concern in Washington, D.C. to pursue work and research in Africa. A political scientist, his work has focused on the political economy of international development. He is co-author of *Social Analysis: Linking Faith and Justice* (rev. ed., 1983) and co-editor of *Catholic Social Teaching: Our Best Kept Secret* (rev. ed., 1988), both co-published by Orbis Books and the Center of Concern.

Mary E. Hobgood teaches religious studies at the University of Maine in Orono. Her doctoral thesis, *Paradigms in Conflict: Economic Theory in Catholic Social Teaching, 1891–1986*, is a forthcoming publication by Temple University Press.

Philip S. Land, S. J. is an economist who has been on the research staff of the Center of Concern since 1976. Previously, he taught at the Gregorian University in Rome and served on the staff of the Vatican's Justice and Peace Commission. He is the author of *Shaping Welfare Concerns: U.S. Catholic Bishops' Contribution* (Center of Concern, 1988).

Maria Riley, O.P. is on the research staff and coordinator of the Women's Project at the Center of Concern. Among her publications are *Wisdom Seeks Her Way: Liberating the Power of Women's Spirituality* (Center of Concern, 1987) and *Women Faithful for the Future* (Sheed and Ward, 1986).

William K. Tabb is professor of economics at Queens College and of sociology at the Graduate Center of the City University of New York. He edited *Churches in Struggle: Liberation Theologies and Social Change in North America*, which contained his essay, "The Shoulds and Excluded Whys: The U.S. Catholic Bishops Look at the Economy" (Monthly Review Press, 1986).

Index